ANAHAREO

A Wilderness Spirit

KRISTIN GLEESON

Published by An Tig Beag Press
Text Copyright 2024 © Kristin Gleeson
Original publication 2012 by Fireship Press
All rights reserved. This is a work of non-fiction. No part of this publication may be reproduced, stored in or introduced into a retrieval system, or transmitted in any form, or by any means (electronic, mechanical, photocopying, recording or otherwise) without the prior written permission of the publisher.
Cover design by JD Smith Designs

WOMEN OF IRELAND SERIES
In Praise of the Bees

Song of the Bees

CELTIC KNOT SERIES
Selkie Dreams

Along the Far Shores

Raven Brought the Light

A Treasure Beyond Worth (novella)

RENAISSANCE SOJOURNER SERIES
The Imp of Eye (with Moonyeen Blakey)

The Sea of Travail

The Quest of Hope

The Pursuit of the Unicorn

HIGHLAND BALLAD SERIES
The Hostage of Glenorchy

The Mists of Glen Strae

The Braes of Huntly

Highland Lioness

Highland Yuletide

RISE OF THE CELTIC GODS SERIES
Awakening the Gods

In Search of the Hero God

At the Edge of the Otherworld

AS K.L. GLEESON

House of **LISTEN TO THE MUSIC CONNECTED TO THE BOOKS**

Go to www.krisgleeson.com/music

Receive a FREE novelette prequel, *A Treasure Beyond Worth,* and *Along the Far Shores*

When you sign up for my mailing list www.krisgleeson.com

To Katherine and Anne

And to Dave, whose original inspiration it was

NOTE
When this book was originally published in 2012, the accepted term in public writing for the indigenous people of Canada was 'Aboriginal'.

TABLE OF CONTENTS

Maps 12

Foreword 15

Introduction 19

Chapter 1: *Childhood & Background* 24

Chapter 2: *Meeting her Jesse James* 37

Chapter 3: *Journey Into the Bush* 48

Chapter 4: *Learning Bush Skills* 56

Chapter 5: *Beaver Kits* 70

Chapter 6: *New Hunting Grounds* 80

Chapter 7: *The Lure of Prospecting* 91

Chapter 8: *National Parks & the Path of Conservation* 98

Chapter 9: *Prospecting & Becoming a Public Figure* 112

Chapter 10: *The New Role of Motherhood* 119

Chapter 11: *Pursuing More Adventure* 131

Chapter 12: *A Relationship Under Strain* 144

Chapter 13: *The Weight of Pilgrims of the Wild* 158

Chapter 14: *Difficult Choices* 175

Chapter 15: *The Backlash After Grey Owl's Death* 187

Chapter 16: *A New Life With Old Problems* 197

Chapter 17: *A Stubborn Vision* 219

Chapter 18: *The Public View Again* 235

Chapter 19: *A Life Recognized* 249

Epilogue 268

Endnotes 273

Acknowledgments 303

Resources 305

MAPS

Western Canada

Eastern Canada

Foreword

When the name "Anahareo" is mentioned, that of "Grey Owl," the pioneer Canadian environmentalist of the 1930s, immediately comes to mind. Anahareo's pleas to save two beaver kits whose mother they had trapped led to his decision to work for the conservation of wildlife. Anahareo encouraged him to write his first articles and to make public lectures. Grey Owl's publications, talks, and the films that the National Parks branch sponsored, made both of their names widely known throughout the English-speaking world.

In his best-selling *Pilgrims of the Wild* (1934) Grey Owl wrote a wonderfully written account of his life with his beautiful young Iroquois bride, he called Anahareo. In her own book, *Devil in Deerskins* (1972), she told her side of their relationship. The Iroquois woman accepted her husband's own word that he was the son of an Apache woman, and a Scot who had been a guide with Buffalo Bill. The fact that she believed Grey Owl's story of his Aboriginal origins reveals how convincingly he explained them. After his death on April 13, 1938, the truth proved otherwise. Swift detective work on both sides of the Atlantic revealed Grey Owl's true identity. Born and raised in England, he was really one Archie Belaney. He had no North American Indian ancestry at all.

The public's fascination with Grey Owl's strange and original story has overshadowed Anahareo's own. The life of this energetic dynamic woman had long merited a full biography of her own. Kristin Gleeson's new book, *Anahareo: A Wilderness Spirit,* adds greatly to our knowledge of Gertrude Bernard, known after her marriage to Grey Owl as Anahareo. With the assistance of family members and the author's own diligent record seeking, Kristin Gleeson brings forward new information on her family and early life. Her father was Iroquois, and her mother Algonquin, but theBernard family did not live on a reserve. Gertrude Bernard was born in 1906. Raised in Mattawa, Ontario, in the Ottawa Valley, she was a town girl who learned her first woodland survival skills from her husband, now revealed to have been born and raised an Englishman.

Anahareo's years with Grey Owl in Ontario and Quebec are fully reviewed; as well as their years together, and sometimes apart, in western Canada. A special moment was the birth of their daughter, Shirley Dawn, in 1932. The previous year they had moved from Quebec to western Canada: first to Riding Mountain National Park in Manitoba, and then to Prince Albert National Park in Saskatchewan. Grey Owl's articles on the North, and wildlife had led to his appointment as a conservation officer, or caretaker of park animals with the National Parks branch.

As Kristin Gleeson explains so well this articulate young woman who loved adventure wanted a life of her own. She could not tolerate the sedentary life her husband adopted in western Canada. He spent his nights writing and days sleeping. In the mid-1930s Grey Owl wrote three books, all best sellers, but his concentration on his writing led to a strained relationship with Anahareo, the name he had given her. The independent adventure-loving woman, still only in her later twenties, left on several extensive prospecting trips on her own. The marriage itself broke up in the mid-1930s.

The final chapters cover the years of Anahareo's life after Grey

Anahareo

Owl's death in April 1938. The author identifies many of the challenges Anahareo faced as an Aboriginal person in a racially conscious Canada in the mid-twentieth century. Yet, in the face of adversity, she continued her fight for animal rights and for greater appreciation of wildlife and the environment. She gained national recognition for her work with her admittance into the Order of Canada in 1983, three years before her death in 1986.

Thanks to Kristin Gleeson, we now have a full and most interesting biography of Anahareo.

> Donald B. Smith Emeritus Professor of History, University of Calgary, and author of *From the Land of Shadows: The Making of Grey Owl* (1990).

March 15, 2012

Introduction

The rivers and lakes of the Quebec bush were frozen over and the snow was thick on the ground. Clad in snowshoes and breeches, her parka hood pulled up over her stylishly bobbed hair, Anahareo, an Aboriginal woman, strode behind Grey Owl in the wintry landscape with confidence, determined to maintain the silence he required. Eventually the pair arrived at an ice-covered creek. Knowing that any current makes ice dangerous, Grey Owl cut a pole to test its firmness. With the snow on the ice only a few inches deep both he and Anahareo removed their snowshoes and Anahareo carried them, leaving Grey Owl free to take the axe and the test pole. In a firm voice Grey Owl instructed Anahareo to keep some distance behind him so that the areas of ice would not have to bear both their weights at once, then slowly he led the way, lifting the pole and letting it fall while he listened intently for the hollow sound that would indicate the ice was too thin for walking. The cautious tapping slowed their pace and appeared entirely unnecessary to an impatient Anahareo. After what seemed an age just creeping forward Anahareo could contain herself no longer and strode out to pass Grey Owl, who shouted at her furiously. Suddenly, the ice broke under her and she fell into the frigid water.

Grey Owl sprung into action and dropped to the ice, then carefully, with the pole outreached, he crawled towards Anahareo until she could grasp it. Once she had a firm grip, Grey Owl pulled her slowly out of the water to safety. Quickly he led her into the woods and set about felling a tree to make a fire. After a time spent warming herself before the crackling flames, Anahareo felt she was dry enough to make it back to camp as she was. Grey Owl agreed but told her to run fast to keep warm. She strapped on her snowshoes and off she went at a rapid pace, certain she would make it without a problem. When she emerged from the woods out into the open, however, a strong wind cut through her and caused a thin layer of ice to form on her clothes. She struggled on, but the ice only thickened everywhere, including the knees. All ability to run had vanished and she could only manage a stiff-legged shuffle as she made her way back. She finally arrived at the cabin door, tripped over the threshold, and fell headlong inside. With some effort she gathered herself up and started to strip off her clothes. She began with her moccasins but discovered that they were frozen solid and impossible to remove, a problem that only standing in a pail of cold water could resolve. The rest of her clothes presented a similar difficulty. After a heroic struggle out of her parka that found her once again on the floor with the bucket of water upturned, she attempted to pull off her breeches and saw that some of her skin came off with them. After more struggle she was able to remove her remaining clothes and wrap herself in blankets.[1]

Like many other lessons, it was one Anahareo, or Gertrude Bernard as she was baptized, learned the hard way. The wilderness in all its beauty and allure was still a dangerous place and even the most skilled at living in the bush know that any little mistake or bad stroke of luck can cost a person's life. Grey Owl, after nearly twenty years hunting and trapping, understood this. Though he was an Englishman he had learned his skills from various Aboriginals and

Euro-Canadians. During his experiences with Aboriginals, he had felt enough sympathy for their culture and their hunting practices that he began to describe himself as part Indian, a remarkable action at a time when Aboriginals were held in low regard. And now Grey Owl was passing on these bush skills to Anahareo, an Aboriginal woman. It was quite an irony.

It was Grey Owl's very wilderness experience and passion for it that first attracted Anahareo, so much so she followed him from her small-town life in Mattawa, Ontario, to the wilds of Quebec where Grey Owl taught her the skills she needed to survive there. The wilderness proved to be everything the stubborn, adventurous and wilful Anahareo hoped it would—exciting, challenging and different from her lonely experience of Mattawa. It was in the wilderness she felt at home. There no one judged her, as they did in her home and the wider community, least of all the animals for which she felt a growing compassion and empathy. It was that compassion and empathy that led her to reject hunting and later convince Grey Owl to rear two beaver kits that they rescued. His ultimate agreement eventually set Grey Owl on the path to become the international voice for wilderness preservation.

Grey Owl wrote the tale of his journey with Anahareo to that goal and published it in Britain, Canada and America. The hugely popular book, *Pilgrims of the Wild,* in which Anahareo's name was coined, successfully captured Anahareo's lively spirit and deep compassion for animals that made Anahareo the darling of Britain. The Anahareo that Grey Owl described in *Pilgrims of the Wild* "was no butterfly," and

> could swing an axe as well as she could a lip-stick, and was able to put up a tent in good shape, make a quick fire, and could rig a tump-line and get a load across in good time, even if she did have to sit down and powder her nose at the other end of the portage.[2]

Who was this woman that captivated Grey Owl and the hearts of so many people? No one at first glance would think the Anahareo Grey Owl described was a town girl, but neither would she appear to be a traditional First Nations woman nor a contemporary image of a First Nations. What kind of woman was she? At the core of this complex modern woman, well skilled in bushcraft, was her passion for the wilderness and her determination to be herself and live life on her own terms. It was a passion that Grey Owl understood and shared.

The path Anahareo chose was not always easy. Except for the brief time when she was a celebrity figure, she constantly fought rejection and harsh judgment as a woman and an Aboriginal. She used many strategies, both conscious and unconscious, to deal with these reactions. She stood firmly and sometimes even brazenly for what she believed and for the most part refused to conform to the established expectations Euro-Canadian society held for behaviour and dress based on the poor images they had of Aboriginal women that portrayed them as either backward, immoral, or both. Anahareo bobbed her hair, wore breeches, high-laced boots and a fringed jacket. As a lone woman she prospected in the bush, paddled canoes hundreds of kilometres and ran dog sleds over mountains.

Not all of the strategies Anahareo used to deal with society's rejection were wise, and some were harmful to herself and others. Excessive alcohol consumption and tempestuous fights with Grey Owl and her later husband provided courage against the hurt as well as a vent for her anger over it, but such actions were not without their price.

Anahareo's passion for the wilderness followed her throughout her life. She never stopped believing in Archie's message about the need to preserve the wilderness, even after his death and events took her away from the bush. She worked for years to get a positive view of Grey Owl's life and his message to the public. Finally, in later life, when the opportunity arose to become active in wilderness preservation and animal rights, she seized it. In the role of spokesperson she wrote letters, gave lectures, showed films and staffed booths to promote the causes in which she believed so strongly. It is a testament to her work that her efforts were finally recognized near the end of her life. It was a long journey from a small-town girl who dreamed of adventure.

Chapter One

Childhood & Background

Anahareo's father called her "Pony" because she always ran, she never walked.1 She ran towards adventure about the house, up trees and along the river behind the house. Unlike her sister, Johanna, Pony preferred to climb, pick berries, or fish instead of playing with dolls or learning to cook and clean. Such wild behaviour eventually caused her aunts to despair and the small-town community of Mattawa, Ontario, to shake its head. Her father was distracted, her mother was dead and no punishment seemed to curb her behaviour.

It was not always the case. From the age of four until she was about eleven Pony lived with "Big Grandma," her father's mother, after her own mother died of tuberculosis at the young age of thirty-six. Big Grandma seemed to understand Pony and the effect such a loss had upon a young child and Pony loved her for it. Her grandmother showered love and attention upon her, teaching her to tan hides, make soap and bead mitts and moccasins. She allowed Pony to examine the contents of her grandmother's trunk and on the occasions her grandmother opened it, Pony would listen attentively while Big Grandma pulled out different items and mementos and shared the history and tales associated with them, slowly instilling in Pony knowledge of and pride in her heritage.

Big Grandma's history stretched back to the early part of the nineteenth century to Oka, an Aboriginal mission immediately west of Montreal, where she was born in 1833 and baptized Marie Catherine Papineau (Pimatanokse). Her father, Francois Kaondinaketch Papineau, eventually became grand chief of the Nippising band of Algonquin whose members sometimes stayed at the mission when they were not hunting and fishing. When Catherine was old enough, she went off to a convent boarding school, where French became her primary language. She returned to Oka a young woman and eventually married a Mohawk, John Bernard Nelson. But John's parents, John Anenha Nelson and Marguerite Kawennonsen Nelson, disapproved of his marriage to an Algonquin. Centuries of warring between the Mohawks and the Algonquins were not easily overcome, despite living in the same mission. John disregarded his parents' wishes, dropped his surname and, with his new wife, left Oka and made his way up the Ottawa River then along its tributary, the Madawaska, to Harcourt Township in the Muskoka district.2

The Bernards lived in Harcourt Township for several years. But the timber industry that supplied Britain's industry, navy and large quantities of Canada's new settlers wrought vast changes on the landscape and the First Nations communities of Ontario. The large stretches of forests cut down for farming and timbering drastically reduced the amount of fish and game available to Algonquin bands that relied heavily on them to feed their families. As the forests fell, with tree stumps or discarded rotting wood the only evidence of their former existence, some Algonquins fled north to the virgin stands of pine, while the timber industry nipped at their heels, ever encroaching. Other First Nations bands that chose not to move north sought help from missions or from the government, choices that meant the end of their traditional way of life. Catherine's own father, Francois Papineau, joined other chiefs on various occasions to petition the government to fulfill the promise to receive income from squatters and loggers who worked their lands. Eventually, they gave up and asked the government to set aside land for them to live.3

In the midst of such dramatic changes John and Catherine Bernard chose to go north, Catherine by train with the smaller children, and John on a barge with the family horses, chickens and cattle up along the Ottawa River, to settle in northeastern Ontario, in the Nippising District at Boom Creek. It was a place just on the fringes of the settlement that would eventually become the town of Mattawa, which was situated at the confluence of the Mattawa and Ottawa rivers.4

At their home in Boom Creek, Catherine cared for their seven daughters and four sons John, Paul, Amable and finally Mathew, born in 1866. John meanwhile earned money through his contracts to bring logs out of the bush which he supplemented with what farming, hunting and fishing he could manage. The timber industry offered many men, including those of the First Nations, seasonal employment in the area. By the fall of 1870 hundreds of timbermen had come up the Ottawa River to cut timber and float the thousands of logs downriver the following spring. Mattawa, as the nearest community, was the natural stopping place for refreshment and restocking and as a result the town boomed.5

In addition to guiding and trapping like their father, the Bernard sons, when grown, took seasonal jobs in the timber industry. Like other Aboriginal men Matt and his brother John had intimate knowledge of the rivers and their tributaries and the bordering bush, and with their skilled balance and understanding of winds and currents from years of canoeing they made natural rivermen.6

Catherine Bernard (Big Grandma), Matt, Paul & Tessie, courtesy of Louise Montreuil

The job of a riverman was tough and required skill and dexterity. Each spring, just after ice break up, these men worked the cut logs, driving them downriver. Clad in spiked cork boots with pike poles in hand they would jump lithely from log to log to raft the timber into groups that could measure acres across. Then they would push the logs over hazardous rapids. It was dangerous work—a dunking in the icy water could be lethal. Unable to swim and clothed in their cumbersome heavy gear the men could only flounder in the raging currents of the icy water that teemed with powerful logs that would easily crush a man. No one knew this danger better than John and Catherine's son Matt Bernard, who participated in drives on the Madawaska River and Amable Du Fond River, and served as a pilot and gang foreman at Patois River, before finally witnessing the death of his brother and the rest of the crew at a place called Rocket Chute on the Madawaska River.7

The Bernards and other First Nations people of Matawa had additional means of earning income. They made goods for sale in the general store owned by Mr. Bell, a man who treated the Aboriginal community with respect. The goods, fashioned mainly in winter, included moccasins, gloves, mittens and jackets from moose and dear hide. The Bernards also earned money by repairing canoes and by making and selling axe and canthoook handles and canoe paddles of ash and maple.8

In 1890, before his brother's death, twenty-five-year-old Matt married seventeen-year-old Mary Nash Ockiping of the Golden Lake Reserve, south of Mattawa. She was the daughter of Amable and Angelique Ockiping (later Benoit) who together with Matt's parents had arranged the match. Matt's brother John married Mary's sister at the same time, after his previous fiancée backed out at the last minute.9

Sometime following his marriage Matt found employment as a carpenter to support his growing family. After their first three children died young, Mary gave birth to a healthy girl, Johanna, in 1901, and a healthy boy, Eddie, two years later. Their third healthy child was born in 1906 and was named Gertrude Philomen Bernard, but "Pony" or Gertie were the names they called her. A few years later another son, Gabriel, was born.

Gertie's memories of her mother were naturally sparse. She could recall some good times when her mother danced and romped with her and her siblings while Matt played the fiddle. Gertie also remembered her mother making pinchberry jelly, an ordinary domestic task. For some reason, though, when her mother went to strain the pulp through a cloth, the sight of the juice running down her arm threw Gertie into a panic because she thought the juice was blood. It might have been her sensitivity to her mother's deteriorating health that caused such a reaction, because it was not long after that her mother's condition took a turn for the worse; making her remaining time comfortable became a family concern. On one occasion, when Matt was carrying his wife out to a cot under the pines, he accidentally banged his wife's arm loudly on the doorjamb. The action upset him badly, and Gertie, witnessing her father's distress, became upset too.10 It was an anguish and pain she continued to share. On the day of her mother's death, Gertie recalled watching as her father, grandmothers, aunts and uncles knelt beside her mother's bed and prayed. When her father finished his prayers, he rose, walked out of the house and down to the lake to be alone. The death of her mother hit him hard.

The loss of Mary Bernard was a severe blow to the family in many ways. Matt's trade as a carpenter meant he was often away for days or weeks at a time so he could not be there to look after his young children. In a few short months the children suffered further upheaval and separation when Matt placed his children amongst various members of his family. His sister Kate Salter and her engineer husband took nine-year-old Johanna and seven-year-old Eddie to their home in North Bay. Angelique Benoit, Matt's mother-in-law, a fun loving, merry woman who eventually outlived four husbands, carried the young baby, Gabriel, back to her home in the bush at Golden Lake Reserve. But Matt kept Gertie close to home, in the care of his mother, "Big Grandma."11

Seventy-eight-year-old "Big Grandma" combined a strong Catholic faith with a fierce pride in her heritage and the skills and crafts of her people. She was a respected member of the community, expert in healing and herb lore and proficient in music, showing her talents in church where she sang and played the organ. Gertie lived with her in a wood frame house by a stand of white pine that overlooked Boom Lake. Around the house was a large vegetable garden, as well as a flower garden of tiger lilies, lilacs and roses, and various fruit trees that included an orange tree her grandmother pampered. Though her grandmother had help with the housework, she looked after Gertie and taught her to sew, embroider, crochet, knit and make soap. Her grandmother also passed on her knowledge of herbs and traditional First Nations crafts.

Gertie, a sensitive but strong-willed child, adored her grandmother, despite the fact she was a strict and somewhat stern woman. Big Grandma shaped Gertie's behaviour with a firm guiding hand that blended her Aboriginal child-rearing practices with her strong Catholic beliefs. Instead of issuing reprimands, Big Grandma told Gertie stories, instructed her firmly or created situations that would teach Gertie the correct behaviour. To curb Gertie's prying hands inside her mother's handbag, before her mother had died, Big Grandma's advice was to place a bee inside the bag. The next time Gertie went exploring she found the bee and it found her. Her mother's handbag no longer seemed interesting after that. Later, when Gertie was still wetting her bed, her grandmother instructed her to dig a hole, wrap a blanket around herself and stand over the hole for ten minutes. Gertie never wet the bed again.12

By the time Gertie was eleven her grandmother was too frail to care for her, so one of the aunts moved in the house, along with her family. The change caused a big disruption to the close and loving twosome and Gertie did not react well to the second major upheaval in her life. She was now expected to work around the house and tend to her aunt's children. They kept her home from school on wash days, scrub days and shopping days and for any other chore that required her help. As a result she started to fall behind in school. Disheartened, feeling lonely and rejected, Gertie rebelled. On a regular basis she crawled out of her bedroom window and escaped for a day in the woods. There she climbed trees, picked berries, swam in the lake and fished. She discovered an old shanty built by the timbermen and created in it her own little refuge. She furnished it with blankets, dishes, cook pots, as well as her fishing tackle and other items to pass the time. The shanty provided refuge for her on rainy days where she might cook and eat the fish that she caught, or one of her aunt's hens that she shot. Vegetables picked from any available garden complemented the meal. Here she could relax; there were no eyes judging her behaviour. She could be herself. Though she relished this freedom she could not escape her loneliness and isolation and the feeling she was a misfit.

Gertie & Lizzie Decaire, courtesy of Louise Montreuil

When Gertie did attend school, she found little to like. The school was attached to the Catholic parish church and under the iron hand of the Grey Nuns and a few lay teachers. Though French-Canadian and Irish-Canadian Catholic children attended the school with the Aboriginal and mixed-race children, they clearly thought the Aboriginal and mixed-race were of the lowest social class, a view they reinforced through bullying and other more subtle actions.13

The existence of these social divisions was mirrored in other aspects of the town. Physically the town was divided in two by the Mattawa River. On the river's south bank, in a section named Mattawan, the Euro-Canadians had their homes and businesses. On the north bank, the site of an original Algonquin settlement, Aboriginal and mixed-race families lived in an area called by the derogatory name of Squaw Valley (the term "squaw" was long understood to mean an Aboriginal woman with loose morals).14 The Catholic Church, school and hospital and some Euro-Canadian families were also located on the north bank, but in a separate area, called Rosemount. Beside the physical divide of races there was the more subtle economic and religious stratification among the Euro-Canadian community that typically found the English and Scottish Presbyterians, Anglicans and Methodists owning the businesses and the Irish and French Roman Catholics acting as labourers. The town was also heavily influenced by the Catholic Church, the faith of the majority of its members. The Church, together with the Euro-Canadian community, exerted pressure on the Squaw Valley inhabitants to conform to Euro-Canadian standards of behaviour and dress. Besides dressing in sober European clothing, the Aboriginals and mixed-race were expected to attend mass, make confession, baptize their children, marry in church and tithe money if they wanted to maintain their good reputations, burdened as they were by the name of their community, with its obvious negative overtones. Their jobs and harmonious existence in Mattawa depended on keeping spotless reputations.

Though First Nations in Ontario had few reserves and usually lived in communities it was unusual for them to be part of a town and the Euro-Canadian inhabitants of Mattawa approached the situation with caution. The Catholic Euro-Canadians mixed with the native population at the Catholic school and other church activities. During mass the priest customarily read out the contributions each family in the parish had made to the church, usually pausing dramatically before the especially low sums given by the Squaw Valley residents who had less to give. The children naturally picked up on these social distinctions and though Euro-Canadian and First Nations children might play together, the differences in race and economic status were usually very clear.

In such an atmosphere and without the support of her grandmother Gertie continued to avoid school. When she did attend she had fallen so far behind she found the work difficult. Occasionally she would deal with the situation in her own manner, such as paying a girl thirty-five cents to do her arithmetic homework.15 For the most part though she chose not to go to school. With her love of the outdoors, she felt very different to other girls at school and even the female members of her family, a situation that only increased her loneliness and isolation. Regular truancy from school could not go unnoticed forever, though. Eventually her day of reckoning arrived and her uncle, a very tall man, confronted her angrily outside the house. Gertie knew the game was up and was so fearful of the punishment to come she impulsively grabbed a nearby axe and, screaming wildly, flung it at him.16

When Gertie's father, who was only home every second week, came to hear of the situation, he decided to make changes. He collected seventeen-year-old Johanna and fifteen-year-old Eddie from North Bay and brought them and Gertie to live in a small little house nearby. Gabriel, now a boy of seven, remained with his grandmother at Golden Lake Reserve. For the sake of the three children under his care Matt managed to secure a contract building a house for a friend so that he could be home every night.

Gertie had only seen Johanna and Eddie on yearly visits to her aunt in North Bay so they were now practically strangers to her. Johanna had grown into a stylish but devout young lady and she now tried to guide Gertie towards more sedate and feminine behaviour, a strategy that only increased Gertie's feelings of being a misfit. Young women in Mattawa generally attended things like church picnics, raffles, and religious meetings as well as films at the Catholic school's large theatre. Or they would have made a trip to the roller rink or to the fairground for the occasional visit of the circus.17 These were very tame pursuits compared to the kind that attracted Gertie.

Prompted by these feelings of difference and isolation, and conscious of her gaps in learning, Gertie continued to avoid school. She visited her old haunts, played sports, swam and camped with the boys. The boys of Squaw Valley engaged in a variety of activities including "bush league" softball and hockey, which was particularly rough and played without protective padding. The boys and young unmarried men in Mattawa also indulged in things like shooting at passing trains from the nearby hill, frightening people at Halloween by rolling spools along their windows or laying ropes across their threshold door and ringing the bell. The need for the boys to join the men in hunting for the family's food supply also meant they had an early introduction to firearms and spent hours at target practice with their small calibre, low powered rifles usually used for small game. In addition to improving their shooting skills, the hours the boys and young men spent at these sessions were also obvious opportunities for them to compete and prove themselves and provided chances to socialize.18

Matt & Eddie, courtesy of Katherine Swartile

Gertie's brother Eddie was among these young boys who learned to hunt and guide from relatives and he often accompanied his uncles or his father on trips to the bush. Gertie joined them on a few occasions when they went berry picking and camping overnight, enjoying the time in the wilderness. Gertie also loved the water and quickly learned to be a strong swimmer. She often swam across to Squaw Valley to visit her cousins and play cards. She would strip out of her clothes and pile them on a board that she pushed along in front of her while she swam. One day, when her father discovered her little escapade, he went after her in a canoe and picked her up out of the water by the scruff her neck while he yelled at her in Mohawk.19 It was scandalous behaviour for any girl at the time, and most especially Aboriginal girls of the community who could so easily acquire a bad reputation for the slightest infraction.20

In the summer of 1925, when Gertie was nineteen and her sister was long married with children, she went to work at Camp Wabikon. Wabikon, located about eighty-six kilometres northwest of Mattawa, was one of the Lake Temagami island resorts opened in the decade after the railway provided access for wealthy city people in search of wilderness vacations. The camp was opened in 1917 for professional people to enjoy various activities that included canoeing, swimming, riding, guided wilderness treks and, on some evenings, dances on Bear Island. Filled with tall pine trees, Camp Wabikon housed about two hundred guests in platform tents scattered along little paths that wound their way from the main lodge.21

Wabikon's social secretary, Isobel "Billie" LeDuc, usually staffed the resort with college girls, but when Gertie appeared Billie found in Gertie an energy and spirit akin to her own. Billie decided to hire Gertie as a waitress and signed as her guardian because Gertie was under twenty-one.22 With Billie's support Gertie had few waitress duties and was able to enthusiastically engage in many of the leisure activities. Gertie blossomed under Billie's support and understanding. At nineteen she was now a beautiful and energetic young woman with bobbed hair who dressed in riding breeches and shirt, though if the occasion demanded she would apply makeup—the very picture of a modern woman.

Such energy and beauty caught the eye of two brothers from New York. One of the brothers, a physician named Jim Howard, was so taken by her quick mind and enthusiasm he was inspired to offer to pay for the fees at any school, college or convent of her choice. Gertie recognized the offer as a significant opportunity and she corresponded with her father about it. He wrote back in favour of the idea and between them they decided she would attend Loretto Abbey, a Roman Catholic boarding school in Toronto. Dr. Howard initiated the arrangements, and while the application proceeded Anahareo remained at Wabikon to finish out the summer. Sometime before the summer's end, Gertie sat one day on the Wabikon lodge veranda, and watched a tall thirty-six-year-old stranger dressed in bush clothes step out from a canoe and onto the shore. His name was Archie Belaney. Later they would call him Grey Owl.

Chapter Two

Meeting her Jesse James

Archie Belaney had come to the wilderness from Hastings, England, but grew up completely enthralled by the North American wilderness and the Aboriginals who inhabited it. He had absorbed every bit of information he could find about plants, animals and life in the bush from James Fennimore Cooper, Henry Wadsworth Longfellow and the nature essays and stories of Ernest Thomas Seton. He practiced wood lore in his garden and the areas surrounding his home, keeping his own menagerie of lizards, frogs, hedgehogs and beetles that he studied closely. Archie's interests and obsession with nature had tended to isolate him from his peers and often put him at odds with the maiden aunts who raised him.1

In 1906, barely eighteen, Archie finally got his wish to go to Canada and go into the bush. After spending a short time in Toronto working in a store, he managed to earn enough money to travel north. His destination was not the silver fields of the Ontario town of Cobalt, on the western shore of Lake Timiskaming, where all and sundry were heading, but to the wilderness, on the Quebec side of the lake. There he became acquainted with veteran woodsman Bill Guppy, who took on the earnest young man. Archie spent the winter with Bill and his family and learned a range of bush skills necessary for trapping and life in the wilderness. When summer arrived Guppy taught Archie how to portage and paddle a canoe through a chain of lakes to Lake Temagami. Despite Archie's growing skills there were few guiding jobs available in Temagami, so Archie took a job as a chore boy at the inn.

Archie returned to the inn the next summer in 1908 and resumed his old job. This time he met Angele Egwuna, an Anishnabe from Bear Island who was working as a kitchen helper. Though she spoke little English and Archie knew only a little Ojibwa, they managed to communicate and form a relationship. She took him to meet her family on Bear Island, and Archie spent many hours with them, furiously taking notes and learning their language, history, culture and bush skills. As Angele's acknowledged boyfriend, Archie met many members of her extended family, one of whom named him *ko-hom-see*, "the young owl who sits and takes everything in."

Archie continued his education in Anishnabe life when he joined Angele's family up in Austin Bay in the winter of 1909-10 and trapped on his own above their family hunting grounds. The following two summers he worked as a guide at an American boys' camp, northwest of Bear Island, teaching Indian wood lore to wealthy preparatory boys, a contrast to his own real-life experience with Angele's people. At the end of the summer of 1910 Archie married Angele and within the year she gave birth to a daughter, Agnes. Domestic life at close quarters, even within the Anishnabe culture, proved too much for the young adventurous Archie. Within a few months of Agnes' birth, Archie departed for new wilderness adventure. Angele, who understood Archie's temperament, did not try to hold him back. In the months and years to come Archie would occasionally send Angele money, but it was her skill in hunting and trapping that largely supported her and her daughter.

Archie found his next home in Biscotasing. A town on the Biscotasi Lake, it boasted industry supported by the forestry, the sawmill, the railway and the Hudson Bay Company, all of which drew both

Aboriginals and Euro-Canadians. In Biscotasing, or "Bisco," as it was called, Archie sported long hair, skin burnt brown from summers out in the open and moccasins. Many took him for an Aboriginal, or at least of mixed-race, an idea that he did nothing to discourage and sometimes even confirmed.

Archie spent the next three summers as a fire ranger in the Mississaga Forest Reserve, among some fifty rangers who worked in pairs, patrolling their areas by canoe or on foot while they looked for signs of fire and kept out trespassing prospectors and hunters. Around the campfire Archie became known as a great story teller and an all-round entertainer. In the winters he trapped out of Bisco, staying at a local boarding house. There he fell in with a boisterous hard drinking crowd who often played pranks in the community that sometimes alienated the more conventional members of the town.

In 1913 Archie met a young woman, Marie Girard, who was working in the boarding house, and he asked her to join him on his trap line that winter. With summer's arrival he resumed fire ranging, appointed this time to the Goulais River region. Archie returned from the bush to Bisco to find that war had been declared in Europe and he went on a drunken tear. Under threat of arrest, Archie went into hiding in the bush, accompanied by the young waitress Marie Girard. The pair emerged in November and a short while later Archie enlisted in the army and was sent overseas, probably before he knew that Marie was pregnant with his child. Marie died shortly after giving birth to a son, John Girard, later known as Johnny Jero.

War did not deal kindly with Archie, neither physically nor emotionally. Trained as a sharp shooter, he was exposed to mustard gas that weakened his lungs and he suffered a crippling wound to his foot. Coincidently he was sent to a hospital in Hastings to recuperate. He contacted his family and they enfolded him once again in the middle-class existence of his childhood. His aunts encouraged his friendship with a childhood acquaintance, Ivy Holmes, a stunningly attractive former dancer who had toured Eastern Europe. Weakened by his injuries and emotionally damaged, Archie found Ivy's attentions soothing to his soul and under the keen and approving eyes of both families, Archie married Ivy, though he knew he was still legally married to Angele.

Recovered enough to be able to limp around, Archie's thoughts turned once again to Canada and his life in the wilderness. He could not settle into the middle-class existence of the sleepy English town, governed as it was by restrictive Edwardian codes of behaviour. Ever the storyteller, Archie entertained Ivy with tales of the Canadian wilderness and mesmerized her with descriptions of its beauty. Much to his aunts' disapproval, three months after their wedding Archie set off for Canada with the promise he would soon send for his wife. A short while after his arrival, Archie wrote to Ivy and explained about his marriage to Angele. Ivy promptly filed for divorce.

The person who returned to Bisco in 1918 was markedly different from the exuberant, inquisitive storyteller who had regaled men with his tales, charmed children with his antics and inspired the name *ko-hom-see*. Archie's lungs were too weak for the long portages required by his previous work and his foot, missing one toe and parts of two others as well as the ball, still swelled on occasion to huge proportions. Prevented from most activity the first year of his return, Archie became morose, brawling often, eating little and drinking heavily of anything available, including his own moonshine in a province that was now declared dry.

By 1919 Archie had recovered enough from his physical injuries to work on a survey party and by the following year he was able to fill the position of deputy under the chief fire ranger. Though his foot still gave him a bit of trouble he could paddle a canoe with skill and some speed again. The men who worked with him found him fair and hard working.

Archie spent the next few years living with an Anishnabe family, the Espaniels. He joined them at their trapping grounds where he completely immersed himself in learning the "Indian way" of hunting. They taught him to keep track of the number of beaver lodges, the age of the inhabitants, and when removing any from the lodge to leave a pair in each lodge. In April 1925, under another threat of arrest for drunk and disorderly behaviour at Bisco Railway Station, Archie boarded the train and went over to Lake Temagami. He stayed a while with Angele and her family, then paddled over to Camp Wabikon in his canoe and took a job as a guide.

A handsome mysterious man, dressed in a buckskin vest, a Hudson Bay belt and moccasins, Archie appeared to Gertie like the dashing daredevil heroes she idolized—Jesse James and Robin Hood. Compared to the bland wealthy vacationers, Archie reeked of adventure and excitement. Gertie found him so fascinating she wasted no time in discovering his name and that he was a guide. Archie was not indifferent to Gertie either. He spotted the young Indian woman immediately and thought she was beautiful, talented and lively.[2] He set about getting to know her, trying to attract her attention by teasing and joking, or disarming her with quirky requests like asking her to treat him to an ice cream, or provide him with "eyeless" potatoes when she was working in the kitchen. Such an approach often annoyed and intrigued Gertie, but she could not fail to notice him. One evening when Gertie and a group from Wabikon went to a night's entertainment on Bear Island, she decided to do her own bit of teasing and danced with one of the resort guests, a sophisticated young man from New York. Gertie smiled and flirted with him while Archie observed them angrily from his spot as the orchestra drummer, until he threw down the sticks and left. This stormy interaction would later set the pattern of their future relationship.

Gertie and aunt at Camp Wabikon, courtesy of Katherine Swartile

Gertie's lively sparring with Archie was cut short when her niece died and she was called home to attend the funeral. Archie was away on a guiding trip so Gertie was unable to say goodbye to him. Back in Mattawa again Gertie saw that her father was taking her niece's death hard so she decided to remain home, but she found she missed the excitement and adventure of Wabikon. The stimulating resort activities and her encounters with Archie had only made Gertie wish for more, while at home the prospect of going away to the convent school loomed large. It held little possibility of adventure, much as she might try and convince herself otherwise. In addition, the gaps in her education and her previous experience of school no doubt added to her anxiety about going away to Loretto Abbey. She would have to make her way in a completely new school and live there with people who, if the past was anything to judge, would surely disapprove of her. Under such disapproval Gertie's sensitivity and shyness would only override her confidence and hamper her chance of success.

Billie LeDuc, Gertie's friend and mentor from Camp Wabikon,

wrote to Gertie to see how she fared. The letter came "in the nick of time," according to Gertie, whose reply to Billie revealed all her restlessness and confusion over the prospect of going away to school. She wrote that "her mind was much wilder than ever" and that following a visit from someone with a motorcycle she was tempted to "hit the trail." The dilemma of pursuing her education or hitting the trail was one that put her head "between the devil and the deep blue sea." She knew "it would surely make papa jump with joy to see me go to school [rather than] turn out loose and wild like my dreams so mostly for his sake I shall go...." She closed the brief letter by adding that Billie should give her love to the gang:

> I feel awfully lonesome for you too and I was just simply wild, did not give a dam for anything yet day by day I try to be myself more careless I get[,] if only you knew how terrible I was going to be when I left here you wouldn't look at me[,] of course it is just like me eh. Well here is hoping all things will be happy and on the right road.3

Adding to her confusion and troubled mind were thoughts of the romantic Jesse James figure, Archie Belaney. Unable to resist any longer Gertie decided to write to him in September and invite him for a visit. Ordinarily it took three days for a letter to reach Camp Wabikon and another three for the reply, so Gertie was surprised when Archie arrived on her doorstep clad in a bulky oilskin the day after she mailed the letter.

Gertie was not the only one who missed the fun and teasing of their relationship. Sometime after Gertie left Wabikon Archie approached Billie LeDuc and asked her about Gertie. Billie told him about Dr. Howard's proposed plan. She could see Archie was really smitten. Archie certainly was, but he told her he did not want to stand in the way of the plan, though he feared he would lose her because of it.4

His fear was strong enough to make him seek out Gertie at her home, only to be overcome with a bout of shyness and uncertainty when he arrived at her door. He regained his confidence quickly enough after he discovered she had written to him, so that when she questioned him about wearing an oilskin on a perfectly dry day, he was able to flip back dramatically one side of it to reveal the gun at his hip. With a certain amount of swagger and the desire to impress, he explained that he was on the run from the law after a knife-throwing incident. The statement succeeded in its goal— Gertie was thrilled to hear something so romantically dangerous.

Gertie invited him in and they wasted no time in reacquainting themselves while Johanna looked on, decidedly unimpressed by Gertie's visitor. She disliked his long hair and thought it strange that he wore an oilskin in fine weather. He appeared to be rough around the edges to say the least in both his manner and his attire. Eventually their father arrived home and during the introductions Archie explained he was half-Apache. Once the two men discovered they were both experienced bushmen they settled down to exchange stories. Though Matt appeared to like Archie, he called him *Windigo*, the Algonquin supernatural cannibalistic figure that lived in the forest and preyed on the unwary, starving and lost. Matt used the term because he thought Archie would be dangerous if he was rubbed the wrong way, an opinion that might have been helped by the gun and Archie's tale that he was on the run from the law.5 Nevertheless, the pair talked companionably throughout the night. Come morning, despite Gertie's efforts to get him to stay, Archie insisted he had to leave. He needed to get back to his preparations for his winter livelihood.

Archie made up for his abrupt departure over the next two weeks and sent letters to Gertie everyday filled with colourful descriptions and tales of the wilderness. With the deft use of his pen he wooed Gertie, pouring out his passion and love for the wilderness in these stories and descriptions that he instinctively knew would capture her interest. The letters were so thrilling and absorbing that even Gertie's brother Eddie would often sit down and read them along with her. But after the two weeks the letters stopped abruptly.

During the next five months there was no further word. Gertie became restless and anxious so that when she received a letter from Loretto Abbey in February stating she would have to wait until the beginning of the next term to enrol, she broke down and wrote to Archie to explain the delay in her plans. Archie's response was to send a round-trip ticket and a telegram asking her to come visit his new trapping grounds in northern Quebec.

Gertie consulted her brother and sister about her answer and they each gave her a different opinion. Eddie, who had found Archie's letters exciting, thought it was a great idea, but Johanna was firmly against it. It was not proper for an unchaperoned single woman, especially a First Nations woman of good reputation, to travel to the bush with a man. Their father, who was working some distance away building a schoolhouse, could not be consulted immediately, so Gertie walked the twenty-two-kilometre round-trip to ask his permission to accept Archie's invitation. It was the longest trek Gertie had ever made. Under the weight of her persuasive powers, her father gave his consent on the condition that the visit last only one week.

After a thirty-eight-hour train journey, Gertie arrived at Forsythe, Quebec, the town nearest to Archie's new trapline. Archie and his friends from Biscotasing had moved there from Ontario because the Ontario government had just banned all non-natives from trapping in the province. Archie and his friends had selected the forested area near Forsythe because they heard it was teaming with pine marten. But they, along with other Euro-Canadian trappers, were invading the trapping grounds of the Grand Lac Victoria and the Lac Simon Anishnabe bands. These lands had suddenly become accessible when the railway was built ten years earlier. Neither Anishnabe band had signed a treaty with the government, and like the Anishnabe at Bear Island, they had no official reserve. Few in number and without the protections of a reserve or a treaty, the bands could do nothing to prevent trappers from stripping the land of all fur bearing animals, so they began to do the same. By the time Archie and his friends arrived there was little game to trap, as they were to eventually discover.6

Gertie spent the first few days after her arrival in Forsythe socializing with the town's four families who were grateful for the chance to break the isolation and monotony of the winter days. After those few days had passed Gertie realized she had to think of her return. She had not understood when she promised to spend only a week that it would take a day and a half to make the journey and the same for the return. When Gertie told Archie she had to leave he protested that he wanted to take her to his trap lines in the bush. Though Gertie was concerned her father would worry too much, she found the idea of spending time in the bush irresistible. At Archie's suggestion she wrote to her father to explain the situation and assure him that she would only stay another week.

In the meantime Archie arranged for a dogsled to take Gertie into the bush the following day. When the dogsled failed to appear, Archie decided they would walk instead, keeping the pace easy. He assumed after discussing bush experiences with her father that Gertie was a seasoned wilderness traveler too, when in fact Gertie's exposure to the bush was limited to overnight trips with her father to collect berries or maple syrup. Archie discovered his mistake soon enough.

Gertie later described her experiences during the next few days with self-effacing humour that revealed the arrogance only a nineteen-year-old can possess. An excited and decidedly ignorant Gertie, dressed in long johns, woolly socks, buckskin mitts, moccasins and snowshoes, set off behind Archie, who toted a heavily laden toboggan. Five hours into the seventy-kilometre trek Gertie was completely exhausted and her Jesse James image had long since galloped off in her mind, to be replaced by a more sinister impression of a cruel torturer. When they stopped for a lunch break on a fallen tree, he gave her a frozen bannock and instructed her to put snow on it to keep the sugar intact. She was not impressed with the meagre fare and the manner of eating it. As they sat there eating, the moon rose and signalled it was time to be off again, a signal that came all too soon for Gertie. They ploughed on towards their goal, stopping only briefly now and again to eat a handful of dried apples.

Finally the pair arrived at the campsite, though the only evidence of its presence was the metre length of tent protruding from the ground and the narrow stove pipe on one side. Archie cleared a path for them to the lodge that revealed the rest of the structure crouched below the snow line. It was unimpressive. Once inside the small dwelling Gertie found little more to recommend it. A hoarfrost covered the canvas ceiling, the log walls and the spruce pole floor. Candles provided the only source of light because there were no windows. The furnishings were limited to a spruce pole table and bunk. Gertie headed for the bunk, collapsed onto it and fell into a sound sleep.

Chapter Three

Journey Into the Bush

It was only the next day, after a thorough rest, that Gertie discovered a second dwelling, a little log cabin specially constructed for her and given the name "Pony Hall." With the help of his Biscotasing friends Archie had fashioned the cabin some months before in the hopes that she might visit.1 It contained glass windows and was furnished with a small oil cloth covered table, block wood chairs, a moose hide rug and a bed of balsam boughs covered with a Hudson Bay blanket. Gertie was delighted.

Her joy was short-lived. After showing her around the cabin Archie announced he had to leave to check his traps. It was not from lack of manners that he went off, but that he knew a sprung trap was not a working trap and could bring in no profit. He had already lost much valuable trapping time meeting her in Forsythe and prior to that he had lain ill and nearly dead for weeks when he had mistakenly sprinkled strychnine instead of sugar on his frozen bannock while out running his trap lines. After such a poor start to a season well underway, Archie had a lot of time to make up.

Archie neglected to explain this situation to Gertie. She only knew she was terrified of being left alone in the bush. Proud and stubborn, she kept quiet about her fears and accused him instead of poor manners. Archie refused to take the comments seriously and kept Gertie busy stowing away sacks of flour, sugar, lard and other supplies in her cabin. When she had finished those chores, she decided to go to see Archie at the lodge, but neglected to put on her snowshoes. With her first couple of steps, she sank hip-deep into the snow. Though Archie thought her appearance hilarious, he told her it was a good lesson. Snowshoes must always be worn outside the cabin.

In the next few hours Archie taught her other skills she would need in the time he was away. He showed her how to look after the water hole, a vital task for all that it seemed simple. Losing a water hole took no effort at all, but creating one was backbreaking. First an area big enough to work in had to be cleared before digging through nearly two metres of snow and then a metre and a half of ice. Then the actual hole would be carved first with an axe and then, when the axe became too short, a two-and-a-half-metre long chisel with a four-centimetre blade. After all that effort it would be foolish to lose the hole by carelessly neglecting to cover it with layers of snow and marking its location with the ice chisel.

After issuing these important life saving instructions Archie could not resist the opportunity to tease her by offering to show her the "bear den." Anxiously she followed him into the woods to a little lean-to building covered in snow. At the cave-like entrance he lit a match and peered inside. After a few moments he told her he guessed the bear was out, reached inside and withdrew a toilet roll and told her that he used it for bear bait. It was only then she realized she was standing outside the entrance to the outhouse.

Later, Archie resumed teaching her other important safeguards. With her limited experience of the bush, he was adamant that she remain in the cabin unless going for wood, water or to use the outhouse. At those times she must, without fail, wear her snowshoes. Under no circumstances was she to use his skinning knives or guns. There was plenty of firewood cut, so she had no need to use the axe. He also told her she must be careful of fires in the cabin, especially when using the lamp, because a trapper was lost if his cabin burnt down. As a final very pointed reinforcement of the dangers of bush living and the importance of following his instructions, Archie drew a map for her to find her way out of the bush in case something happened to him.

After Archie left early the next morning Gertie soon forgot her fears and concerns in the light of the crisp clear air that was so appealing she spent the day playing in the snow after her chores were done. Gertie was no better at obeying Archie's instructions on the second day when she lost herself in the woods and managed to find her way home only as darkness fell. Not to be outdone, on the third day she decided to prove to Archie she could be of some use and spent all day felling, chopping and splitting dead trees. Besides the outdoor pursuits she also occupied herself in various activities in the cabin. She made curtains out of her pyjamas, combed the moose hide rug and when she exhausted all other ideas, she decided to try her hand at making bannocks, an effort that ended with smoke pouring out of the cabin door.

Gertie managed to make it through to Archie's return on the evening of the third day without any further mishaps. She welcomed Archie back eagerly in part because she enjoyed his company, but also because she had discovered the solitary boredom of living alone in a cabin. With all the great energy and enthusiasm of her youth, she could not stomach the inaction required by the small confines of the cabin with only herself for company, a situation that could only remind her of the isolation of her school years.

That night, flushed with the joy of each other's company, Archie and Gertie made up for their time apart and talked of their past experiences. Archie weaved a tale of his Apache origins, the maiden aunts and his many trips into the bush. Though he told her well-embroidered tales, Archie also revealed to Gertie some deep truths of his life and explained about his past relationships with Angele and Ivy Holmes. If it was a bid to make her jealous, he was clearly disappointed. Gertie found these disclosures further proof that he was an intriguing and dangerous person who was full of adventures of the wilderness life. It was an irresistible recipe.

At the time of Archie's return Gertie's week was nearly over. Before he could take her back to Forsythe Archie explained he still had some traps to check. When Gertie asked if she could go with him, he refused. The trip would be too rough and he would have to sleep outside. Undaunted by what appeared to be negligible reasons Gertie launched a campaign of persuasion until Archie finally agreed she could go.

The next morning, before light, they headed out to the trap lines in a driving snowstorm, the wind whipping in all directions, stinging their faces and eyes. The wind dropped once they went deeper into the bush and the thick trees blocked out the storm's fierceness. They came across a large furrow in the snow made by a moose. Archie jumped into the furrow to examine the print in order to identify the animal's sex and direction. After turning the toboggan on its side to prevent the bottom from icing over Archie retrieved his rifle and went after the moose. Eventually he killed it and skinned it. Slitting the belly in a cloud of steam, he removed the innards, cut up the meat, then wrapped it all in hide and packed it in snow. Gertie watched the whole procedure in all its gory detail with growing horror. There were sides to bush survival that were not so appealing to her.

With the meat stored they resumed their journey to Archie's traplines. At the first stop Archie found the trap had sprung early and caught a pine marten, an animal with the same red hue as a fox, but much smaller in size. The pine marten was still alive, but it was pulling on its caught leg, dragging the trap as far as the chain that fastened it to the ground would allow. Archie quickly assessed the situation and dispatched the marten with a blow across the head from the blunt side of his axe. Appalled, Gertie watched as the animal struggled in its death throes. Once it was dead Archie packed the animal away and moved on to check the rest of his lines. Gertie followed in numb silence as he picked up another marten and two lynx that, much to her relief, were dead when they arrived.

Gertie was glad when Archie finally decided they would make camp for the night. It was a joy short-lived when he explained they could not erect their camp on the surface because the fire would soon melt its way out and leave them in the cold, submerged in a cloud of smoke. They would have to make a dugout. So Archie shovelled and Gertie packed the snow to form walls, the two of them creating a pit of cleared ground big enough for two beds, the grub box and a large fire. Over the hole Archie erected a tarpaulin for a roof, supported by poles, and laid a carpet of boughs on the floor. Despite its rough nature Gertie was surprised to find the dugout cozy and comfortable.

The next day they returned to their main camp so Gertie could prepare for her journey home. She was distinctly unhappy about leaving now, her keen sense of adventure awakened fully, despite the distress of the day before. The magic of the wilderness had taken hold of her, challenged her and excited her restless spirit.

The following morning Gertie announced she would stay another week. She was too ignorant of bush life to understand the impact such a decision might have on Archie's stores or his livelihood. He agreed to her extended visit, but continued to check his traps every day while he left Gertie to amuse herself in the cabin. Bored to tears in the confined space, by the end of the week going back home suddenly seemed more attractive. Archie recognized her desire to leave but he persuaded her to stay a few more days. After that she said she had to go. Holy week had arrived and she needed to make her confession for Easter.

As promised, after the few extra days, Archie took her to Forsythe. By this time it was a full two months since she had left home, and there in Forsythe, she found letters from her father waiting for her. The letters revealed her father's growing concern over her prolonged absence. In the final letter, however, her father was reproachful and warned that her reputation was in shreds. But ultimately he would not abandon her; she always had a home with him if she did not marry Archie. As Gertie wrote later in her autobiography she was surprised and upset by her father's words. In her mind she had done nothing wrong except stay longer than she had originally promised. She still did not accept or believe that her behaviour was improper, though by the Euro-Canadian standards of the time, her actions were immoral and would be strongly condemned.

Many Euro-Canadians, especially those with a recent frontier past, viewed Aboriginal women who did not conform in a harsh light and fostered various negative stereotypes: the squaw who hung around town enticing men into immoral acts, with the drunken squaw, and the backwards blanket-clad squaw who lived at the fringes of the community hindering the progress of civic minded citizens.2 These were the images that underpinned many Euro-Canadians expectations of and beliefs about Aboriginal women. Any Aboriginal woman or girl who did not follow the Euro-Canadian codes of behaviour and dress to the letter was in danger of strong condemnation.

Deeply upset, Gertie showed Archie the letters and Archie told her in frank words she must either return home immediately or marry him. Piqued at such unromantic behaviour, she argued with him as they both boarded a train for Senneterre, the nearest place Gertie could make her confession to a priest. Far from easing her mind, the priest berated her severely when he discovered she was the woman rumoured to have spent two months in the bush with a man. Gertie stormed out of the confession box and decided to go back to the bush with Archie.

The pair returned to the camp and Archie resumed his trapping while Gertie remained at the cabin bored and stifled by inaction and the solitude. Archie had taken particular care in selecting the campsite for its beautiful surroundings, as he did with all his campsites, but Gertie was in no mood to appreciate it. He tried to keep her occupied with hidden notes and little games; he read books to her and expended as much charm as he could muster to enable her to settle. Archie also continued to hunt and check his traps in the hope he might collect enough furs to clear his debts. Gertie waited for his return, still confined to the cabin. She tried to persuade Archie to let her go with him, an effort that often ended in heated arguments and led nowhere. He remained firm. Gertie was clearly not experienced enough to be anything but a hazard to him while he practiced his livelihood. By the end of six weeks, they were hardly speaking. Despite this tension it was at this point Gertie realized how much she cared about Archie and missed his company when he was gone.

The spring hunt ended by the beginning of June, as did their stores, a situation that frightened Gertie. But Archie was adept at extracting food from the wilderness, and as they made their way out of the bush to Forsythe, he kept them fed on fish and the little bit of tea they had left. In Forsythe Gertie found another letter from her father. Though this one contained no recriminations; it was filled with a coolness that upset her. Still ruminating on the letter, she boarded a train with Archie for Doucet, the place he had bought his supplies on credit the previous fall and where he had to take his pelts to clear his debt. In Doucet other trappers joined them, all dirty and reeking of the bush, ready to celebrate the season's finish. They arranged for a dance and asked Archie to play the piano. As the opening chords struck for the first dance of the evening everyone moved onto the floor. All except Gertie. No one asked her to dance. Though the women were welcoming to their newly returned husbands and sweethearts, they were distinctly cool towards Gertie and under the glaring eyes of their women the men dared not ask Gertie to dance.

If Gertie had any doubts over the truth about her damaged reputation the reaction of the priest and the people of Doucet dispelled them. Though she felt their reaction unfair it still upset her badly. She felt unjustly judged and rejected. Shortly after being shunned by the women at the dance, she took whiskey to her room and drank the whole bottle in a dogged determination that her first experience with alcohol would produce the promised oblivion. While she drank she managed to get hold of Archie's gun and brandish it around like a gunfighter. Archie tried to reason with her and eventually was able to calm her and persuade her to give him the gun. Such behaviour no doubt did little to help her image with the people of Doucet and did nothing for her bruised feelings.

Gertie's distress over the priest's and town's rejection and her father's letters was compounded by the approach of her birthday, a day usually spent at home with her doting father. Up to this point Matt had given her love and support no matter what scrapes or tangles she got into, the only person beside her grandmother to do so. Now, among strangers, and in possession of her father's harsh letters, Gertie's anguish made her act impulsively. It was a reaction that Archie seemed to understand. In the days that followed the dance he tried to reassure her of her worth with words and actions. He told her he loved her, flattered her and showered her with attention. Such a demonstration of love and support enabled Gertie to decide to abandon her faith, her education plans and her life back in Mattawa. She rejected the Euro-Canadian codes of behaviour by which her family and the inhabitants of Mattawa lived and went into the bush with Archie, a person who clearly loved her and offered her adventure and excitement.

Chapter Four

Learning Bush Skills

Still in Doucet, Archie continued to make a great effort to woo and amuse Gertie. He played the piano and talked about books, reading Robert Service's poetry of the Yukon and James Fennimore Cooper's *Last of the Mohicans*. These works illustrated his love for the wilderness and had been part of what inspired him to come to Canada and he hoped they would equally inspire Gertie.1 The works, both nostalgic and romantic, reflected some of Archie's own romanticism.

While they were in Doucet a few men from the Lac Simon band of Algonquins approached Archie and asked for his help. Like the band at Temagami, the Lac Simon had never signed a treaty with the federal government and so they had no reserve or any recognized control over their hunting grounds. With such limitations, when the railway arrived and brought with it hoards of Euro-Canadian hunters, the land was soon depleted of game and their ability to feed themselves. Disease added to their problems of food shortages and wiped out many of the band members and left them with only 180 people to protect their land at the time they approached Archie. It was an impossible situation. Their chief, Ingace/Nias Papaté, had written a letter in Algonquin to the Department of Indian Affairs in 1927 and explained the situation. But there was little response.2

With the band's difficult situation, it was no surprise that a conflict arose. Two of their members stood accused of burning down a shack belonging to two trappers and pouring coal oil on their traps to discourage animals from going near them. The accused men faced a court appearance and members of the Lac Simon approached Archie to ask that he act for the men. The Lac Simon explained to Archie the reason for the men's actions was that the winter before the two trappers had used strychnine as bait for wolves and foxes and neglected to remove the unused bits at the end of the season. Many of the band's huskies had then eaten the bits of leftover strychnine and died. Given such a plausible explanation Archie agreed to their request. While Gertie remained in Doucet Archie traveled the 100 kilometres west to Amos to argue the case for them and was so persuasive the judge handed out only a thirty-day sentence instead of the maximum two years. Nias Papaté credited Archie with the reduced sentence and invited him and Gertie to visit his summer encampment at Lac Simon, southwest of Doucet.3

Archie and Gertie went to the encampment in early June, traveling first by train and then by the canoe they launched at Senneterre. It was a typical encampment crowded with tents, lines of washing and airing blankets and stretched hides. Curing fish and meat were arranged on racks while huskies wandered among the clusters of women sewing, tanning, preparing fish or tending other chores. A short distance across the lake was the church and the Catholic priest's residence. All the band attended mass there, especially the deeply religious Papaté.

Archie and Gertie could see the poor state of affairs the Lac Simon endured. Though the welcome was warm, the food was meagre, a clear indication of the lack of game. Through a mixture of Cree, French and English Archie and Gertie learned the exact nature of their problems. It seemed that the government had sent Papaté and his people farm implements and a number of horses in an effort to encourage the band to support themselves through agriculture. In the government's view agriculture would provide the band with a better living than the effort it would take to preserve the band's hunting grounds and continue to try and provide food and support for themselves through hunting and trapping, practices and customs the government deemed backwards. But the Lac Simon were not convinced that it was best to switch to farming, something they knew little about. They preferred to stick to their own customs and skills. With farm implements stacked away and the horses treated more or less like pets, it was clear to Archie and Gertie the Lac Simon were not interested in farming.

Over the course of their visit Archie and Gertie also helped the band solve a dispute with the priest, witnessed the burial of the chief's daughter-in-law after she died in childbirth, and celebrated the chief's fifty years of marriage to his wife. In her early autobiography Gertie expresses how moved she was by her experiences there and sad she was when it came time to depart. "We had grown very fond of these people, and heartily hated having to leave them," she wrote.4 She particularly loved "the tiny, wee babies":

> They looked so sweet, laced in their Indian cradles. And how fancy they were! The young mothers in their attempt to excel each other had introduced the most startling variegated designs. But in spite of their beauty, I do not believe in those laced cradles for everyday wear, for the babies' movements when in them are so limited that they can scarcely move at all. They should, I think, be used only when travelling, as they are very convenient to pack.5

Though the Lac Simon's traditional existence would have been familiar to Gertie's mother and more especially her grandparents, as a town girl this was something new for Gertie. She knew nothing of their language, and though she lived a wilderness life in the bush with Archie, her outlook was more modern and even radical. There was no careful division of chores. Archie shared the cooking and sewing as she shared the paddling and portaging. She had proved herself just as capable of hunting and trapping as Archie was. As she viewed the life of the Lac Simon Gertie felt no romantic notions of a return to the traditional life of her ancestors. They faced too many difficulties. Besides the lack of game, the Lac Simon also suffered from tuberculosis, glandular fever and alcoholism. Several of their members had ended up as vagrants in the nearby town. Such problems prompted Archie to offer his own insights, phrased in a good-humoured statement. "Get rid of your outboard motors," he told them. Canoes, he felt, allowed the band to become chilled on the water and more susceptible to illness.

Gertie holding sturgeon with John Papate, courtesy of Katherine Swartile

Following the chief's wedding anniversary celebration, just before Archie and Gertie departed, the pair decided to mark their union as a couple and asked Papaté to give them a marriage blessing. It was a ceremony not recognized in Euro-Canadian law, under which Archie was still married to Angele, but it was binding and real to Archie and Gertie. A short while later, at the close of their visit, the chief also presented them with a wolf pup that they dubbed "Hingy," a shortened form of the word "wolf" in the Cree language. The chief gave the wolf to Gertie when she became upset after Archie told her that he had to leave for Quebec to take up his post as fire ranger, while she spent the summer in Doucet. Women were not allowed at the fire ranger post. Gertie was delighted with the pup, but was adamant she would not stay in Doucet, even with Hingy. Archie was equally adamant that they could not stay with him in Quebec. After much arguing the pair reached a compromise. Gertie would go to Rouyn with Hingy and try and find a job there for the summer. She was determined to keep busy during their three-month separation rather than twiddling her thumbs in Doucet, the town that gave her little welcome.

They parted the next day, Archie heading northward to his fire ranging and Gertie taking Hingy in a crate on the train to the mining town of Rouyn. Gertie arrived in Rouyn anxious and scared, greeted as she was by a bustling town crowded with modern buildings that obscured the few older shacks that hung on in the town's fringes. Despite such modern advances the roads were still rough and deeply rutted and during Gertie's taxi ride from the station Hingy's crate jolted open and he escaped and ran off. After a fruitless search Gertie found a room for the night. With no sign of Hingy the following day, Gertie managed to secure a job as a waitress in a diner, despite her distress over the wolf cub. The job was to prove doubly lucky. During the next few days, while serving customers Gertie met a journalist who found her tale intriguing enough to publish in the local newspaper. The story was so moving it prompted many people to visit the restaurant and her tips mounted. Eventually, through all the publicity, Hingy was found and the pair reunited. But the wolf cub had not fared well during his separation from Gertie; he was sickly, dying of starvation. After a night of nursing him, but still fearful of his recovery, Gertie decided to abandon her summer plans and seek out Archie's help. The pair boarded a train and headed for Oskélanéo,

560 kilometres east of Rouyn. The journey proved too much for the little cub and he died just before they reached their destination.

Distraught over Hingy's death, Gertie went directly to the ranger's office to discover Archie's exact location. When the chief ranger told her that wives were not allowed to join husbands on duty, she became so upset he relented and arranged for two Aboriginal men to take her the 256 kilometres into the bush to Archie's cabin and watchtower. They spent the rest of the summer together, he tanning moose hides and she making mitts, moccasins, leggings and shirts for them for winter clothing, employing the skills her grandmother taught her.

In the years that followed Gertie made all their clothes, fashioning them from skins, canvas and other materials at hand, to construct practical pieces tailored to fit their needs in the bush. For the most part Archie wore canvas shirts and canvas or buckskin pants and a buckskin jacket. Gertie sported buckskin or canvas breeches, jackets and vests, and cloth shirts. On her feet she wore tall lace up boots or moccasins. She was not without flair in her style of dressing but when practicality was in demand she opted for comfort, as she revealed when she described the outfit she wore when she traveled to Rouyn:

> I slid into a pair of black breeches and a mildly chequered shirt, without any qualms whatever as to what the best-dressed waitress should wear, waiting table being the work that I was going to look for. But when it came to donning my high-cut boots in my usual fashion, I stopped and puzzled awhile, for I always wore them partly laced, just tied about the ankle to allow free circulation when kneeling in a canoe, and only four eyelets at the top were laced to keep twigs, leaves and other such annoying things out.6

But the journey to Rouyn left room for a little style. Over the chequered shirt Gertie also decided to don a spotted sealskin vest. It was a vest Archie bought at a Hudson's Bay post, and though she thought it was pretty she felt it smelled, but not enough to prevent her from wearing it. She topped off her outfit with a wide hat and a Hudson's Bay belt.7

Such outfits were a far cry from the usual skirts, blouses and dresses seen in towns and rural communities across Canada at the time, or even the traditional skirt and printed blouse commonly worn by Aboriginal women. Women mountaineers and explorers had trekked remote areas early in this century and in the previous century clad in skirts and dresses for the most part. Shorter, divided skirts were also worn on occasion. A few intrepid adventurous women who were tour operators, park officials and prospectors wore pants or knickerbockers as the twentieth century progressed, but for the most part they were worn only while in the bush.8 For Gertie it was the choice wherever she was, a choice that raised eyebrows that lifted higher once they saw she was an Aboriginal.

As the fall of 1926 approached the decision loomed about where to head for the winter's trapping. Eventually Archie decided to go to the Jumping Caribou River area and keep moving until freeze up forced them to build. It was a 112-kilometre canoe trip, Gertie's first excursion of any length with supplies and packs and a real challenge. Mistakes could be very costly and even result in the loss of life. She was under Archie's tutelage and there was much to learn and on one particular point, he was adamant. On no account should she stop and let the paddle drag while she talked. She must paddle smartly, keeping strokes at both bow and stern in perfect unison. Archie abhorred aimless chatter on the trail.

At their journey's first portage, which was by a set of rapids, Gertie naturally assumed she would help, but Archie only allowed her to carry the tea pail and the tomahawk, despite her insistence that she do more and her unmistakeable growing temper. Ignoring the temper, Archie made it clear that he felt women should not attempt what was clearly a man's job. Those sentiments were a red rag to a bull for Gertie. Impulsively she launched the canoe, headed for the rapids and plunged into them shooting each swell. It was a foolish and risky move and by mere luck she survived unharmed, with the canoe intact. Though she did not realize it, wrecking the canoe meant miles of high banking around deep bays, burns and windfalls, a journey that could easily mean starvation. Archie, who knew all these disastrous possibilities, was furious. But Anahareo had made her point. She did not want to be protected and coddled unaware in the bush—she wanted to learn how to do her fair share.

The pair arrived in the Jumping Caribou region and quickly built their cabin. Archie went off each day to set and check his traps, while Gertie waited at home for his return. Archie still thought hunting and trapping was men's work. and he also was aware of Gertie's limited bush skills and did not want to have the responsibility of looking after an impulsive novice while working under the increasing financial pressure to get as many pelts as possible. Despite the sense behind the need to stay in the cabin, Gertie found it very confining. She grew restless and lonely. Archie saw this and created little games to keep her amused. He hid notes in various places around the cabin and wrote her entertaining letters. Though these gestures helped they did not completely alleviate her loneliness and boredom. She continued to try to convince him to take her with him, but he was adamant that she remain behind. When he finally did relent and took her with him on his traplines she disobeyed his instructions and ended up plunging through the ice into the water. Though it reinforced the lesson that it was vital she obey Archie's instructions in the bush, it did not lessen her desire to accompany him on his traplines and learn to hunt.

Gertie continued to badger Archie to teach her to trap and finally, when the spring trapping season arrived, he relented. With a fair degree of patience, he taught her the skills she needed to earn her way as a trapper in the bush. It was not an easy life as Gertie later described bluntly:

> Trapping is a tough life at best, and as hunting is done in the winter, naturally the hardships of the trail are more severe.

Hunger, cold and fatigue are constant companions, and stir a sense of kinship toward all living things, especially towards those that have seen more mealtime than meals.9

Archie also described the life of a hunter in more detail in his first book, *Men of the Last Frontier*. In his view it was a cycle that began in summer when the hunter made long trips by canoe and portaged into wilderness interiors in search of suitable hunting grounds "whilst swarms of mosquitoes and black flies make life almost unendurable." In late summer or early fall, with canoes laden with little less than half a ton of supplies, the trapper paddled down or poled up rapids, paddled across lakes in all kinds of weather to make his way to the selected territory. At every portage he unloaded supplies and carried them to the next stage by tump line (a leather headpiece attached to two-and-a-half-metre long thongs) in loads from 100 to 300 pounds per trip. Once the trapper reached the hunting ground he built a log cabin, laid out the trails and distributed provision caches to outlying points for later use when he needed temporary shelters. The trapper then set traps that could number 200 or so, spread out over forty-eight to sixty-four kilometres of lines. Once the snow arrived the trapper worked to maintain the trails and after every storm, he examined the traps to ensure they were still intact. The trapper completed these essential jobs while also constantly cutting wood, cooking, tanning hides and doing other routine work.10

Gertie in buckskins, courtesy of Katherine Swartile

Despite its hardships, in Archie and Gertie's view, a person could be "soaking wet, half-frozen, hungry and tired, landed on some inhospitable neck of the woods, vowing that a man is a fool to so abuse himself," yet once he has "sat before a fire drinking tea, with a canvas sheet between himself and the elements, all the misery fades and there is only joy and contentment for such a life."[11]

Gertie worked to master the skills Archie taught her even as she experienced its hardships. Though Archie did not always make it clear the reasons behind each of the instructions and cautions he explained them in such an engaging manner that the wilderness came alive for her. She learned about the habits of various animals, the falls of new snow, how to throw a knife, to set a trap by herself, and, if necessary, how to weald the axe handle to deliver fatal blows if the animal still lived. It was an action that always caused Gertie great anguish. On one occasion when she checked a trap she found that a captive marten had clawed and gnawed the trap box:

> Every bit of bark was stripped off the sticks. And behind the tree-trunk almost hidden was the poor creature in the trap, trying desperately to keep out of sight. In this he didn't succeed, even though he was stretching his foreleg as well as the chain which held him to its full length. He was unable to hide from us, for I could plainly see his little pointed nose and beautiful orange-coloured throat. It was his eyes, though, that I shall never forget; two unblinking eyes shining with pain and terror.[12]

Gertie pleaded with Archie to spare the marten, but he refused and gave its nose a firm wallop with the axe handle instead. The incident brought home to Gertie the pain and torture the traps could cause, but she was still determined to do her share of the trapping and contribute to their income. So she doggedly gritted her teeth and set aside her revulsion and continued to learn trapping skills. She rationalized that it was a business and it was their livelihood. She also reassured herself that Archie was not one of the inconsiderate trappers who thought only about the preservation of the hide. Archie did think about the animals' pain and had some doubts about his choice of livelihood, as Gertie was beginning to discover. Over the years he had created his own little rituals and tributes that alleviated some his remorse, such as removing the shoulder blade of a freshly killed moose, cleaning it and tying it to a tree limb on the west side. And when Hingy died he had removed a little bone from his hind leg and kept it as a memento.

In the year they had spent together Gertie had come to realize that Archie was a complex person. She discovered that beneath his bluff exterior Archie had little self-confidence and he was extremely sentimental. He could also sometimes be high-spirited, happy to tease, joke with schoolboy humour and play pranks.

Physically Archie was not as strong as he initially appeared to Gertie. His damaged lungs continued to affect his energy levels and his severely injured foot would sometimes swell so much he could not walk. His heart, no longer strong, made him subject to occasional fainting fits if he became overexcited or exerted himself too much. These problems contributed to his periodic episodes of moroseness; brooding moods that left him silent and unapproachable that were also symptoms of an underlying depression. Gertie would try and coax him out of these moods, but her own temper and stubborn spirit meant that her approach was not always the best kind and her patience easily wore thin. Archie could be as stubborn as Gertie and arguments arose that could get very heated and take physical form with a passionate Gertie coming out swinging. Despite his own short temper Archie disliked conflict with Gertie and he was miserable when they argued. He often tried to please her and understood her high-spirited nature that he, in part, admired.

Drinking also figured into the equation of their relationship. Many people who worked and spent lengthy periods in the bush drank alcohol and, during this period of prohibition, even made it. When they arrived in town or at a trading post, after a season or two in the bush, facing danger and sometimes hunger, they were anxious to unwind and "whoop it up." Archie was no different. He had been drinking for years, going on occasional drunken sprees when arriving in town with his friends after months in the bush. Archie was not a confident person at heart, and drinking initially gave him the courage to socialize and interact with other people. Later it also helped him for a time to forget his increasing ill health and growing struggle to earn money. Gertie, his companion in hunting, trapping, paddling as well as his friend and sexual partner, became his companion in drinking. Shy by nature, she too found that alcohol gave her courage to face a roomful of strangers and talk to them. She also found that it could help her temporarily to forget or dismiss the hurt and rejection she felt when she encountered strong criticism or harsh judgment. Eventually it became a crutch for the both of them. They were both crack shots and when they drank it was not unusual for them to go haywire, Archie on occasion firing his gun and playing deadly games like shooting a cigarette out of Gertie's mouth, or Gertie and he throwing knives.[13]

By the end of the spring hunt Gertie was skilled enough to contribute to the pelt count, but the fur prices had dropped, so they were still unable to meet their debt and pay for their grubstake for the coming winter. In the past, a good season's trapping had netted Archie $1500 to $2000, but now it only paid him less than half that amount.14 With their funds so low Archie was forced to spend another summer fire ranging in Quebec.

Following that second summer the pair returned to the Jumping Caribou region and Gertie reluctantly resumed running her own traplines. As she checked her traps through the winter of 1927-1928 catching mink, marten, fisher and lynx she never could quite shake off her revulsion for the whole process. Gertie later recounted that she cried shamelessly when she caught anything. Finally, in March, during the spring season, Gertie came across a live lynx in one of her traps. In her judgment it had been there ten days. The weather had not been cold enough to kill him so, after stripping the bark from everything within his reach, he had resorted to gnawing his trapped paw to the bone. To release him in such a poor condition was certain to cause a slow painful death so Gertie decided to take the kinder choice and kill him. It would be the last time she trapped.

Her decision to stop trapping and her feelings about it caused tension with Archie. Though Archie often showed his kinship with the wilderness, he also knew how close they were to starvation and felt the pressure and difficulties of earning a living that would support them both. His only additional income was an army pension that was too small to cover their costs. To compound matters game was still scarce. Despite Gertie's misery, Archie continued his hunt, trying to increase his meagre pelt count and the two squabbled often. Gradually Archie concluded that the Jumping Caribou region was as barren as the one he left behind in Ontario.15

While he mulled over matters Archie still set traps until the season finished. At the end of May, as Gertie accompanied Archie while he checked the lines, the pair paddled along and came to a fair-sized beaver house where Archie had set a trap a few days before.

When they neared the set they could see the drowning stone was missing, indicating that something was caught in the trap. On closer inspection they found that the beaver had cut the anchor line and made off with the drowning stone and the trap and consequently died at the bottom of the pond. A few minutes after they discovered the missing stone two young beaver kits poked their heads out of the water and Archie and Gertie scooped them up. They were funny looking creatures with their baby fur, little scaly tails and exaggerated webbed hind feet. They weighed less than 226 grams each, small enough to fit into Gertie's hands. Gertie described their terrible state:

> They were a pitiful sight, terrified, wet and weak from starvation, their poor drooping bodies too filled with fear to tremble or cry. They remained so still that even though I carried them inside my shirt I couldn't tell whether they were alive or dead.16

After a fruitless search for the mother, Archie and Gertie made their way back to camp with the kits. There the kits came to life, scrabbling inside her shirt with their claws. Archie cleared out the grub box, lined it with moss and leaves and placed the kits in it while Gertie worried over them. Gertie had tried and failed to save a beaver kit before when another trapper had brought the sickly creature to her. She had attempted to feed it milk with a spoon, but the peculiar shape of the beaver's mouth made it impossible and the beaver died. She was determined she would not fail this time.

Chapter Five

Beaver Kits

By 1927 Beaver had nearly disappeared from the Canadian landscape. Ever since the Europeans had discovered that the beaver pelt was perfect for hats and other fashionable items, their voracious appetite for the pelts had led to over-trapping and plunging numbers. At various times since the seventeenth century officials had noted the decline in beavers. By 1821 the situation was critical enough that Governor Simpson implemented a number of conservation measures. He reorganized and reduced the number of trading posts, initiated a quota system, banned anyone from accepting beaver trapped during summer and barred the use of steel traps. He also established several beaver sanctuaries.[1]

For a variety of reasons these approaches were unsuccessful and in 1841 the governing council noted the continuing alarming rate of beaver decline. A few years later the situation was remedied only marginally when Europeans switched to silk hats. But trapping for other commercial needs and to supplement food supplies continued. By the 1890s the situation reached a critical stage and some provincial governments began periodically passing legislation to protect the beaver until the 1920s. Measures included prohibiting trapping for a stipulated number of years, establishing a quota limit, charging royalties on each pelt, restricting the length of the trapping season, regulating the methods of capture, and establishing licensing fees. Violators were fined. Destroying a beaver lodge or using poison for bait became illegal. Poison posed a problem because of its effect on the skins and its far-reaching destructive effects on all the wildlife, which in turn badly affected the Canadian economy.2

The beaver was not the only animal suffering from over-trapping and disappearing habitats. Other fur bearing animals were feeling it too. To combat their decline as well, legislation sometimes extended to such animals as marten, otter, fox and muskrat. Some provinces created parks and reserves or leased crown lands as reserves to individuals, naturalist clubs and fish and game clubs with the hope that these organizations would help enforce the regulations.3

Though many lamented the decline of the beaver all the measures implemented in the various provinces were motivated from a desire to increase the supply of furs that supported the nation's economy, rather than to protect the wilderness. Regardless of the motivation, the measures each government attempted had little effect in most areas for a variety of reasons. The wilderness covered a large area and animals could be caught and transported over large distances without detection. Trappers spent most of the year out of reach in the bush and were difficult to trace. There was also the problem that regulations differed in each province and could change year to year which caused confusion to the trapper and sometimes the enforcer. And finally, the beaver's scarcity brought high prices, and they were so easily captured, that the temptation to break the law was very strong. For the trapper there was no incentive for conservation. If one trapper did not take all the available beaver someone else would.4

Regulation became more difficult with federation, when each province controlled its own regulation. Under the Hudson's Bay Company regulation had been difficult because of the laxity of post managers, but under federation, there were not enough effective game inspectors, game keepers and wardens to regulate the law effectively. Improved transportation and trapping methods also contributed to the decline of beaver and other fur bearing animals, as more trappers hopped on trains north, swelling the ranks, and bringing with them more sophisticated equipment. In the past, Aboriginals had used simpler hunting methods like pit falls or dead falls in which a heavy log would tumble over and break the beaver's back. Or they would drain the beaver dams and use spears, clubs and bows during the ice-free periods. The advent of guns and the introduction of steel traps and snares made trapping much easier. Traps could be set under the ice, increasing the catch. Large scale standardized production of lighter steel traps made it possible to take more traps into the interior. These traps brought ever-increasing numbers of Euro-North Americans who tended to be more systematic in laying their traps than the Aboriginals. They were also generally motivated solely by profit, in contrast to an Aboriginal who trapped and hunted to supplement his food.5

In the years from 1700 to 1800, the number of pelts taken annually was in the range of 300,000. By 1900 it had dropped to less than 50,000 per year. Massive exploitation led to near elimination of the beaver not only in Canada, but also in the United States. By 1890 there was only one known native beaver colony in the whole of New York State. More than ten years later, in 1904, at the St. Louis World Fair, New York purchased seven of the beavers Canada exhibited.6 Despite the dropping numbers, the railroad continued to bring to the bush increasing numbers of part-time hunters who had little knowledge and skill and who laid traps often baited with poison that wiped out whole beaver colonies.7

Archie had long been aware of the decline in fur bearing animals, especially the beaver. In 1925 he and his Bisco friends had left their trapping grounds in Ontario for Quebec after the provincial government had limited trapping to resident Aboriginals. But in Quebec Archie found an even greater decline in beaver.8 It was a fact that could not have escaped Gertie as she checked her own traplines and also as she saw Archie struggle to repay his grubstake debt. But Gertie's main concern was not the general peril of the beaver, but the desperate plight of the two little kits. Their situation summoned all her protective instincts. In contrast Archie could not see past their own desperate financial state and the hefty price the kits might bring. But the heartrending cries from the grub box and the baleful eyes fixed on him as they stood on their hind legs softened Archie enough to try and solve the feeding problem. The situation required a little ingenuity. They had no baby bottle and the kits could not eat from a spoon or dish because of their fur-covered extra lip behind the large front teeth. The lip closed to prevent water from entering the mouth while cutting and carrying branches underwater.9 After some thought Archie devised a method with a small stick. He dipped the stick into condensed milk and managed to insert it around the large front teeth and into the mouth while Gertie held the inner lips apart. Because the kits resisted Archie and Gertie needed great speed to get the stick in and clamp their mouths closed over it so that the milk would remain when the stick was removed. It was a messy but effective method.

Eventually, when the kits were satisfied, they sat back on their tails and began to groom themselves. After the grooming, as with every meal afterward, the pair demanded to be picked up and fondled and afterwards fell asleep inside a shirt, halfway up a sleeve, or draped around a neck. If either Archie or Gertie removed them from their chosen place and attempted to put them in their box they would awaken and demand to be returned to their spots with piercing cries. If Archie and Gertie disregarded the cries the kits would eventually fall asleep.

Within a week of regular feeding the kits gained strength, their voices ringing louder and longer, baleful cries that broke any silence Archie might have wished to impose. Eventually the crying ceased as they got to know Archie and Gertie's voices; the kits grew very gentle and affectionate, their manner and behaviour wholly naïve.

Archie continued with his spring hunt and Gertie stayed at the camp with the kits who were now allowed the freedom of a small pen. With little hesitation they had accepted her as their missing mother, an important step because normally female beavers nurture their kits for the first two years of their lives. Being nocturnal animals they would awaken around 5pm and begin their activities. They ate, had a splash in the washtub, then carted firewood all over the place or wrestled with each other, after which they would go to Gertie to play or be petted. Since they cried when Gertie was out of sight she had to sleep on the floor. They became much like babies, providing Gertie with an unexpected opportunity for mothering and closeness.

Though the kits may have won over Gertie, she was not so certain about Archie. Live beaver brought in a higher price than dead beaver and initially Archie had spent too little time in the kits' company to become attached to them. But it was not long after the kits' arrival that Archie finished the spring hunt and returned to the camp to wait for the remaining skins to finish drying and stretching. Within a few days Archie was captivated by the kits, watching them race up and down on the blankets, galloping, tripping, tumbling and colliding with each other, screaming with delight. Archie described their antics around the tent:

> We allowed them to roam around the tent at will, and occasionally on their rambles they would become lost and parted. Their bold self-confidence would then quickly desert them and they became lonely and would call frantically for help, and on being placed together they would throw themselves on their backs with wiggles and squeals of joy, and lie down together holding tightly on to each other's fur.10

Archie's true feelings about the kits were put to the test when one of them went missing just before they packed up the camp to leave. While the remaining kit howled for its missing companion Archie and Gertie frantically hunted the camp. After many hours of searching, the missing kit was finally located and restored to its companion.

Archie's concern gave Gertie reason to hope that he might not decide to sell the two kits after all. It was a hope she nurtured as they packed up to go to Doucet to sell their winter's catch and decide on the fate of the beaver.

Archie wanted to make the journey quickly because food supplies were low. The grub box, now empty, was put to another use—transporting the beaver kits, a plan that seemed sound enough, until they got underway in the canoe and the kits began a terrific racket of wailing, screeching and clawing. These actions would not help win Archie to their cause, especially when he preferred silence on the trail. After paddling sixty-four kilometres while enduring a great cacophony it was a great relief to all when they stopped to make camp. Archie and Gertie fed the kits and returned them to the battered box for the night in the hope they would settle after such an exhausting and distressing day.

Early the next morning Archie and Gertie were rudely awakened by two very wet beavers who were grooming their coats madly to keep them waterproof. The kits had broken through the box and, with their unerring instinct, headed straight for the nearest water--the lake. Despite the wet blankets and abrupt awakening, Gertie and Archie realized the benefits of the kits' bad behaviour when the kits promptly fell asleep after the grooming. Archie and Gertie needed no further hints and for the rest of the journey they ensured the beavers were well fed and allowed long nights of swimming before they set out paddling for the day.

Gaunt from a diet of nothing but fish Archie and Gertie arrived in Doucet with the beavers. Gertie was still anxious about the beaver's fate, but her fears were groundless. Though their earnings from the season's hunt did not completely clear their debt, Archie decided they would keep the beavers. As he wrote later in his book, *Pilgrims of the Wild,* the kits won him over:

> Their sneezes and childish coughs, their little whimpers and small appealing noises of affection, their instant and pathetically eager

response to any kindness, their tiny clinging hand-like forepaws, their sometimes impatiently stamping feet, and their little bursts of independence, all seemed to touch a chord of tenderness for the small and helpless that lays dormant in every human heart.11

Gertie greeted the decision with relief and joy and it was with a good heart that she could join Archie and the other trappers whooping it up with drink and carousing to mark the end of the hunting season.

With the arrival of summer, Archie once again took up a position as a fire ranger. He chose to work the lookout tower, rather than patrolling, so he and Gertie could remain stationary and keep an eye on the beavers, now called McGinnis and McGinty. Gertie and Archie had chosen those names after some initial false starts because they thought the kits resembled industrious Irish railway workers.

The beavers were now over two months old and nearly weaned. Most beaver kits would be weaned at two-and-a-half months, but Archie and Gertie began mixing the kits' milk with water and porridge even before they left camp, in order to extend the milk supply. The kits soon settled into the new environment, and over the course of the summer created a den on the banks of the lake near the tower in which they slept during the day. By the end of the summer, they had even started building the beginnings of a feed raft and a lodge of sticks and mud on top of their den.

Normally beavers build their lodge in either the centre of the pond or on the bank of a lake or stream. Many have tunnels ending in chambers in the bank where a beaver might spend time without using the lodge. They place mud and old sticks in a pile that protrudes well out of the water. Then they chew and dig underwater and hollow out one or more tunnels that lead into the house and end in a chamber slightly above water level. The outside of the lodge is plastered with short sticks and mud from the bottom of the pond until it is a smooth conical shape. Most have a hole directly on top of the house that serves as an air vent. Building such a lodge serves as a protection against predators and keeps the beavers warm in winter.12

Most beavers will generally remain in the lodge until the evening when they emerge to eat, groom themselves, and cut fresh trees for lodge repairs. If the tree they select to cut is too large to manage alone, they will take turns cutting it down, though in practice they usually work alone. Once the tree is down, several beavers may participate in cutting off the branches and dragging them into the water. If it is October, they stick the butts into the mud in front of their house to make a food pile for the winter. The trees are also cut into shorter lengths and dragged into the water, or the bark may be eaten from them where they fall if they are too large to move.13

When Archie and Gertie were away up the lake for any length of time McGinnis and McGinty met the canoe, answering Archie's call with long high-pitched cries until they arrived. The kits would then reach up to Archie and Gertie with outstretched hands and grasp their fingers. Archie and Gertie made a practice of giving them tidbits and then watching the kits lie on the water eating the bits, smacking their lips loudly. Afterwards the kits would often try and board the canoe and clamber all over Archie and Gertie.14

The kits were extremely eager to assist in all activities around the camp, a notion that could be as destructive as it was entertaining. Gertie described McGinnis, who seemed to favour Archie in particular, as "a great one to help":

> He'd look on with searching interest while Archie cut down poles with which to put up the tent. And he never missed a chance to cut one down as well. But unfortunately, when he got around to it, the said pole would then be bravely serving us as the sole support of our humble home.15

McGinty, who favoured Gertie, and was perhaps not as energetic as McGinnis, found her own type of helpful mischief, such as taking Archie's mackinaw out for a nice long swim in the lake while Gertie and Archie chased her frantically. Another time, after Archie had poured a heap of flour into a bowl to make bannock and turned to rummage for the baking powder, McGinty decided to gallop across the floor and dive into the bowl. Archie shouted and tried desperately to pull her away, but McGinty gripped the rim of the bowl firmly and would not be moved, as her hind feet paddled furiously in the flour. Flour filled the air, coating everything, before Archie was able to remove her.[16]

Scolding the kits could often produce dramatic dejection worthy of the stage. At other times, when a threatening finger was shaken at the guilty kit, the other one would come tearing out to join in the fracas and the two would hop around like jumping beans, then fall on their backs to whirl and wriggle violently, thumping the ground with their tails.[17]

As the summer came to a close, Archie and Gertie were faced with some hard decisions about their future. Archie still had to make his living trapping, though they both knew that the grounds he had formerly used were exhausted. He was also growing increasingly uncomfortable with trapping, an inclination Gertie encouraged. The physical limitations from his war wounds that still plagued him also added weight to his reluctance to trap. But trapping remained their main source of income, though he was uncertain where to find an area with enough game but that was still safe for McGinnis and McGinty. It was becoming increasingly important to Archie that the kits thrive and hopefully eventually produce their own young. He was forming an idea that the two could be the foundation of a beaver colony, one that might be a means to help preserve them before they disappeared entirely. Gertie heartily endorsed the idea.

In Senneterre, where they had laid in their grubstake before they left for the winter's trapping, Gertie met Dave Pelon, an old friend of her father's. In his early fifties and originally from Golden Lake, Dave had spent much of his life trapping, guiding and prospecting, using Mattawa and North Bay as his base. In years past he and Gertie's father had gone on river drives together.[18] It was a happy meeting for Gertie not only because he was an easygoing likeable person, but also because he was a connection to her father, whom she missed sorely. Archie found him likeable and the pair quickly formed a friendship. It was through Dave Pelon that the pair met a Micmac who gave Archie and Gertie disastrous advice about where to spend their winter trapping that was to prove fateful for them both.

Chapter Six

New Hunting Grounds

As the fall of 1928 approached Gertie and Archie prepared to head several hundred kilometres east to Cabano, by Lake Témiscouata, on the New Brunswick border as the Micmac man had recommended. There, he assured them, they could find wild beaver to start their colony as well as enough game to earn a living trapping. With Dave promising to follow later, Archie and Gertie packed the beavers in a crate and traveled to Cabano by train. They stayed with the beavers in the baggage car along with their packs and all the poplar branches and the water basin for the beavers. Gertie was oblivious to Archie's worries that he only had

$3 left in his pocket.

The group finally arrived in Cabano. Clad in their sweaty, smelly buckskin Gertie and Archie toted the noisy beavers and a canoe through the town, ignoring all the stares that came their way and launched their canoe in Témiscouata Lake and paddled for an inlet Archie spotted and camped there. Soon after their arrival the beavers fell sick, scratching and pulling out their fur and moaning continuously from the rash that covered their bodies and showing little energy and no appetite and no interest in the water. Archie and

Gertie were worried enough to take them to a doctor who gave them ointment for the rash and advised them to feed the beavers pablum if they refused their natural food instead of porridge and bread.

Generally once beaver are weaned, they subsist wholly on bark, small twigs, tree leaves and various aquatic plants like duckweed or pond lily leaves. Porridge and bread was not something beavers could reasonably digest, though Archie and Gertie had little understanding of their diet.[1] Raising beavers was an entirely new experience for them both. Though they knew to some degree about a beaver's habits and life cycle, they had no idea of the harm that could be done feeding a beaver a human diet. There were no written resources or wildlife experts to advise them on wildlife preservation, just their own experiences and instincts. Up to this point wildlife preservation had focused on increasing animal numbers for trapping for sale of the pelts, as a supplement to the larder, or for recreational hunting. Never had it been done for the sake of the animal alone.

Archie and Gertie wanted to preserve the beavers for their own sake and the sake of the wilderness they could see was disappearing. During the many years Archie had been in the bush he had seen drastic changes. Later, in his book *Men of the Last Frontier*, he would talk about witnessing "noble forests reduced in a few hours to arid desert sparsely dotted with twisted, tortured skeletons of what once were trees, things of living beauty...."[2] He also mentioned a lake he once knew that had been circled by a pristine sandy beach, set in a valley of ancient spruce and birches near a wooded mountain transformed into a barren wasteland, the lake polluted and the mountain "a pile of sterile rocks."[3] Even Gertie expressed her horror at the sight of mile upon mile of forests devastated by clear cutting, describing it as "ravaged, timberless land."[4]

Archie and Gertie shared an affinity for the wilderness that included the landscape as well as its wildlife. For Gertie that affinity extended into an empathy for the wildlife that slowly transformed into a certainty that all wild creatures, with their individual personalities, had as much right to an existence as humans. This empathy gradually became a conviction that it was important to reclaim and preserve some wildlife from the onslaught of urban development and exploitation.

These issues confronted Archie and Gertie in Témiscouata, an area they discovered was no longer pristine and in fact so heavily logged that there was no wildlife habitat left to support their venture. The Cabano locals recommended they travel 60 kilometres northeast to Birch Lake where they thought the lumbermen had not yet cut. After managing to buy over $100 worth of winter's provisions on credit at a store in Cabano Archie and Gertie made their way first by truck and then canoe to the lake. In the heavily laden canoe, they poled and paddled for miles, passing slashed trees and stumps while snow fell and piled on the ground and ice formed on their paddles and poles, until they found a place suitable for a temporary camp. Archie went on to search the lake for a permanent site and returned to collect Gertie and the beavers. The group then made a gruelling portage on an overgrown trail through muskeg and cedar swamps until they arrived at the site he had found. Then together they felled trees and chopped out frozen moss to build their cabin for the winter.

The spot they chose was set in a magnificent grove of birch and pine. They fashioned their new home from frozen wood that took a week to thaw and furnished the cabin with chintz curtains, a cupboard, table and stands that Gertie had built and draped with new oilcloth coverings. On the floor she scattered deerskin rugs. They collected frozen moss to chink the cabin and Archie put it around the stove to thaw before inserting it. The next morning he awoke to find that the beavers had removed some of the moss from the stove and, following their natural instincts to plug any air leaks of a lodge, had attempted to stick it in all the crevices they could reach. Later, Archie and Gertie found that this compulsion to plug air leaks extended to windows and doors.

Though they were finally settled Archie was still worried. It was now December and he knew the provisions would last them only eight weeks, if they were careful, and he had seen little sign of any fur bearing animals that could go towards paying off the bill at the store. Without wasting any time Archie took off with his traps. Gertie meanwhile traveled back to a cache of a 110-kilo box of books, magazines and some vegetables they had left along their journey in their haste to make their camp before winter closed in. Friends had given them the magazines and they used them first to pass the time and once read, to light the stove. Among them were copies of *Country Life*.5

Only a week later Archie returned deeply discouraged. The area was barren, there was nothing to trap. The only animals evident were the beaver family they had recently spotted in a lodge when McGinnis and McGinty had gone exploring. Archie had hoped to begin his beaver colony with them. After much reflection he decided not to trap them and try to live off his monthly pension check of $15.6

Since Archie no longer needed to check his traplines daily he had plenty of time on his hands. Entertainment was often readily available by watching the beavers who could be endearing or frustratingly mischievous. They communicated with little cries and signals between themselves and with Archie and Gertie. Weighing a healthy seven kilos each they had fully recovered from their earlier sickness. Despite their size they still cuddled up to Archie and Gertie in bed, often picking at Archie and Gertie's eyebrows and lips, among other things, when they were ready to rise. The kits had no tub of water to play in, just a washbowl nailed to the floor for drinking. They expressed no real interest in the water, and they made no attempt to go to the lake when the weather permitted. When Archie and Gertie took them to the water hole, they both refused to enter it or even drink from it.7

The pair did have a great fascination for what lay beyond their reach on the table. They had tried various methods to explore it and once succeeded in pulling down the tablecloth, with all the tin dishes crashing down around them. One day when Archie and Gertie returned from a brief trip to a lumber camp, they found the beavers had piled blankets up against the door preventing their entry. After they finally managed to open the door, Gertie and Archie saw the beaver had levelled the table by cutting off the legs and had removed most of the utensils and dishes to their den. The washstand was also pulled down and the soap had disappeared. The floor was covered with wood chips and other bits and pieces from their lumberjack efforts.8

Besides occasionally rearranging the cabin and carrying objects from one place to another, the beavers embarked on an engineering scheme under the bunk and created their own private chamber. Using the entire contents of the wood box they erected a barricade all down the outside between the bunk and the floor, with an opening at the end. Inside their chamber they cut a hole in the floor, dug a tunnel under the rear wall, which eventually served as a bedroom. The dirt they removed they used to plaster the wooden barricade under the bunk. Gertie and Archie only discovered this great engineering project when it was nearly completed. This structure eventually became McGinnis and McGinty's bedroom and private chamber.9

Some of their antics were not so benign. McGinty discovered a new pastime: thieving various items, then creeping stealthily with her booty to a hiding place. It was entertaining at first, until she stole some tobacco. After eating half of it she became dangerously ill, wailing and clutching Gertie until she fell into a coma. Desperate to save her, Archie and Gertie immersed her in a mustard bath and rubbed her vigorously. Eventually she showed signs of recovery and after a while was restored to her usual self, though she abandoned her brief career as a thief.10

With their lives so closely involved with these two wild creatures Archie and Gertie began to regard the other wildlife around them with a new intensity. Gertie made friends with a muskrat that visited the water hole; she and Archie named him Falstaff. Later the pair watched a half-grown fawn that fed across the lake from them and occasionally went by the cabin. After a while the fawn became tame enough to pass Archie and Gertie quite close as they sat outside waiting for him. They also had two squirrels that visited the cabin who learned to come when called to be fed bits of bannock. Such free handouts soon attracted the whiskey jacks who made the area around their cabin their permanent squatting ground, giving Archie and Gertie an opportunity to study their individual personalities.11 Through observing all these new visitors Archie and Gertie became increasingly aware of the variety and number of animals the wilderness housed, each of them unique.

In addition to watching the wildlife Archie and Gertie passed their time during the day reading the magazines they had brought. At night they would talk or tell stories, Archie recounting his various experiences or telling numerous tales. Gertie suggested he write down his experiences but he was not particularly interested in the idea. A while later when he was reading an article about dropping strychnine pellets to destroy wolves in Algonquin Park in Ontario he became so incensed he started writing notes in the margins. The notes became so long that he grabbed sheets of paper and continued. The notes became paragraphs and the paragraphs pages of ideas that countered the article. Gertie encouraged him to take these pages and create his own piece and send it off to *Country Life*.

It was not long after that the Christmas season began. Archie and Gertie celebrated Christmas in 1928 in a simple but innovative fashion, hanging a Chinese lantern from the rafter, distributing coloured candles and making a Christmas pudding from ingredients Archie had hoarded. They erected a Christmas tree for the beavers and Gertie tied on it pieces of apple, seeded prunes, pieces of bannock, chocolate, and other bits. Gertie later described the beavers' reaction:

> McGinty was the first to spot this windfall. She stood and sniffed cautiously, then sampled a piece of chocolate and went completely haywire. Greedily she tried to take everything all at once. Then what she least desired happened. McGinnis arrived on the scene. She planted herself solidly between him and the tree, but McGin-

nis, out to get his share of the goodies, gave her a push that sent her sprawling. McGinnis plucked a big fat prune from the tree just as McGinty came bounding back. With a quick flip of her short little arm, she whisked the prune from his grasp and it sailed across the floor. Caught unaware, McGinnis looked positively comical. While he stood there considering what had happened, McGinty ran after the prune, but before she could pop it all into her mouth McGinnis made a flying tackle, sending them both tumbling. McGinty, with the prune still clamped in her mouth, tried desperately to free herself, but McGinnis held tight and forced her backwards. McGinty found a firm toe-hold and pushed him away. Back and forth they went until it looked like some sort of dance. Then suddenly, as if by some signal, they raced together for the tree.12

Christmas was made for Archie and Gertie, not through any great efforts of feasting or decoration, but through the entertaining antics of the two beavers.

When spring arrived Gertie and Archie went to the local settlement to pick up a few supplies and the pensions checks. There they found a packet for Archie from *Country Life* containing a check for his article, a copy of the magazine in which it was printed, and a request for more articles. With such good news it made little difference they were unable to return to the cabin immediately because the sudden mild weather had made the trail too muddy to negotiate. They waited a few days and made their way back, mildly concerned that the beavers had been left alone all the while. On their arrival at camp, they found Dave Pelon waiting and, with a view to being helpful, he presented them triumphantly with the wild beaver from the lake, freshly killed. Though they were upset they could hardly blame Dave who was only trying to be a good guest and had no idea they had planned to use these wild beaver to start their beaver colony.

With the plans for Birch Lake beaver colony in ruins all three decided to move on as early as possible, Dave to join them when they had found a new situation. They relocated thirty kilometres south to

Lake Touladi. As Archie and Gertie made camp, the beavers went off to explore the lake. They returned briefly for some bannock before leaving again. That was the last that Archie and Gertie saw McGinnis and McGinty, though they searched widely including the lake and every tributary they could find, but no beavers. Gertie and Archie feared the worst. Being so tame and used to humans the beavers had no fear of any trapper who might come upon them and decide to take them for their pelts. Gertie was devastated.13

Gertie had become very attached to the beavers. She had rescued them, coaxed Archie to keep them, patiently fed them with Archie using the feeding stick and then worried and nursed them through their scrapes and illnesses. They were like children to her, naïve and affectionate and full of endearing antics. They also kept her company when Archie was writing. Gertie's distress over their disappearance was compounded by the toll the extensive search had taken on Archie's injured foot. In June, a month after they had returned from their search to the camp, Archie could still hardly bear to put any weight on it. By this time Dave Pelon had joined them at their camp and offered to secure more beavers for them from a lodge he had spotted while hunting. Since Archie's foot made it impossible for him to accompany Dave, Gertie decided to go instead.

They returned a week later with two beaver kits. One they named Sugar Loaf, after the mountain where they found them, and the other they named Jelly Roll. The two were very small and delicate. Less than three weeks after their return Sugar Loaf died. Jelly Roll fell sick a short while later, refusing to eat the canned milk and bread Gertie offered her. She just lay unmoving, with her head in the corner of her box.14

By this time they had moved to Hay Lake, only seven or so kilometres from Cabano. The local community came to hear of the plight of the little beaver and tried to help, offering advice and food. On the doctors' instructions they accepted fresh cow's milk that was offered and, thinning it down, administered it to Jelly Roll every two hours with a glass syringe. After a few days the desired effect took hold.

Jelly Roll recovered. She grew and thrived and began her own series of antics that amused the visitors from the community who had come to get news on her progress. Grey Owl later recounted that groups would set up a picnic on the beach and watched Jelly Roll amble by, "with such a look of disdain about her rear exposure, that her departure was always a source of great merriment, and perhaps some relief."15

Despite the series of setbacks Archie and Gertie were determined to continue with their plans to start a beaver colony. While Archie's foot healed, Dave Pelon assisted them when he could by sharing meat from his hunting and his stores. This valuable aid helped them in the short term, but it was clear they would have to find some alternate means of support. It was with this aim in mind, towards the end of the summer, they made a long and expensive train journey to Metis-sur-Mer, on the south shore of the St. Lawrence River, where Archie hoped to get a job as a guide.16

The idea proved a mistake. The resort was too much of a leisure resort for pursuits like fishing to require a bush guide, so Archie found work as a gardener's assistant at a place that he had heard contained a freshwater pond suitable for Jelly Roll. Despite the job, they still had enough money problems that Archie felt the need to charge ten cents to the many who came to view the "tame" beaver at their campsite.17 And Gertie, as usual, wanted to contribute her fair share so she answered an ad for a Swedish maid that she had seen in the post office. Dressed in her boots, breeches and buckskin, shirt she applied for the position in person. The woman, Madeline Peck, explained she needed a Swedish-speaking person to converse with her own Swedish maid. Gertie obviously lacked the necessary skill, but in the course of their conversation, Gertie described Archie's article in *Country Life* and that interested Madeline Peck very much. She was so intrigued she visited Gertie and Archie at their camp. There she was so impressed by the pair and Jelly Roll that she eventually succeeded in persuading Archie to give a lecture about his conservationist views in the ballroom of the Seaside Hotel.

An extremely nervous Archie, feeling like "a snake that has swallowed an icicle," appeared before a crowd of about a hundred. Despite his fears he was a success. Everyone who attended liked the lecture, among them, Colonel Wilfrid Bovey of McGill University. He was impressed enough to arrange for Archie to give more talks at the hotel that summer. Eventually Bovey would become one of his strongest supporters.18 There were others who were impressed too and called on Archie to share his knowledge further. A scoutmaster asked Archie to give his troop pointers on woodcraft. The boys showed up at their camp and listened attentively while Archie talked to them and demonstrated basic bush skills.

At the summer's end Archie and Gertie had enough money to solve their financial problems temporarily. The pair returned with Jelly Roll to their former cabin at Hay Lake and found a letter from *Country Life* asking Archie to write a book. Though somewhat unnerved by the offer he agreed to try. They all settled in for the winter and Archie threw himself into his writing. He became so immersed in the project that he erected a table alongside the bunk so he could just and reach out at any moment and jot down ideas.19

Visitors gave him an occasional break from his writing. In early November a Quebec City newspaper editor, Jean-Charles Harvey, while on a hunting trip, called in to see "the beaver man," as Archie was becoming known in the county. A lover of the wilderness, Harvey later described his time with Archie and Gertie as some of his happiest days. He found Archie, whom he took to be Aboriginal, educated and cultivated and was impressed with Archie's ability to call Jelly Roll to him when she was out on the lake. He was also impressed with Gertie's beauty and later wrote of her that for Archie she was "son inspiratrice, sa passion et son tourment," his source of inspiration, his passion, his anguish.20

Still only twenty-three, Gertie was full of energy and eager for more adventure. She was also conscious that they needed more income and she wanted to do her part and earn money in some way. Previously, Archie had supplied the stimulation, instruction and support that met her need for adventure and reassurance in a setting that, for the most part, was away from the judging eyes of small-town communities. These experiences allowed her to build her bush skills and form a confidence that bolstered her sense of independence. Though they sometimes had terrible arguments and fights, underneath it all Gertie knew Archie loved and supported her. He was protective of her, calling her "poor ting" when some ill had befallen her, or other endearments like "Pony"

– her father's name for her – or "little insect" or "reptile." But now his declining uncertain health and injured foot meant that he was no longer able to spend long periods of time in the bush paddling canoes, his lower legs immersed in the water that pooled at the bottom. Nor was he able to tramp through the long, wet muskeg portages carrying heavy loads. His lungs, heart and foot could not take such treatment. His new potential source of income, writing, drew him into a completely different, sedentary lifestyle that, on the surface, might have seemed better for his health. He began to spend long periods inside the cabin, virtually uncommunicative, working at night and sleeping in the day. For Gertie it was "like living with a zombie."[21] Not only was her main source of adventure and teacher unavailable, there were long periods when his emotional absence meant her main source of support had vanished too.

In view of these considerations, it was hardly surprising that when Harvey came to call, Gertie decided to accept Dave Pelon's invitation to them both to prospect at Opemiska Lake. It was an opportunity for more adventure in the bush where she could use her now excellent bush skills and there was also a possibility of earning money. So when the time came for Harvey and his friends to return to Riviere-du-Loup, Gertie and Dave accompanied them. From Riviere-du-Loup the pair traveled to Quebec City and boarded a train to northern Quebec for an autumn prospecting at Opemiska Lake.[22]

Chapter Seven

The Lure of Prospecting

Dave Pelon was no stranger to prospecting. His wish to go to Opemiska was inspired by his visit there a few years before when he had located a very promising spot but had no money to pursue it. Now, with Archie supporting him financially, he was returning with Gertie to stake the site. Gertie made the journey filled with excitement and anticipation, easily overlooking the minor hiccup along the way when Dave went missing in Quebec City and ended up on the wrong train. After searching widely for three days she found him hobbling down the track. It was ninety kilometres before he had realized he was on the wrong train and he had gotten off and walked back. Reunited, they traveled to Oskélanéo, launched the canoe in the St. Maurice River and paddled north for three weeks, before arriving at Lac Doré, ninety-six air kilometres from Opemiska Lake.

Prospecting had never been a uniquely male undertaking in North America. In the nineteenth century, out of the thousands who prospected, perhaps as many as a hundred or more women went to places like California, Alaska and Nevada. By the turn of the century, however, the numbers dwindled, though they increased

slightly during the Depression years. Most women prospectors were Euro-North Americans, born in Canada and the
United States, and only a handful of them made fortunes, but many earned decent money.1

Though the type of women attracted to prospecting were often removed from the mainstream of society, they were usually interested in the world at large and more often than not had radical views and were not shy to speak their minds. The women were also marked by their obsession with prospecting, an obsession supported by some technical knowledge and varying degrees of false science. Many came from the working classes and tended to be solitary, fiercely individual and strong-minded figures who rejected society's values in almost absolute terms, so disdainful of convention that a few led very flamboyant lives. They were often rough, daring, indefatigable, and lavish in their generosity, placing little value on money and continuously pursued new excitement. They generally had no social ambition whatsoever and tended to spend their profits, usually in a grand spree.2

Like Gertie, the women who prospected all invariably rejected popular ideas of appropriate feminine behaviour. Mining gave them a sense of freedom from any restriction and an unconscious pride in their survival skills. They were attracted to the adventure and the challenge of the rugged conditions, the lack of monotony on the trail and even the ever-present empty landscape. It was not riches they cared about, but the adventure and all the possibilities the search provided. They disliked society and reveled in the wilderness that gave them strength. The attraction of the wilderness was like an addiction, a feeling bordering on the sacred, fed by the challenge of adventure. Prospecting became a reason to go into the wilderness and to remain there. For some the wilderness was a place to heal, a place to hear the "pulse beat of the universe," where it was possible to "journey inwards to wisdom and serenity."3 These were women with whom Gertie would feel at home.

Aboriginal women prospectors had a rather grim experience.

Whether they were on their own or with an Aboriginal spouse, their efforts were less likely to produce results, in part because they were usually hired to labour for Euro-North Americans for tasks like panning or digging. If they were labouring for themselves other prospectors or lawyers were apt to exploit their lack of legal knowledge or their inability to read and write. In these situations they were tricked into signing documents waiving their rights. Aboriginal women who assisted prospectors with their local knowledge of the land fared poorly too. Shaaw Tláa, or Kate Carmack as she was known, a Tagish woman, used her experience and traditional skills to ensure the survival of her Euro-Canadian husband in the Klondike when they made the now famous gold strike. With the pressures of wealth and accompanying alcoholism Kate's husband left her, leaving Kate penniless, to eventually die in the influenza epidemic of 1920.4

It took a bit of skill and several steps to prospect successfully. First it was important to find a promising area and make camp. Then the search intensified. The prospector panned streams and rivers, searching all the while for dull yellow flecks. He broke chunks from ledges hoping to find signs of mineralization: the white threadlets of quartz, the yellows and browns of iron often associated with gold; the greens and blues of copper, silver and turquoise; the black of manganese; lilac of cobalt and the pale yellow of molybdenum or lead. The prospector also roamed the hills hunting for "float," a chunk of mineral-bearing rock broken from a lode and carried away by water. If he found any float he tried to trace it to its origin, a difficult, time-consuming and exhausting task that could often lead to dead ends. Anything he found he gave a crude field test and, if satisfied with its value, he staked the claim by putting up a notice in the middle of the area and marking its four corners and the centre of the end lines with posts, blazed trees or stone cairns. Then, within a stipulated period of time, the prospector had to register the claim with the authorities in the nearest town. The prospector usually used the opportunity to take the samples to an assayer for more definitive testing.5

For many the next step was to sell the claim, a process that took the prospector to a variety of places that ranged from a saloon to an office. Claims worth little they might retain and mine just enough ore to keep them fed. Or they could keep the claim and develop it to prove its value and sell it for a higher sum later. To attract investors a prospector could either persuade a shopkeeper to put a sample on display in a window, interest a newspaper editor to write about it, or ask an assayer to use his mining company connections to secure a buyer. Or they might find some wealthy men eager to invest in it. Women prospectors often found this step the most difficult because of the general scepticism about their prospecting skills that greeted their proposals. The profit from selling the claim was usually modest and grew more modest still if she owed grubstakers. Any money left from this, women prospectors usually blew in spectacular spending binges.6

By the time Gertie arrived at Lac Doré she had some understanding of mining from her discussion with Dave Pelon. With his prospector's enthusiasm infecting her she was anxious to get started. Set in rocky, rugged country, Lac Doré was some 320 to 420 kilometres southwest of inland Labrador. When Dave and Gertie arrived, it was a busy hive of tents and buildings, filled with prospectors and drilling companies, a sight that Dave greeted with dismay. On his previous visit, less than two years before, Lac Doré had been deserted, but now, as he quickly discovered, a strike was on at Opemiska. This news alarmed Dave so much he accepted someone's offer to fly himself and Gertie to an area nearest the site and paddle the remaining distance in their canoe. The next day the made their way there to find it was too late. Two brothers who had spotted the outcropping from the air had just staked the area. The claim, when eventually sold, made a big profit.

Dave was heartsick. All that time and money for nothing and now he had to repay Archie's generosity. To complicate matters ice was forming on the smaller lakes and they were a long distance from any railroad. It was too late in the season to get out of the area before freeze up. Even if they waited until the ice froze enough to snow shoe out their provisions would not last long enough for them to reach the railroad. Disheartened, they both flew back to Lac Doré. Dave immediately secured a job hunting and providing meat for the crew of the Three Diamond Drilling Company and offered to support Gertie through the winter. Too proud to accept the gesture Gertie refused and established herself in an old trapper's shack instead and decided to trap once again, but after a few days she found it impossible to allow herself to do it and removed them all. She decided instead to toboggan down to Oskélanéo and work her way back to Cabano. When she made the perilous twenty-eight-kilometre trek across the glaring ice to Merril Island to inquire about the winter route south from the staff of a drilling company, Chibougamau Prospectors Ltd., they were so appalled at her idea that they offered her a job on the site running dog sleds to haul supplies, wood and the freight from any incoming planes.

Gertie accepted the job gratefully. Living in a shack tent they built for her, she worked each day supplying wood for thirteen stoves and three drills with gas and hauling tons of freight from the planes. The first plane that landed after freeze up contained several letters from Archie filled with worry. Gertie had not mentioned her job or how she was managing at Merril Island in her letters to Archie because she knew it would upset him to think she was working and camping among a group of men. Despite the omissions her situation still concerned him and he promised that when he could he would send her the return fare from Opemiska. Despite the offer of money, he wrote her that he had not received any money from an article he had written for *Canadian Forest and Outdoors*. He also mentioned that he had moved to an abandoned lumber camp and he was working hard on some articles as well as his book. He noted sadly that there was still no sign of McGinnis and McGinty. The possibility of their return was a slender hope they had both shared, though they knew it was unrealistic.

As unconventional as Archie might appear to some, he still found it worrying and even inappropriate for a woman to mix among strange men in the bush without the presence of a spouse or partner. Some of his concern was no doubt based on his own observations and experiences and also some leftover sensibilities from his Victorian middle-class upbringing. The men on Merril Island were in actual fact protective towards Gertie, and they respected her pluck, a common enough sentiment among their kind.7 Male prospectors and miners were inclined to admire the courage of their female counterparts and the mining camps tended to be free and tolerant, especially in the early stages of a mining boom, when weak social controls and the camps' fluid populations meant there were few or no clearly defined roles, and this gave women more freedom than usual. As one woman prospector declared, "a woman is safe among miners as at her own fireside. If a woman complains of her treatment from any of the boys she has only herself to blame." Another woman stated they would "die in a pinch for their companions. There are no embarrassing circumstances for me as a prospector. I am as safe in camp as I would be at home."8

The drilling company staff's respect for Gertie did not stop them from joking around with her. One evening she stopped at the bunkhouse wearing a lady's blouse, a change from her usual flannel or canvas shirts. The men teased her and chased her around wielding talcum powder, eventually nearly drowning her in it. Other opportunities for light-heartedness arose with the arrival of Christmas and New Year. The staff celebrated the season in great style, drinking and playing cards. Though Gertie joined the New Year celebrations, at the evening's end she was still sober enough to lace those who were not into their toboggans to prevent them from falling off and return them to their bunkhouses.9

The days of January 1930 brought with it the terrible news of the stock market crash, so it was no surprise that in late January, the company's promoter flew in to shut down operations. Everyone left the island on the plane except Gertie. She had been paid only two weeks of her wages to date and so could not afford the plane fare.

Gertie was appointed caretaker and instructed to sell everything. She felt it a laughable instruction since it was clearly obvious there were no buyers.

    Besides the radio, books and the dogs, Gertie's only company that winter on the island was the three prospectors who lived on the north shore. Eventually, a plane arrived bringing a man who informed her that his company had bought all the gas and drill rods. He asked Gertie if she could haul them to Antoinette Lake since it was impossible for a plane to land there. There was no danger she would lose her way because the three prospectors had often made journeys to the site to work their claims and had marked the route clearly. On her first trip she loaded and hauled over 1,320 kilos weight of equipment. As she pushed and pulled the dogs up the first steep hill she realized that it was a mistake to take such a huge load. The realization was affirmed when she reached the top of the hill and saw the descent was just as steep. Gertie unhitched the dogs and reversed the sled and used a pole as a brake while she took the load down backwards, the dogs jumping and barking all around the load and Gertie. Finally she arrived with the load, the dogs and herself intact. Having learned the best approach the hard way, she hauled the rest of the equipment without any problems.

    Gertie earned more than enough money from the hauling job to pay for her journey back to Cabano, but since there were no more planes, she was forced to remain on the island. It was not until June that a plane arrived and was able to take her to Quebec where she could take a train for the rest of her journey. While she waited for the train Gertie went on a shopping spree and bought a pipe, tobacco and whiskey for Archie and some clothes for both of them. After making these purchases she treated herself to a movie, her first talkie.

Chapter Eight

National Parks & the Path of Conservation

Gertie returned to Cabano armed with a new confidence given her by the money and respect she had earned using her bush skills on Merril Island and found someone to guide her to Archie's new home at the abandoned lumber camp. There she was reunited with Archie and Jelly Roll, and Archie introduced her to their new companion, another beaver. Named Rawhide, Archie found the beaver caught in a trap he had set to capture an otter that threatened Jelly Roll. Archie brought the beaver home to tend to an injured foot and the gash on his head that happened when the beaver had tried to escape the trap. The gash healed but a piece of skin that hung from the wound and was later clipped, inspiring Archie to give the beaver his name, Rawhide.

While Gertie was on Merril Island that winter Archie and Jelly Roll had forged a strong bond. At the beginning of the season Jelly Roll had built a little lodge on the lake and stayed there each day until Archie came down in a fit of loneliness and carried her back to the cabin in a box. After a while she would find her own way back to her lake lodge. Jelly Roll joined him in the cabin once freeze up occurred and the hard winter set in. Archie sunk a galvanized tank for her in the floor and dug a niche out under one of the walls in imitation of a beaver house interior. He changed the water in the tank daily, a task that required five trips carrying two water pails. Once Jelly Roll moved into the cabin she proved quite an entertaining companion as she made her own modifications to Archie's efforts, covering the floor with heaps of dirt, raiding the wood box for materials and completely rearranging the place.[1]

Jelly Roll had her quiet moments with Archie too. He described sitting on the deerskin rug before the stove with Jelly Roll's head on his lap, as she moaned and appeared to sing contentedly. It became a regular activity, contributing to the strong bond that was forming between the two of them. Archie even speculated that it was possible that Jelly Roll thought Archie belonged to her, as if he were her beaver companion. When he left the cabin for a few days, on his return she would attack his legs, as if to punish him for being away.[2] She was headstrong, full of mischief, artlessly childlike in Archie's view, and there was no doubt that he grew very attached to her as he watched her antics over the winter. Despite all of Jelly Roll's amusing behaviour Archie could not shake off his loneliness. He missed Gertie. After spending Christmas day in the cabin he decided to accept various invitations to celebrate New Year in Cabano.[3]

In the months leading up to spring, Jelly Roll took to the water again, inhabiting her old lodge, but always returning to visit Archie. It was early spring when Archie discovered a skittish Rawhide caught in the trap he had laid for a suspected otter, and Archie spent over two weeks desperately trying to save Rawhide's injured foot. Rawhide rewarded Archie's efforts by his extreme devotion to Archie, hobbling around at Archie's heels, and crying mournfully when Archie went out. Jelly Roll's reaction to this new dynamic was clear. She attacked Rawhide aggressively, or as Archie put it "she at once decided that here was somebody who, being disabled, would be perfectly easy to beat up, which kind and chivalrous thought she immediately proceeded to put into execution." Archie was eventually forced to remove a loudly objecting Jelly Roll from the cabin and take her down to the lake.4

After Rawhide's foot was sufficiently healed Archie released him back into the water. But Rawhide refused to go. Despite Jelly Roll's attempts to see him off, he stubbornly returned, visiting Archie in the cabin and swimming nearby in the lake. Rawhide followed Jelly Roll around and did everything she did, almost desperate to join the little group. Archie recounted that he "somehow gave the impression that he was starving for companionship, and Jelly refusing his advances, he turned to me." Archie, not immune to such favouritism, took Rawhide's part in any squabble between the two beavers.5

With Jelly Roll and Rawhide possessing such distinct personalities it was not surprising that Archie's relationship with each one differed. He felt Jelly Roll regarded him as an equal; they were rough and tumble playfellows, while his relationship with Rawhide was based on gentleness and kind gestures. Between Jelly Roll and Rawhide there eventually emerged a devotion and harmony, a situation created after Rawhide saved Jelly Roll's life when, according to Archie, they were attacked by an old aggressive beaver.6

By the time Gertie returned and found Archie installed in his cabin with Jelly Roll and Rawhide, the three had formed a close relationship. Nine months earlier when Gertie had left to go prospecting Jelly Roll had only been a small kit. Now she was nearly grown and had a companion, Rawhide, who added another dynamic to the mix. Gertie later wrote how glad she was that Jelly Roll remembered her, a sentiment that gave some hint at the anxiety she must have felt about the current situation and her place in it. In view of Jelly Roll's relationship with Archie, Jelly Roll could have easily regarded Gertie as a rival. It was perhaps because of Rawhide's presence and Jelly Roll's memory of Gertie that there were no real problems with the beavers.

Archie had also been busy writing over the winter. He had worked on his book but his need for money had made him write magazine articles that he submitted to *Canadian Forest and Outdoors*, published by the Canadian Forestry Association. These articles he authored as Grey Owl and described himself as the son of a Scot and an Apache. The name he fashioned was a loose translation of the Anishnabe name given to him when he was with Angele on Bear Island. Once published the articles were brought to the attention of James Harkin, Commissioner of National Parks, who shared Archie's concern about the disappearance of the wilderness. Intrigued by Archie's efforts to preserve the beaver, Harkin sent his publicity director, J.C. Campbell, early in the year to secure Archie's agreement to make a film with Archie and the beavers that would create a visible argument for their preservation. The result was the film *Beaver People*.7

The film crew arrived in the summer after Gertie's arrival and provided a bit of excitement for her. She was feeling frustrated with the silent and uncompanionable Archie who was still absorbed in writing and editing his book and she welcomed such an interesting distraction. The crew filmed Jelly Roll and Rawhide swimming, diving, walking, running and hauling sticks around, as well as climbing in and out of the canoe. They also caught the beavers in their final preparation for winter, going in and out of the cabin, opening the door with one hand while carrying sticks with the other. The film crew showed great patience and fortitude as they stood in the water unmoving, for long periods, awaiting the beaver.8

Gertie holding one of the beaver, courtesy of Katherine Swartile

Archie and Gertie also featured in the film. Archie took the canoe on the lake, beat the paddle on the water to call the beavers. Wearing a hat, his hair long past his shoulders, he moved through the water like the expert canoeist he was. Gertie, in separate shots, laughed and played with the beaver, a beautiful woman with her hair stylishly bobbed, wearing breeches and shirt and sometimes her fringed buckskin jacket.9 Though the beaver were the centrepiece of the film, it also subtly underscored the idea that Archie and Gertie, presumably a First Nations couple, were authentic voices of the wilderness. Archie appeared to fit the image with his long hair and buckskin, a noble savage straight from the pages of James Fennimore Cooper. Gertie, however was different. With her bobbed hair, breeches and laced up boots she was unmistakeably modern and unconventional. She did not conform to established expectations of Euro-Canadian women, but neither did she fit the current images of

Aboriginal women. Her hair was not in braids and the fringe and beads were on her jacket, not on a dress. She did not wrap herself in a blanket looking dishevelled and seedy or seem like a vagrant from the edges of town. She did not fit any of these images of native women common during this time.

The film crew left and with them the excitement and stimulating activity. By this time the summer was drawing to a close and for Gertie, the prospect of a gloomy winter loomed with Archie wholly engrossed in his book. She knew he would be writing all hours of the night and sleep during the day while she tried to make as little noise as possible. Archie told her the book would not be ready before January at the earliest. Gertie rebelled at the thought. She later wrote, "I had to admit to myself that I couldn't face another week let alone two more months of this morgue like atmosphere."10

With the promise of such torture only two months away Gertie took matters in hand and decided to go to Montreal to see Mr. Gilman, the man who had handled the closure of the operations on Merril Island and appointed her caretaker when the crew departed. She was convinced Gilman would have another job for her up north and she would pass the winter busy on another adventure. She was sorely disappointed when Gilman explained he had no job for her, but he did suggest she try an exclusive new resort in the Ottawa Valley called Montebello, later to become the Seigneury Club.11

His tip proved successful and Gertie was hired to assist with the skiing, riding, tobogganing, and bobsledding. Gertie later described Montebello's lodge as very plush, with six impressive fireplaces, mounted heads of buffalo, moose, elk, and caribou hanging on the walls, along with pelts of wolverine, badger, lynx, fox and wolves. Navajo blankets draped the chairs and lounges and buffalo and polar bear skins covered the floors. The décor was carefully chosen to evoke the images and ideas of the wilderness for the select guests whose normal urban environment was a far cry from anything remotely wild.

Besides the duties for which she was hired, Gertie also convinced the management to let her run dogsleds for anyone who wished to tour the countryside in a different and exciting way. It became a very popular activity among the guests, with its lovely scenery and unusual transport, and it gave Gertie a chance to show off her skill. She seemed not to mind the social life either, revisiting a situation not dissimilar to her time at Camp Wabikon.

Gertie was thrilled that her skills could once again be put to good use earning money. That she was an Aboriginal woman seemed not to matter, or at least not in any negative way. She happily passed another Christmas without Archie, and when New Year's Eve arrived, she threw herself into the celebrations, an evening she described as "very gay" during which the champagne "flowed like moose milk." The lodge was filled with guests, some of them from as far away as New York and Vancouver, eager to see Nels Nelson, the world champion skier, take the 263-foot (over eighty metres) ski-jump, scheduled for the next day. As midnight approached, Nelson headed the staff parade into the lodge, with Gertie in tow at the back with her dogs and a curly headed infant representing the New Year tucked in her sled. An old bewhiskered man representing the Old Year greeted the staff, took the baby and handed it to Nelson, with the idea that the old man would then sit in the sled and Gertie would guide the sled out the door, "taking the Old Year out." Just after the baby was handed over, the lights went out and the year 1931 was announced amid shouts, singing, blaring horns and whistles that sent the dogs wild. As Gertie later described it, the dogs "circled the room to beat old hell, the cariole barely skimming the floor, then out the door we went—leaving the 'Old Year' behind."12

In late January Gertie received a telegram from Archie requesting her to go to the Windsor Hotel in Montreal and ask for Grey Owl. The Canadian Forestry Association had invited Archie to show the new beaver film and address their annual convention of nearly five hundred delegates. Anxious about such a big event, Archie needed her moral support so Gertie left her job and joined him in Montreal. There she worked to reassure him about his performance and possibly soothe fears he might feel that he did not have enough experience and knowledge to answer all the questions the conference delegates might ask. The illness McGinnis and McGinty had suffered because of their poor diet also could certainly have undermined his confidence. In addition to that, at this point Archie really had no idea that Jelly Roll was a female because he referred to her as a male during the lecture. It was an easy mistake to make, since it is almost impossible to tell a beaver's sex until it is two years old. Archie also announced at the end of the lecture that Jelly Roll and Rawhide were dead. He thought it was the truth because the beavers had not reappeared since taking to their quarters under the ice that winter. Both beliefs proved wrong that spring when Rawhide and Jelly Roll emerged, proud parents-to-be.13

All of Archie's worries were for nothing. The lecture was a wild success. The next day the *Montreal Star* carried the story, "Grey Owl Devotes Life to Protection of Beaver," and other papers soon picked up the story. The *Star* article explained briefly about Archie's "beaver farm" and the accidental nature of its founding. The main focus, however, seemed to be Archie's background. The reporter called Archie "Grey Owl," and described him as a Jicarilla Apache who had lived along the Rio Grande and later joined the Buffalo Bill Circus, performing war dances twice daily in America and London. Following the stint with Buffalo Bill he moved up north and trapped until he created his beaver sanctuary. The article concluded with a description of Archie sitting with an empty beer bottle and a headache remedy nearby which the reporter felt demonstrated that despite his Aboriginal blood he "knew the ways of the white man as well as any redskin." The reporter also added that "his outlook was that of an Indian, even though he is fluent in speech. He has a vocabulary that would put many of his paleface brethren to shame."14

Since Archie's death in 1938, many people have expressed various views and explanations for his choice to present himself as

Grey Owl with either Apache or half-Apache heritage. In making these choices Archie could not help but be aware of the significance of presenting the face of an Aboriginal to the public as he challenged and persuaded his audiences to join his cause and preserve the beavers and the vanishing wilderness. He understood and to some degree sympathized with the European idea that First Nations were authentic voices of nature.15 Archie had spent his childhood immersed in his passion for the wilderness, reading such authors as James Fennimore Cooper and Ernest Thompson Seton, as well as Longfellow's poem, *Hiawatha*. Seton wrote over twenty volumes of animal and nature essays and animal stories for children. In his animal stories Seton presented animals from their viewpoint, as did Rudyard Kipling and Jack London, but unlike them, Seton's animals were realistic and did not talk and think like humans. Seton's style reflected his support for the rights of animals and his influence became heavily apparent in Archie's books.16

Though Seton's depictions of animals might have been more accurate, he was like Cooper and others in portraying nostalgic and unauthentic Aboriginals, showing them as "noble savages." Underlying these portraits was the idea prevalent among some British, Canadians and Americans that Aboriginals represented a purer and more virile time in colonial history that a rapidly modernizing society had lost.17 Archie had absorbed many of the underlying sentiments he found in these books and was a young teen when Buffalo Bill's Wild West Show had appeared in Hastings. The show gave dramatic live performances of Aboriginals and Euro-North Americans re-enacting events. It was only a few years later that he left Hastings to go to the Canadian wilderness, a place he viewed as unsullied by modernization. Later, he loudly lamented the disappearing wilderness, something he witnessed at close hand over many years. And finally, another element that factored in Archie's new identity, like others before him from Europe, Archie reinvented himself, slowly taking up the persona as a woodsman and then an Aboriginal, a person from a group in his view that was inextricably linked to the wilderness, a group that he admired.

Following his speech, as Archie emerged as a spokesperson for the wilderness, he understood urban society's perception that the Aboriginals were linked to the wilderness and made use of it to present his passionate desire to preserve what was left of it. With his sympathy and connection to First Nations people, he did not hesitate to identify himself as First Nations too. He wanted to be an Indian. He identified with them, a rejected outsider. He chose this course despite the fact that there still existed a great deal of discrimination and prejudice against Aboriginals, especially in rural areas and towns. Archie had witnessed it personally.18 He had also "played Indian" before while drinking with his trapper friends, enacting made up war dances and songs. At Metis Beach someone photographed him with a buckskin jacket and hair in braids and a feather. By the time of his lecture at the Canadian Forestry Association he had evolved into Grey Owl, a Jicarilla Apache who had joined Buffalo Bill's Wild West Show. When Gertie, who believed him to be half-Apache, questioned him about presenting himself in full Aboriginal regalia with buckskins and feathers, he replied "he would do anything to make people listen to him." During his public appearances he stood tall and stoically, his expression grim, his face turned to show his hawk-shaped nose and his dyed hair plaited in braids.19

Following the presentation to the Canadian Forestry Association, Grey Owl and Gertie accepted an invitation to dine at the home of one of Montreal's prominent families. Grey Owl was reluctant to go and insisted they dress in buckskins. Once there, he behaved rudely until he was certain they were sincere about their interest in his work and did not think he and Gertie were "ignorant savages" there only to entertain them. After the dinner Gertie went off upstairs with their hostess who offered Gertie a gown to change into so the hostess could try on Gertie's buckskins. Gertie styled her hair and made up her face and the pair presented themselves to the other guests who, after overcoming their astonishment, exclaimed over Gertie and said how well she looked.[20]

Just as Grey Owl insisted that he and Gertie dress in their wilderness clothes to reinforce the commonly held image of an Indian as a wilderness representative Gertie was keen to challenge any mistaken notions and ideas held by the small group of Anglo-Canadian dinner guests. That she could "look well" and carry off modern evening wear and makeup like any Euro-Canadian was certainly a surprise for these people whose own idea of women Aboriginals was more likely to be confined to Indian princesses in buckskin tunics and hair in braids or wearing blankets and lurking at the edge of town. Her initial appearance in trousers and buckskin contradicted this image, but it was still different from the Anglo-Canadian women's garb and as such still kept that boundary between Aboriginal women and Euro-Canadian women. In the evening gown Gertie met them in their own territory, wearing clothes familiar to them, further challenging any deep-seated notions about Aboriginals. Though Gertie's impulse might have been a desire for fun, she was letting them know, for all her bush skills, she was a modern woman who could appear as sophisticated as any Euro-Canadian woman it she chose.

The day after the dinner Grey Owl fell ill with pneumonia, a life-threatening illness in these days before antibiotics, especially with his weak lungs. Gertie, unable to leave Grey Owl, sent for her things from Montebello but then returned to the cabin when Grey Owl insisted she go check on the beavers while he recovered in Montreal. Grey Owl joined her a short while after he left the hospital against the doctor's orders. He hitchhiked his way back and then snowshoed the remaining three-kilometre distance from the highway and finally collapsed at the cabin. After some extensive rest he finally recovered.

Grey Owl's success at the Canadian Forestry Association raised his profile considerably and the Parks Branch commissioner, James Harkin noticed it. Aware of Parliament's reluctance to grant money to support a parks system that did not generate income, Harkin emphasized the parks' profit potential from the numerous tourists who would visit the parks. He thought that if Grey Owl were to pursue his beaver program in one of the parks his presence would attract a greater number of tourists. With that goal in mind Harkin offered Grey Owl a post at Riding Mountain National Park. Formerly a favourite hunting and fishing ground of Aboriginal groups including the Cree, Anishnabe and Assiniboine, by 1929 it had been designated a forest reserve.21

Early North American conservation efforts began in the U.S.A. in the late nineteenth century with John Muir, who later established the Sierra Club, and others who saw the frontier's disappearance as a death knell for the wilderness.22 The Canadian government initiated conservation efforts to preserve some of the natural beauty of the wilderness when, in 1885, it set aside for public use twenty-six square kilometres of Cave and Basin Hot Springs, later known as Banff National Park. The Rocky Mountain Park Act, passed in 1887, officially established it as a park. A few years later, in 1895, the government set up Yoho, Glacier and Waterton Lakes as parks, followed by St. Lawrence Island's National Park in 1904. In 1906 the federal government bought North America's last wild herd of bison from Montana and installed them in Elk Island and Buffalo National Parks in an attempt to prevent their decline. The herd thrived to such an extent in Buffalo National Park they suffered from disease and over-grazing. Finally, in 1930, Parliament set the guiding philosophy for the management of the national parks, recognizing that they were "dedicated to the people of Canada, for their benefit, education and enjoyment."23

Appointed to the parks in 1911, Harkin shared Grey Owl's concerns about the endangered wilderness and, as the first to oversee Canada's national park system, he established many new parks and initiated steps that protected wildlife. He had already worked to protect the wood buffalo, the muskox and caribou. Even in the 1930s most Canadians still believed the frontier was endless, and as the Depression and drought pushed thousands to leave their farms in southern Canada and head north to start over, the wilderness shrunk ever more quickly. Few people in public positions other than Harkin understood this threat until Grey Owl arrived on the scene. As others have said, "half a century before real conservation movements had existed in Canada [Harkin] fought for both wildlife and wilderness preservation within Canada's national parks."24

Harkin knew that many of the people who read Grey Owl articles and responded to his talks were middle-class, city and town dwellers, who were able to access the newly laid roads created in the wake of the arrival of the automobile. The invention of the low-priced assembly line car meant that suddenly a large number of Canadians and those further afield could travel into areas that previously had been out of reach. With this new technology came also a yearning for the wilderness, a place where life was simpler and where men could test their courage against the elements. Easy access made the newly opened parks places to visit and experience the wilderness. And at the very least cars provided a freedom for the individual to journey to areas so lately inhabited by danger.25

Over the decades of the nineteenth century, the journey into the wilderness of the west had come to represent a journey of self-discovery, of transformation, but always with the attendant danger of the wild animals and threatening Indians. Now there was the opportunity to make that self-discovery without any serious threats. This romantic view was emphasized in the images adorning the touring atlases, travel posters and guidebooks of the day that depicted Aboriginals in full regalia amid tall pine trees while a car ambled along the mountain path, or the maps that showed cowboys roping steers alongside a car.26 When Harkin offered Grey Owl a position as "caretaker of park animals" at Riding Mountain National Park, in a quiet wooded area about fifteen kilometres north of park headquarters, he was using the idea of the wilderness and placing what he thought to be real Indians alongside wildlife—the beavers—in an accessible setting with virtually no danger attached. He also felt that Grey Owl's articles, books, films, interviews and presentations would further publicize the parks and their conservation efforts, drawing many who would come to see Grey Owl, Gertie, and the beavers, thereby increasing the park's income. It would also enable Grey Owl to start a beaver colony without the pressures of making a living. It seemed a winning plan.

Chapter Nine

Prospecting & Becoming a Public Figure

Grey Owl accepted the appointment to the Parks Branch, but even as he and Gertie packed up Rawhide and a pregnant Jelly Rollin the spring of 1931 to make the move, Gertie was forming other plans. She had not given up the dream of striking it rich. While she worked at Montebello she had met a miner who had told her that Elk Lake, in Northern Ontario, was the best place for prospecting. With that aim in mind, she laced up her prospecting boots and with the canoe, parted company with Grey Owl and the beavers when they reached Toronto and headed north. Grey Owl continued on by train to the prairies, the beavers housed in their metal box.

With her goods packed in her canoe Gertie traveled 480 kilometres up to the Elk Lake area in Northern Ontario. The usual kit for a prospector at the turn of the century was no small bundle. Provisions for one person included things like flour, hardtack, rice, spit peas, dried fruit, lard, butter, coffee, tea and a hefty amount of sugar and salt, laundry soap and toilet soap and of course matches. Besides food supplies a prospector usually carried a rifle, knife, prospecting picks, shovels, hatchet, hammer, handsaw, spikes, rope, pitch and plumb level as well as the cooking equipment, water bucket, and plate, cup and utensils. All these items plus a tent, sufficient clothing, and for some a stove, made up the basic kit of most prospectors.1

When Gertie arrived in Elk Lake she located a promising site and established her camp. Though she possessed the stamina, strength and determination necessary for a prospector it still did not guarantee her a strike. For weeks and weeks she pounded her chisel and broke rock, looking for the tell-tale signs that meant a possible vein but to no avail (though later she was to claim she had made eighteen strikes). She led a basic existence that focused entirely on the prospecting tasks. Meals were simple. Housekeeping details like washing were kept to the minimum—she only laundered her socks, underwear and the occasional shirt.

Then, one of her fellow prospectors who was camped a few portages away from Gertie, rushed home when he received word that his infant daughter was seriously ill. While he was home he heard news of a recent gold discovery in northern Quebec. Hoping to stake a claim there as soon as possible, he wired Gertie and asked her to meet him halfway with his gear. Gertie made the four-day trip and returned to find that lightning had struck her own camp and burnt it to the ground, leaving her with only her canoe and the clothes she wore.

It was early October. She sent word to Grey Owl and he instructed her to go immediately to Winnipeg where he would meet her. Gertie paddled for three days to the nearest train station and boarded the train for the additional three-day journey west to Winnipeg. There she met Grey Owl dressed in her rumpled, unwashed bush clothes with her canoe in tow. She was not home yet —their cabin in Riding Mountain National Park was another 320-kilometre train ride north and then fifty kilometres by road.

While the pair broke their journey in Winnipeg, a Manitoba *Free Press* journalist interviewed both Grey Owl and Gertie. Since his lecture in Montreal in January, Grey Owl's fame had grown through his magazine articles, the Parks Branch publicity and the various newspaper accounts of him. A Winnipeg *Tribune* columnist had traveled to the cabin at Riding Mountain National Park and a warm and welcoming Grey Owl. While Gertie had prospected the previous June the Parks Branch had commissioned another film of Rawhide, Jellyroll and the four new beaver kits that had been born while she was away. The result delighted the Parks Branch and they commissioned more. Schools, church groups, and service clubs across Canada showed the films.2 Grey Owl's celebrity status and the couple's distinctive dress meant they were easily recognizable in Winnipeg and would naturally attract the attention of a journalist for the Manitoba *Free Press*.

The result was an article entitled, "Quest for Gold to Buy Airplane Takes Mohawk Girl Prospecting Alone," with a subtitle "Mrs. Grey Owl Aids Husband to Found Beaver Haven But Keeps Eye on Pots of Gold and Freedom to Roam." The journalist placed it in the woman's interest section, alongside the news of the charity and club work, the "brave women" who carried on missionary work in northern Manitoba, a description of members of the amateur theatre group, as well as a bit on science's influence on fabric colours in clothes fashion.3 Placing a story about an Aboriginal woman prospector in the woman's section reflected the newspaper's view on women prospectors and Gertie in particular. Though occasionally journalists viewed women prospectors as unwelcome intruders in a man's world, for the most part they tended to write about them as curiosities in language and a tone that contained an awkward mix of sexism and admiration.4 There was no doubt Gertie was a curiosity.

The reporter described her as "a winsome lassie with bobbed and wavy hair, eyes in which laughter twinkles and a smile that invites friendship even before she extends an eager hand. Mrs. Grey Owl combines the graces of civilization and the charm of the wilds, choosing what seems best to her from each to make her own life rich and good..." and she possessed a "fine choice of diction, a soft voice and intellectual ideas." A photograph headed the article and showed

Gertie with her bobbed hair, shirt and knotted kerchief around her neck.5

What to make of her? In the initial paragraph the journalist stated that Gertie's dreams had taken her "alone into the hinterlands of Quebec on prospecting trips which few men would dare face without companions...." Further along in the article Gertie recounted her experience as caretaker on Merril Island, as well as the recent lightning strike on her camp while prospecting, and the eighteen claims she staked. Only a few lines later, as if to reassure the reader, the article explained, "the Indian girl is not without her feminine moments. She confessed to a love of nice clothes..." but, with Gertie's typical sly humour, she declared she had given up trying to buy dresses because the fashions changed so quickly that every time she looked she would have had to "get a complete new outfit so not to look dowdy."6

The article also claimed that Gertie, a "Mohawk girl," and descendant of Mohawk warriors, prospected in order to acquire enough money to buy an airplane to travel the world though she also harboured the "deep racial hope that civilisation's latest gifts may give back to the redskin some of the glorious freedom he has lost." The "modern independent" Gertie believed her husband should have "the right to whatever freedom he needs to carry on his work" but such freedom extended to her:

> [she should] have the right to indulge her own tastes when they differ from his but do not infringe on his rights; she wants to make her own way in the world and at the same time she wants to help her husband make a success both of his writing and his chosen work among the beavers.7

To illustrate the point the journalist wrote, "when the urge to write is upon Grey Owl and he seems to need solitude, Mrs. Grey Owl packs her kit, puts away the ways of domesticity and turns again into Paharomen Nahareo (Flaming Leaf), the name under which she trod the wilds with her father and her brothers."8

Despite the article's initial description of Gertie as a curiosity further on in the article the journalist painted a more complex picture of her that challenged many prevailing ideas of Aboriginal women. She was a radical, modern yet feminine woman that could still possess the "charms of the wild," was proud of her heritage and had considered, informed opinions. The journalist wrote that Gertie believed she had as much right to pursue her own interests as Grey Owl did. She was not portrayed as an "Indian Princess," dressed in a buckskin tunic and braids or a drunken vagrant, the common images the public held of Aboriginals. He did not write that she trailed after Grey Owl wrapped in a blanket tending to his needs, or tramped the wilderness as her "mother and sisters," but as her "fathers and brothers" did.9

Grey Owl's interview with the journalist had a very different result. During the exchange Grey Owl reinforced his role as a wilderness champion and condemned the Winnipeg's zoo for their treatment of the beaver, describing it as "a refinement of cruelty," which would cause them to die within the year. His remarks caused quite a stir and prompted zoo officials to issue a statement that revealed Grey Owl had based his opinion on the word of friends. Grey Owl eventually withdrew the condemnation when he personally visited the zoo.10

In this and other interviews Grey Owl was conscious that because they regarded him as Indian he was perceived as the authentic voice of the wilderness and crafted himself to their expectations. To succeed in recruiting the sympathy of these groups Grey Owl increasingly promoted an image that he thought would gain the most acceptance. His literary skill and talent for public speaking at times contradicted his attempts to appear authentic as reporters quizzed him about his ability to speak and write so well. He answered these queries by simplifying his writing and speech to conform to their low expectations of Aboriginal writing and speaking skills.

Following the newspaper interviews Grey Owl and Gertie left Winnipeg for Riding Mountain National Park. Shortly after their arrival Sir Charles G.D. Roberts and his son Lloyd visited the couple at their cabin. Roberts was one of Canada's leading men of letters who, along with Seton, developed the realistic animal story. Lloyd was much struck by Gertie and described his first meeting:

> A young girl, slim and straight as a boy and dressed in fringed buckskin breeches and a blue flannel shirt, shyly shook my hand. Grey Owl introduced her as Pony, but her Indian name was Anahareo. She had bobbed black hair, large dark brown eyes and a wonderful complexion. She was really pretty.11

Grey Owl showed them the beavers and discussed future plans. He was concerned because the continued drought there had left the water levels so low it seemed certain the lake would freeze completely through in winter. The beavers could not survive those conditions. Recognizing this danger Grey Owl asked for a new location. Gertie was reluctant to give up their new spacious cabin with its wonderful veranda, but when she saw the beaver emerge from the stagnant water covered in slimy sludge she was convinced that Grey Owl's decision to move was right.12

In answer to Grey Owl's request the Parks Branch officials suggested he search for a place in Prince Albert National Park, some 720 kilometres northwest of their current location. Grey Owl made the journey and scouted for the best site for the beavers while Gertie stayed at Riding Mountain to look after Jelly Roll, Rawhide and the four kits now named Wakanee, Wakanoo, Silver Bells and Buckshot. He returned ten days later and told Gertie that he had found a site some 169 kilometres north of Prince Albert, by Ajawaan Lake.

They planned the move carefully. Since a beaver's inclination is to build, Gertie and Grey Owl decided to keep them in captivity until the lake froze over to prevent them from working on their lodge, building their feed rafts and creating storage areas in case a sudden drop in temperature froze the shallow lake and trapped them beneath. At the end of October 1931 Gertie and Grey Owl and the still healthy beavers left Riding Mountain National Park and headed for Ajawaan Lake.

It was in the next month that *Country Life* published Grey Owl's book, calling it *Men of the Last Frontier*. Published on both sides of the Atlantic it attracted a lot of attention.[13] The book gave a lyrical account and insight into the life of woodsmen, provided moving descriptions of the wilderness and told of his early experiences with McGinnis and McGinty. The book left no doubt as to his great writing skill and his instinctive talent for storytelling.

Reviews for *Men of the Last Frontier* were favourable in Britain and North America. *The New York Times* praised it, calling Grey Owl, "real and honest," and predicted his book would "outlast its season and many another season." The *Reader's Digest, Toronto Star Weekly* and others ran excerpts of his beaver stories. *The Saturday Review* praised his talent. One professor who reviewed it cast doubt on Grey Owl's authorship and suggested it was the work of a ghostwriter because it was so well written.[14] Grey Owl's power to captivate an audience through the power of his printed and spoken words contributed to his growing fame as one of Canada's pioneer conservationists, crusading for the conservation of Canada's natural resources and wildlife.

Chapter Ten

The New Role of Motherhood

P rince Albert National Park in Saskatchewan Province was part of a new generation of Canadian national parks that hoped to attract the growing number of tourists who had taken to their automobiles to explore the countryside beyond the reaches of the railroad. With its 5,000 square kilometres of forests, valleys, rivers and lakes placed between the southern prairies and the northern boreal forests, the park seemed the perfect spot for recreational tourism.1

The area was originally the hunting and trapping grounds for Cree and a Hudson's Bay Company fur region, with the town of Prince Albert only a small mission among a fledgling agricultural community. In the late nineteenth century the railroad arrived and opened up the region to a timber and fishing industry boom. The boom lasted until just after the First World War when overambitious plans to build a hydroelectric plant left the city bankrupt.2

The Prince Albert residents wanted to continue to develop the fish, timber and mineral resources of this northern wilderness while the prairie inhabitants further south wanted to use the land for agriculture. In the end the government decided to establish a forest reserve, a move that delighted Prince Albert as they began to foster the idea for the government to establish a buffalo herd there. The plans collapsed when the government declared it unsuitable for buffalo.3 These hopes were revived in 1925 when permission to build a new cottage subdivision on Red Deer Lake in 1925 was approved. The Prince Albert residents approached the Parks Branch again and requested the government establish the area as a national park there, with the idea that the buffalo would eventually be installed there. The timely assistance of Prince Albert's MP to solve Prime Minister Mackenzie King's political crisis, prompted the prime minister to grant the request. In 1927 the region, covering 3,570 square kilometres, including the area within the forest reserve and other lands to the east and south of Montreal Lake, became a national park.4

Though Parks Commissioner James Harkin was a conservationist, he was not a preservationist, and so had no plans to keep the park in its wilderness state. His vision for the park was to establish a recreational tourism that would provide enough income to satisfy Parliament. To further this plan the government established Montreal Lake Indian Reserve on the park's eastern edge for the Cree and other tribes who were still trapping, hunting and fishing in the area. They also prohibited them and any other locals from hunting in the park. Not everyone was happy with the situation. A well-known Metis and acquaintance of Gertie and Grey Owl, Louis LaVallee, remained in the park until 1934 when he reluctantly agreed to relocate after receiving compensation.5

The park included three important lakes, Waskesiu, Kingsmere and Crean. In 1929 LaVallee Lake was added, increasing the park's size. Waskesiu Lake, 169 kilometres north of Prince Albert, with its large number of white, sandy beaches, became the park's main base site for its facilities. To build the park facilities the Parks Branch decided to create work camps and employ the growing number of jobless that gravitated to Prince Albert and wandered their streets in the wake of the Depression. These government workers built tennis courts, golf courses, a clubhouse, kitchen shelters, a band shell, a recreation field and a children's playground. They also constructed internal roads linking the buildings. Such promising facilities attracted shops and other private businesses. By 1931 Waksesiu boasted ten rows of shack tents (wooden walls and a tarp on the roof divided into a bedroom and living area), at least three hotels, a grocery story and a dance hall, The Terrace Gardens. The Terrace Gardens featured bands like the Singing Rascals and The Terriers and in the week hosted jitney dances where ten cents was charged for each dance.6

The park administrator, James Wood, established a park warden patrol system. The wardens worked six days per week, ten hours a day during the summer, nine hours in spring and fall, and eight hours in winter. They were on call at all times and earned

$1200 to $1500 per year. Each had a district to patrol of about 427 square kilometres and patrols could last anywhere from a day to a week and were accomplished by freight canoe, snowshoe, horseback or dog team.7

Grey Owl and Gertie arrived in the middle of this extensive development and made their way with the beavers to Ajawaan Lake, just north of Kingsmere Lake, to their newly built cabin, Beaver Lodge. Given the state of the economy, Grey Owl's appointment was fortunate for them both. The Depression had badly affected park attendance, despite the staff's efforts to build more attractions. It was with hope of improving these statistics that Superintendent Wood welcomed Grey Owl and built the cabin to his specifications to provide the best home possible for the beavers. The lodge, (6.6 metres by 7.6 metres) included a living area for Gertie and Grey Owl, as well as living quarters and a plunge hole for the beavers. The plunge hole was a submerged tunnel under the cabin's foundations that led out to the beaver's feed-raft in the lake. Gertie and Grey Owl's side of the cabin floor was made of adzed log, while the beaver's side was simply earth. There was also a gateway for the beaver to come and go as they pleased through Gertie and Grey Owl's part of the cabin.8

Though the group quickly settled in at the cabin Rawhide was in a frenzy of worry over the lack of winter preparations because it was early November. Confined to the cabin, he chewed away at the house while the beaver kits created mayhem around him. Once the lake had frozen Gertie and Grey Owl opened the plunge hole and Rawhide was able to discover that the feed-raft was already in place and his worry was needless. The beaver's provisions satisfied, Grey Owl turned to the chore of stocking up the human winter food supplies; he packed his gear and headed north of Pelican Lake, outside the park boundary, to hunt game. Once he completed that task there was little to do but settle down for a winter without financial worries, pressure to write, or the need to search for lost beavers. With so little to occupy him, and with the beavers more or less holed up for the winter, Grey Owl became restless and moody, thinking his remaining life would be very inactive. To counter his feelings he went out on exploring expeditions, frequently staying overnight, and occasionally extending his stay to two or three days. Gertie remained at home with the beavers, listening to the radio they had purchased.

Gertie could not always charm him out of his moodiness when he did return from his expeditions. His restlessness continued until January when he made a decision. He would write another book. Gertie was appalled. Despite his claims he would only "dabble" in it, she knew the dabbling would consume him and make him "like a zombie." Gertie imagined a dismal winter confined to the very small cabin, with few things to occupy her time as she tipped-toed around to perform chores while Grey Owl slept after a long night of writing. With the Depression in full swing Gertie knew there was nowhere she could go easily and find employment. For as she put it, "in good times and in bad, how many openings are there for a trapper, dog-musher or prospector?"[9]

Grey Owl began his book and, as Gertie feared, all she heard from him that winter was the "scratch, scratch of his pen," along with arguments against taking a bath. Grey Owl loathed baths and would offer any number of lame excuses—he had a cold, there was no privacy—or he would recount events from history to illustrate the dangers of baths. It was all said humorously but it did not lessen Gertie's frustration at dealing with a man inhabiting a world she could not share, the world of writing. Tempers flared and arguments erupted. Gertie was not one to endure such behaviour quietly or without complaint.

Eventually Gertie decided to take more positive action and study mineralogy. On her previous prospecting trips she had often lamented her lack of knowledge about the various rocks and their formations and felt this was a perfect opportunity to do something about it. In addition to her study she corresponded to four or five of her former fellow prospectors. While she worked away, her table scattered with mortar, pestle, magnifying glass, books and some 200 rock specimens, Grey Owl, surrounded by piles of paper, wrote his book.

Rawhide was also busy at his own project creating a house for his brood. Initially it had begun with a few paltry sticks leaned against the wall over the plunge hole that Gertie and Grey Owl had only pitied. But Rawhide was working thriftily and patiently, only using peeled sticks left from the bark given to his family. The house took shape gradually, its opening right off into Gertie and Grey Owl's living room so the beaver could continue to bring in more mud and sticks later on if it was necessary to enlarge it, and also of course to obtain snacks of apples, rice or the whole wheat bread treats Jelly Roll usually ate.

With everyone so absorbed in various projects it came as a surprise when Gertie became ill. Convinced she had contracted tuberculosis like her mother before her, she persuaded Grey Owl to take her as far as Waskesiu, and from there she went by truck to a sanatorium in Prince Albert. The sanatorium staff x-rayed her and questioned her. She was not ill at all. She was pregnant. Early in their marriage when Gertie had broached the subject of having a baby Grey Owl had adamantly refused. "No babies," he told her categorically. Learning she was to have a baby was unexpected to the both of them but Grey Owl seemed happy to hear the news.

As the winter passed the pair continued with their respective projects, though the prospect of a child did not always mean a harmonious environment between Grey Owl and Gertie. She had never found it easy to control her temper and the fluctuating pregnancy hormones made it even more difficult now. On one particular occasion, when Grey Owl returned from a trip to Waskesiu and forgot to bring back the greens she craved, she flew into a rage and went after him with a knife.10

Despite these hiccups the winter and spring passed and when the tourist season arrived the visitors began to find their way to Beaver Lodge. Waskesiu, the park's headquarters, was 112 kilometres from Prince Albert. Once arrived in Waskesiu the visitor could launch a canoe onto Kingsmere Lake and paddle the ten kilometres to the old warden's lodge on the northern shore and then portage the small distance to Ajawaan Lake. There they could re-launch the canoe to cross the remaining distance (canoe was the only transport Grey Owl permitted once he arrived; he banned the use of motorboats on the lake). Alternatively, the visitor could make the fifty-six-kilometre trek around Kingsmere Lake to the warden's cabin, then on by canoe to Beaver Lodge which was tucked among a dense forest of aspen and pine trees, water lilies floating by the shore.11

Grey Owl delighted in showing off the beavers. In the years following, visitors to the lodge were treated to a memorable spectacle, one created to some degree with conscious deliberation by Grey Owl in order to win others to his work and also because he welcomed the company. He was the perfect host, saluting them "like an Indian" as they arrived, his hair in braids, dressed in buckskin trousers and a red flannel shirt, or, if he wore his hat he would doff it, bow slightly and help his visitors ashore, fix his piercing blue eyes on them and impress them with his command of English. Sitting on logs or blankets on the ground, Grey Owl would chat amiably until he called the beavers or they appeared on their own. One visitor described the experience following the arrival Jelly Roll and the other beavers:

> The Old Lady turned up first. She swam around a bit and then came ashore, looked the visitors over, walked to the cabin door and banged it open and went in. After something to eat she went off on various jobs and we managed to see something of them. They have workings all over the place. They cut down stuff and drag it to the water and swim it to the lodge. Sometimes it goes on the outside part and other times, they land it, drag it through the cabin and put it on the part of the lodge there.[12]

In the cabin there were boxes of apples and bread. Rawhide was known to come out with a loaf of bread in his arms and dive into the water, kicking his back feet madly in an attempt to go below the surface, until the loaf was soaked enough to sink and allow him to go lower. In addition to the apples and bread, the beavers were also provided with canned milk, Jersey chocolate bars and peanuts, mostly for Jelly Roll. A typical shipment of stores the park provided contained a box of chocolate bars, five boxes of apples, forty loaves of whole wheat bread, ten pounds of peanuts and a bag of rice.[13]

At the opening of the 1932 tourist season Gertie seized the opportunity to escape the cabin and go to Prince Albert to buy clothes to accommodate her expanding waistline. Dresses were the only available maternity wear and since it was five years since she had worn one, she had no idea what size to buy. But now, with a new shape and motherhood looming, putting on a dress was more than just a change of clothes. It was a reminder that she was heading into new territory and one that led her away from the bush, where all her abilities and confidence resided. This new territory of motherhood was completely new to her and there was no one to guide her in it.

Gertie was not the only one considering the implications of a newborn. In view of the baby's imminent arrival at Beaver Lodge, the Parks Branch made plans to build another cabin just above it for Gertie and the newborn. Beaver Lodge, where over one third of the space was devoted to the beavers who tripped in and out at all times in the summer months dragging saplings, scattering peanut shells, or carrying loaves of bread, was not the safest place for a newborn baby. A separate cabin seemed a practical solution.

In August, two weeks before the baby was due, Gertie returned to Prince Albert and stayed in a hotel to be near the hospital in case she gave birth early. As she passed the time before the birth, thoughts of her new role as mother prompted her to perm her hair and shop for a dress to wear following the birth. It was a tentative exploration, an experiment, far removed from the woman dressed in buckskins. There was only Grey Owl to help her, but unlike his previous mentoring in bush skills, Grey Owl had no experience in motherhood.14

On August 23 Gertie gave birth to a daughter. In the haze of sedation after the birth Gertie called her daughter Rita Ellen, a name later changed to Shirley Dawn. Grey Owl visited the pair just after the birth, and perhaps uncertain how to react when presented with his newborn daughter exclaimed, "Holy Mackerel, she looks like a maggot!"15

Maggot became one of the many names like "reptile," "insect" and "wee ting" Grey Owl used as endearments for Dawn and sometimes Gertie. Though he could not instruct Gertie directly on baby care, he did understand she might need some help. She had purchased no diapers, clothes or any of the necessities for the arrival of a baby. In the light of these worries and on the recommendation of one of the game wardens, Grey Owl arranged for Gertie to stay for a time in Prince Albert with Mrs. Ettie Winters, an Englishwoman. She and her family had recently arrived from the parched prairie lands of southern Saskatchewan and had established a boarding house. Mrs. Winters came highly recommended by many of the wardens who stayed with her and her family when they were in Prince Albert during their time off.16

Mrs. Winters shopped for all the necessities for the baby and met Gertie at the hospital. With newly permed hair Gertie donned her dress, a lovely fitted black one with a flared skirt. She wrapped the baby in a shawl and accompanied Mrs. Winters to her boarding house. The Winters, spending all their time in south Saskatchewan, had never seen a "real Indian" before and had imagined a large woman with her papoose. Gertie surprised them all with her styled hair and modern dress. But Gertie's experiment with a more feminine motherly image was short-lived. The dress donned for her departure from the hospital she quickly set aside for her more familiar shirt, breeches and high-top boots and the determined use of the iron on her hair removed most of the traces of the perm until it grew out and she could shape it once again into her usual bob. This view of Gertie was even more surprising to the Winters family, but they could see she became more relaxed and at home, eventually becoming very close to the family that included a daughter and three sons. Gertie found Mrs. Winters' patient coaching helpful and reassuring and saw her undoubted attachment to Dawn, something that might have caused her a few twinges of envy. Under Mrs. Winters' eye Gertie continued to learn and grow more confident about caring for Dawn. She even knitted her booties and other jackets. Ultimately though, her role as a mother would be defined on her own terms and not dictated by society.17

While learning amid the Winters all that caring for her new daughter entailed, it would have been natural for Gertie to think about her family back in Mattawa. Though she had not visited them since she left for the holiday years before, she had kept in touch with them. Grey Owl wrote them letters and Gertie, never one for corresponding, would include her message at the end. She missed her father the most and spoke often about him to the Winters. Back when she and Grey Owl were confined to their cabin in Quebec, she had even fashioned a figure of her father from the cabin's clay floor.18

The Winters family did their best to make her and Dawn feel welcome. Fourteen-year-old Margaret Winters was delighted to have the baby in the house and fell in love with her. She found Gertie interesting and exciting, lots of fun, with a great sense of humour. Gertie showed her how to knit and soon had her making a garment. When it was finished, Margaret was so anxious to show off her first efforts at knitting, she washed it and put it on the oven door to dry, until the smell of burning wool caught her attention. To her horror she saw a gaping hole in her new garment. This was no problem for Gertie, who knitted a patch right into it.19

From Beaver Lodge Grey Owl wrote many affectionate letters to Gertie filled with plans for Dawn as well as news of the progress on the new cabin. Gertie was impatient to return, so when he wrote that furniture was the only remaining thing to construct, she decided to speed up the process and purchase the furniture in Prince Albert without a word to Grey Owl. She bought a Chesterfield sofa bed, chairs, a rug, a mirror and two tables, as well as curtain material. Following her shopping spree, she phoned the Parks garage in town and told them to pick up the furniture and send it on to Beaver Lodge. She asked that they send it as soon as possible so that it would arrive before her, to ensure she would not be present when Grey Owl was presented with the bill.20

Mrs. Winters was concerned about Dawn living so far in the woods and at Grey Owl's prior instruction she arranged for a companion named Alma to accompany Gertie to Ajawaan Lake. Gertie was not enthusiastic about the idea and felt it was a waste of money, but she agreed. With Alma in tow the small group made their way back to Beaver Lodge to surprise Grey Owl. On the way, to Gertie's dismay, they passed the furniture at the Kingsmere portage and later arrived at the cabin, where Gertie faced her own surprise: a man perched on one of the bunks filming the beavers as they scurried busily across the roofless cabin with armloads of sticks and mud to shore up the two-foot hole created by the film crew. The Parks' publicity person, Bill Oliver, and his crew had returned to make another film of the beavers to be shown in schools across the country.

With Grey Owl running madly between the crew and Gertie and the baby there was no time to discuss the furniture. It was not until after the film crew had departed the next day and Grey Owl had retrieved the carpenter in the boat that Gertie confessed to her shopping spree. Despite her fears, Grey Owl accepted the seemingly reckless use of their money with calm and even entered into the excitement of arranging the new purchases when the furniture finally arrived.

Gertie with baby Dawn and Louis LaVallee, courtesy of Katherine Swartile

Once the thrill of her return and the filming of the beavers had passed, Grey Owl resumed his writing and his habit of sleeping during the day, writing at night, intolerant of any disturbance. Gertie's new quarters, the upper cabin, had no food storage, dining or cooking facilities, an arrangement that meant every time Alma or Gertie needed to prepare or eat a meal, they disturbed Grey Owl's sleep. It was not long before Grey Owl's lack of sleep began to tell and he became irritable and unsociable and at odds with Alma. After a few encounters Alma borrowed Grey Owl's canoe and paddled to one of the warden's quarters, returning the next morning with a nasty hangover. Since Grey Owl was known to drink, he could not quibble with her actions, but he nonetheless felt that it was time for her to go, thereby eliminating at least one person who might disturb his peace.

Following Alma's departure Gertie went to Beaver Lodge only when absolutely necessary. She started bringing the next day's lunch and breakfast up to the cabin with the evening meal. She did the wash only when Grey Owl was awake. Other than meals and washing, her day primarily consisted of bringing in the wood and the water and taking care of the two-month-old baby who slept most of the time. Increasingly the cabin seemed too confining, so as soon as the lake froze and the beavers went to their quarters, Gertie and Grey Owl scrubbed Beaver Lodge, covered the beaver house with a tarpaulin to keep the dust down, then brought a rug, chair and curtains from the upper cabin, and Gertie and Dawn moved down to Beaver Lodge.

They passed a quiet winter; just before spring was upon them and travel became very difficult in soggy snow and melting ice, Gertie and Grey Owl decided it would be safest for Dawn to be in Prince Albert in case she became ill. Wrapping Dawn in a rabbit-fur robe Gertie had won in a poker game when she was up North, Gertie traveled by toboggan to the Winters' home in Prince Albert. Grey Owl returned to the cabin to write, attend to the beavers when they emerged from their winter quarters, and prepare for the tourists that might arrive when the park's summer season began.

Chapter Eleven

Pursuing More Adventure

Gertie and Dawn were still in Prince Albert in May when Gertie received a cable from a prospector she had met in Elk Lake advising her to go immediately down to Chapleau, Ontario, and stake an area where a new discovery of gold had just been made. Such an expedition would take a month, including traveling time. Dawn was not even a year old but the temptation to go out in the wilderness and try again to strike it rich proved very tempting.

Other women prospectors faced similar dilemmas when torn between the lure of the mineral field and the tug of children. Many left their children behind, sending them to school if possible, or placing them in the care of a family member or friend. An occasional woman prospector took her children along with them.[1] The depth of the obsession for both the promise of riches and the wilderness itself led many women prospectors to remain in or return to the wilderness. Gertie was no different and could not easily shake off the addiction, the draw of such a challenge. Later in life when she was asked how she could have contemplated leaving her daughter she said, "I had to go," then added, "but you don't leave your child like that."[2]

The inhabitants of Waskesiu came to recognize Gertie's love of challenges and taking risks. She once accepted a bet with some "old timers" around Waskesiu that she could cross the lake with an open box of matches in the bottom of the canoe on a windy day and never get the matches wet. As she later recounted, she shot from the pier at Waskesiu into the white caps with the matchbox open, and an hour later she nosed into shore, laid the paddle across the gunnel and began to light the matches.3

Still undecided, she wrote to Grey Owl for guidance, and he replied with a letter filled with encouragement and advice, as well as a post-dated check for $71. "Let no moss grow on that offer," he told her. "This is the only Gambler's chance you get to make a few thousand for the Great Bear [Lake] stake." Despite the small size of the prospect he urged her take it seriously:

> "Stake, if you go, under Gertie Bernard otherwise it will not be legal, you know what I mean. Use me or your dad or both [proxies]. Make this a serious business."4

He explained the enclosed money was to purchase her prospecting license and to hire an Indian girl to accompany her. In this way he thought she would only be dependent for help from the other prospectors for a grubstake and transport in from Chapleau and then only if they suggested it. Help should be accepted when she was in a position to return favours. That said, Grey Owl suggested she look up his old friend Bill Draper, as well as the policeman, Mr Anderson, and his former mentor, Alex Espaniel, and ask his daughter Jane Spaniel to be her companion:

> Look up Mr. Anderson, a policeman in Chapleau. He and I had some dealings. ($50 and costs) he is a good fellow. Find out if Alec Spaniel is up there. He will give you very wise counsel; heed him. You might get Jane Spaniel; she is very intelligent and good company.5

Gertie's adventure had also inspired Grey Owl to form his own hopes and dreams about venturing into the bush. He told her "If I am able to save enough a year from this fall I will spend the Winter in the [Spanish River?] and you could come down for Xmas."6 Spanish River was "40 miles in" from his old stomping ground, Bisco. Such a desire may have only been wishful thinking initially, but it was one born of his fond memories of his time near Biscotasing, when he was active in the bush. He closed the letter with some additional advice about switching Dawn over to formula milk before she left and ended with his love to the "wee ting," then signed it "Archie."7

Grey Owl understood the need that drove Gertie to prospect—the lure of the wilderness and the potential it held for riches. He knew what it was like to yearn for the adventure and challenge the wilderness held and the frustration of a fixed and limited daily life. Gertie's immersion into motherhood was not yet able to satisfy her curious mind and thirst for adventure. Grey Owl realized that and let her have her wings, in as far as he was able.

After consulting with Grey Owl, Gertie talked to Mrs. Winters and she agreed to look after Dawn while Gertie tried her luck. With Grey Owl's support and Dawn safe in the care of Mrs. Winters, Gertie decided to seize the opportunity to prospect at Chapleau. Grey Owl met her at Prince Albert before she left, and though they had some cross words, possibly over finances, there was still no doubt that he supported her decision. Such support was important to her and she was grateful.8

Before her arrival at Chapleau a newspaper reporter filed a story about her. It appeared first in *Christian Science Monitor* in a shortened version under the headline, "Indian Squaw Turns From Kitchen Duties to Gold Prospecting," but the next day a longer piece appeared in the Calgary *Herald,* with the headline, "Grey Owl's Wife Leaves Alone on Search for Gold." Though the *Herald* headline played on her connection to Grey Owl, both articles focused entirely on her. They portrayed Gertie as an expert in the bush, "entirely capable of the arduous tasks necessary for prospecting."

These tasks included "wielding a tomahawk," and easily carrying a pack weighing as much as 120 pounds [54 kilos] "when she is hardened to the trail." Her kit included 500 pounds [227 kilos] of supplies and equipment, besides her canoe, which she would have to port at least six times to her destination. This posed no problem for her, capable as she was of "swinging her canoe up for a portage as nonchalantly as another woman would stir the morning porridge." Though she might proclaim that it was easy, there was no doubt that such a journey would try "the courage of the sturdiest of men."9

Despite the use of "squaw" in the headline of the one piece, the article steered away from the negative imagery associated with it. Gertie was described in masculine terms that emphasized her capability and strength; a woman who could carry out the arduous tasks necessary to prospect. It was only in equipping her with a "tomahawk" instead of a hatchet, putting "squaw" in the headline, and stating "Nahareo" as her Mohawk name, that the journalist drew attention to her as an Aboriginal. These terms carried with them the "noble savage" sentiments that suggested her natural purity and connection to the wilderness, but they were not central elements of the article.

Gertie also explained some of her attraction to the wilderness. "I'm very lonesome in town," she told the interviewer. "It's different in the bush and I feel more at home packing and paddling than I do standing beside a kitchen range." Though she was noted as the first woman prospector to travel alone in the Swayze area, being alone in the wilderness did not equate to her being lonely, a quality she experienced only in town.10 The wilderness was her home, support and strength. There she felt independent, strong and capable, and that was the person she presented to the world. Her image was convincing and confident enough that she could momentarily successfully challenge the codes of conduct for women in general and Aboriginal women specifically.

In the end Gertie's endurance and capabilities and love of the wilderness were tested in a different manner. She arrived at her destination, but after five days and nights of a drenching rain that prevented her from going into the woods, Gertie succumbed to an overwhelming longing for Dawn and took the next westbound train. Before she left, Grey Owl sent her another letter, addressing it, "Madame the Woman Prospector of Algona." Still encouraging, he mentioned the wife of a friend who was also prospecting (though he assured her that she would go further) and passed on news of another find. He also told her not to "take foolish risks" for Dawn's sake because, "a girl raised without a mother's love is often unhappy or a misfit in later years and we don't want our Reptile to be miserable do we." He hastened to reassure her that Dawn was not presently miserable and was in good hands with Mrs. Winters, but added again that, "a girl child needs a mother; you poor kid know how it feels to be without one."11

Tones of recrimination eventually crept into this letter, something he tried to counter in mid-sentence, or in the next line. He wrote he was sorry that neither he nor Gertie would be present at the celebration for Dawn's first birthday but then in the next breath he apologized.

> I feel pretty bad having been cross with you, not knowing when I might ever see you again. Try and forget it if you can. My nerves are not as they should be and there has been quite a strain this last year, and a person alone and a wee bit discouraged is inclined to brood over things.12

He also mentioned that he had originally thought her ungrateful for his help:

> I felt a big cloud lift when you told me that you appreciated whatever help I have been able to do to help you at times....What I felt to be lack of appreciation was what made me impatient a lot, and I am glad it is not so, because it is good to give, and a privilige[sic] to be able to do so, even if every so little, and gifts

small or large, should encourage good feeling and not cause dispute.13

Besides apologizing for the argument, he also wrote he was sorry that he only sent her $70, but it was all he could afford. Grey Owl still had money worries despite his regular salary from the Parks Department. Never good at managing his finances, he often over spent his pay in bouts of generosity or drinking sprees. He even sent money to Gertie's father at least on one occasion. Often he would postdate checks, banking on his future pay. He still worried enough to explain himself to Gertie and question her purchase of a canoe, but it did not prevent him from expressing the hope that the profits from the book's sale would enable him to stay at Beaver Lodge only in the summer and go back east during the winter, after arranging for someone else to look after the beavers in that time period. Grey Owl felt that he could not remain at Beaver Lodge the year round for if he did he would "become nothing at all." He too understood the frustration of being stuck in one place with little to do, harbouring his own dreams of more adventure, and as a consequence accepted that Gertie might be away for a long time in pursuit of her dreams.14

Though absent from Prince Albert both Grey Owl and Gertie still gave thought to their daughter. Grey Owl wrote to Mrs. Winters on a regular basis, enclosing money and directions for Dawn's care. Before she departed for Chapleau, Gertie had left instructions with Mrs. Winters for the doctor to call on Dawn every month, but Grey Owl countered that idea because he could not afford it and felt it unnecessary, though he asked Mrs. Winters to refrain from telling Gertie who would only worry.15

By the end of September Gertie was back in Prince Albert, at Dawn's side, and Grey Owl was requesting that she knit socks for him for the upcoming winter. All thought of knitting was put aside, though, when a short while later she received another letter from a prospector. He was at Great Bear Lake in the Arctic where the biggest discovery of a variety of radium ore had been found. The letter urged her to "join the big doings" and come and blanket stake the area.16

Despite her previous disastrous experience Gertie was anxious to try her luck. She felt that armed with the knowledge she would miss Dawn, she could manage it better. The problem this time was the $5,000 necessary for the trip that included a return plane ticket from Edmonton to the Arctic, proper equipment, clothing and sufficient provisions. Though she knew they had nothing like that amount of money she went to Beaver Lodge and showed Grey Owl the letter. He bought her a ticket to Toronto to approach three miners whom she thought would sponsor her. The only person she managed to locate strongly disapproved of anyone venturing into that area, especially a woman. Undaunted, Gertie used her "eating money" to journey to Buffalo to see a man she had met in Elk Lake country while he was on a holiday canoe trip. He refused to finance her because "the thought that he would be responsible for sending a girl there would drive [him] nuts." Disappointed, Gertie returned to Prince Albert and then on to Beaver Lodge with Dawn, where Grey Owl was still hard at work on his book.17

This time before she had left for the east Grey Owl wrote her and instructed her not to ask the park administrator, Mr. Woods, for permission to go prospecting. Though they could not stop her, it would be best not to "open up any ideas." It was not just his concern that she refrain from asking the park's permission but that she "keep mum[,] tell nobody except the Winters when and where you are going…"

> All this news is getting out through "friends" of ours in the park. Warn Mr. Walrod if you see him, he is a careful man, tell no one from the highest park official down. If the press come for a story tell them nothing that they can use but be careful do not antagonize them[,] the Prince Albert papers are hostile to the park officials.18

Grey Owl was already aware of the need to control his public image and Gertie's.

Early in the winter, after her return from the fruitless journey to secure her grubstake, Gertie and Dawn returned to Prince Albert to board with the Winters. Despite his declared loneliness without her, Grey Owl was so immersed in his writing that Gertie found Ajawaan "indescribably dull," confined as she was to the cabin and its immediate surroundings with a young baby. In Prince Albert there would be some diversion and people to talk to, though, as she described it, "boarding out wasn't exactly a satisfactory way of life either." Gertie was still young, only twenty-seven years old and full of restless energy. All that she had wished for back in the Jumping Caribou River area she now had, but it did not seem to be enough. As she herself explained:

> Now I had two homes at Ajawaan, and I found neither joy or contentment in either of them; I had the baby I had wanted so badly, whom I loved more than anything in the world, yet I had to fight an urge, almost unbearable at times to go north again….The expression 'the call of the wild' is hackneyed and a joke with most people, but with me it was a disease, and by spring 1934 I knew I would have to make one more trip—out there.19

Unaware of her strong feelings, Grey Owl wrote to Gertie often that winter, nostalgically discussing the past events that they had shared as he wrote the book, *Pilgrims of the Wild*. He had set aside his earlier writing, *Tales of an Empty Cabin* to work on this book, recapturing at least on paper the idyll they had shared in Ontario and Quebec, while the present space between them was increasingly becoming a physical and emotional reality. "Of course I can't keep you out of it, & I describe vividly how we fought five fast rounds to a finish over a tub of moonshine. (Ha!Ha! and again Ha!)…There will be none of that bitter hatefulness…If there was anything beautiful in those days, and there was a lot of it." He also wrote, "I have captured some of it."20

Ettie Winters' husband spent February and March with Grey Owl, typing up the manuscript, compiling his drawings and arranging for them to be printed, then sending the manuscript to the publishers. It was a companionable relationship, Grey Owl near in age to Mr. Winters and sharing some of the same interests. That he valued Mr. Winter's assistance was clear when he called on his help to compile and post his later book, *Tales of an Empty Cabin*.21

In May Grey Owl wrote to Gertie in Prince Albert after his return to Beaver Lodge from a trip to town for supplies and to see her and Dawn. The journey had been tough going and he had sweated so much he caught a cold in his weakened lungs. Despite his ill health Jelly Roll greeted his arrival with a dressing down as she vented her dismay over his neglect. It was all wearing on him. The growing number of beavers, compounded with the demands of the book, made him contemplate a request to have a friend, Albert Berube, to help him in July and August, because he was getting no regular meals or sleep and felt in need of company. He also hoped to figure a way to have Dawn spend some time at Beaver Lodge during the summer. As he speculated about the possibilities, he also advised Gertie not to be too harsh with Dawn during her tantrums, but to keep her own self control.22

Though his letter was full of parenting advice it was also clear that his visit with them had not gone without a hitch and he and Gertie had argued:

> What got into me that night? I can't quite remember what it was all about, my mind seemed to lapse and I have only a hazy idea. I remember walking up and down some road howling. Hope I didn't make too many breaks.
>
> Say Gertie—I mean -rude [sic], where did you spend that night out? And part of the next day? You must be careful. Hope you are not slipping kid. I would be disappointed for our daughter, and for

old times too. This is not an accusation but I was and am a little worried over it.23

He now knew she was thinking of going away again and it might have been that which caused his "roaring." But after the heat of the moment he tried to make a bit of amends and asked that if she was going north, would both she and Dawn come and visit before she left. In his closing page, he apologized for his mood, explaining it away by war pictures he had seen:

> these past days kind of weigh heavy on a person's mind at times, which I suppose is why I talk of them now when I'm drinking, a kind of defence or escape complex. It plays hell with me at times. Don't take too seriously some of the things I say. I am sometimes very worried.24

Though his letter was full of mixed feelings, he still sent her $35, all he could manage at the time after their bout of drinking and expenses.25

Such was the distance between them that when Gertie finally resolved she had to make one more trip, she refrained from telling him until she was well underway. She knew that he worried about their lack of money and any prospecting venture required it. She also sensed perhaps that Grey Owl's patience with her unproductive prospecting trips was wearing thin. But Gertie was determined to head out. She decided to go to God's Lake in sub-Arctic Manitoba, some 640 kilometres away as the crow flies and much longer by canoe. She knew that if she returned to Ajawaan to collect her gear Grey Owl would learn of her plans, so she decided to order new equipment on credit at the hardware store in Prince Albert. Axe, cooking utensils, tent, mosquito bar, sleeping bag, rifle, dynamite, prospector's pick and a prospector's license were all added to Grey Owl's store bill, an amount she recalled as $900 but Grey Owl later stated was $160. The canoe she hired at $25 a month.26

Though she may not have informed Grey Owl, others easily got wind of it, including a journalist who interviewed her. In the news article he called her "Mrs. Grey Owl, the wife of the widely known beaver conservationist" and described her decision to head north as the "lure of gold." The bulk of the article focused on her capability and strength as she embarked on a difficult journey:

> Hardships of the outdoors hold no terror for the Indian women, Mrs. Grey Owl pointed out, citing the case of Mrs. Blood, 90-year-old Indian woman of the Little Black Bear Reserve, found last Saturday after being lost for two and a half days in the wind and rain swept bluffs near her home. Almost blind through old age, Mrs. Blood burrowed into the bluff and weathered the rainstorm. When she was returned home by searchers she called for a cup of tea and her pipe, and chuckled over concern felt for her safety....
>
> Muscular from her life in the open, Nahareo is 5 feet 5 inches tall, and when on the trail wears a red flannel shirt, khaki breeches and top boots, with her jet-black hair bare to the weather...[27]

This was Gertie at her best: a prospector, proud of her Aboriginal heritage, about to embark on an arduous journey that held no fear for her, like the old Aboriginal woman to whom she compared herself. She was a woman capable of handling the elements in adverse situations, alone and independent, not a squaw subservient to her mate as she trudged after him in the wilderness, laden with supplies, a common image among Euro-Canadian society.

In the years since she first appeared in newspapers Gertie was able to hone her own ideas about herself, and as a result, gave responses to journalists that countered many of the prevailing ideas and images of Aboriginal women. She came across increasingly as an independent, articulate and capable woman who could possess progressive ideas and behave in a modern manner while still negotiating bush in a way that represented her contemporary views rather than the past of her ancestors.

Though Grey Owl had many Aboriginal acquaintances he chose to promote his message cast in the romantic mould of the noble and pure Indian, the idea that held sway in the England of his youth. Despite creating an image for himself that included beaded buckskins, braids, and, even on occasion, a warbonnet, Grey Owl's portrayal of Gertie in *Pilgrims of the Wild* contained very little of the romantic ideas gleaned from Longfellow or Fenimore Cooper. He certainly drew a romantic picture of the story of their relationship, but the Gertie he portrayed was no Indian Princess. His only nod to any hint at romanticism was the statement that she was a direct descendant of hereditary Iroquois chiefs, a claim that was in part true, and his decision to call her "Anahareo." He explained that "Anahareo" was her tribal name, but more likely Grey Owl, in his usual manner of loose translation, chose to modify the name of her great-grandfather John Ananenha Nelson.28

Anahareo, courtesy of Katherine Swartile

Besides giving Gertie a "tribal" name and recounting her parentage, Grey Owl depicted no Indian stereotype; he remained true to the image that she presented to the journalists. "She was strictly modern," he wrote, "as modern went at that time, a good dancer and conversationalist, and, a particular dresser herself...." Though he could praise her style and modernity he was not shy of pointing out her contradictions:

> I speedily discovered that I was married to no butterfly, in spite of her modernistic ideas, and found that my companion could swing an axe as well as she could a lip-stick, and was able to put up a tent in good shape, make a quick fire, and could rig a tump-line and get a load across in good time, even if she did have to sit down and powder her nose at the other end of the portage.29

Strong and stubborn, eager to follow him on the trap line, she "was not very much of an expert at out-door cooking," but she was still a "first class needlewoman." She was also a woman who was emotional and temperamental who "could sleep out in the rain with a smile and cry over a lack of ceremony at meal times," one who demanded to be included in his everyday life in the bush but required curtains and decorations in the cabin. It was only such a woman as this who could persuade him to give up his trapping and rescue the beaver kits to raise them. And it was this Anahareo that would capture the imagination of the multitude of readers when the book, *Pilgrims of the Wild,* was eventually published.

Chapter Twelve

A Relationship Under Strain

Anahareo launched her hired canoe from Waskesiu Lake, paddled the seventy-two kilometres of shallow rapids to Montreal Lake. She had packed to account for all possibilities, even added some books to read, but had miscalculated the capacity of a sixteen-foot canoe. With her canoe top heavy and sitting low in the water, she was forced to wade and guide the canoe down the swift water to avoid ripping it on the rocks. Once she reached Montreal Lake an invitation to a poker game with some Cree women soon solved the extra weight problem. Throwing anything from a bar of soap to a bag of beans on the blanket as a wager, she soon found her canoe sitting higher in the water.[1]

Before she departed on the next stage of her journey, Anahareo finally wrote to Grey Owl and told him about her trip, then headed off for the 128 kilometre stretch to Lac La Ronge. To keep her thoughts from running riot about her actions, Anahareo paddled as much as possible, no matter the weather, resting only when necessary, often too tired to put up her tent. By the time she arrived at Lac La Ronge she was soaked to the skin. She handed over a letter of introduction that she had to two miners to ensure a warm welcome and she was soon dry and well fed.2

Her arrival coincided with a wedding dance celebration. Anahareo joined in with enthusiasm and had a good sampling of the plentiful food and the illicit moonshine. She was soon brought down to earth when she received a letter from Grey Owl filled with a mixture of envy, disapproval and admiration, its borders punctuated with a scowling fanged owl, exclamation points, jagged arrows and "x's." He was not mad, he told her, she was doing what she thought was right. But he was worried about the finances because the park had cut all wages, and he had been already overspending. Despite his worries about the money, he still expressed envy over her journey:

> Gee but when I heard that you were out into clear and free with a canoe and an outfit, bound for the big waters, I felt sick and hungry to be out again, going, going with the old axe and teapail and canoe and away.3

Grey Owl also wrote that he was disappointed because he was not to have Albert Berube to help him that summer, so all his dreams of traveling were put on hold. The idea had little practicality, not just because of the beavers but his health was poor and his foot was causing him pain. Even he conceded that his foot needed surgery, removing "the front part so I have no more bother with it, and can walk flat footed, and not stoop the way I do...." He dreaded the operation since he was not as strong as he used to be, but he told her he would undertake if the book was a success. It was with the publishers at present and if all went well, he would not miss the money she spent. He closed the letter with some sympathy:

> ...somehow I always feel rotten when you go away like that, poor ting, trying to get somewhere, doing the best you can, like some beaver starting away in the spring, pitiful some way, and yet reminds me of my own young days.4

Though Grey Owl's patience with Anahareo's prospecting trips was disappearing he could still find it in himself to express sympathy and understanding for her need to go into the wilderness by tapping into his own desire to return to the bush and forgetting for a moment that his physical ailments made it impossible. When he wrote of his dream to return to the bush, he did not assume she would go with him. If was as if he already knew that those days were in the past and could only be relived through writing about it.

Money was still a problem when Archie wrote again. Humorously addressing her "The Indian Woman (Ojibway) Prospector" because he had read a newspaper article in which they labelled her "Ojibway," he explained that his finances had reached such an alarming state he had handed them over to Mr. Wood, the park administrator, who had told Grey Owl not to post date checks any more, among other things. Despite these concerns Grey Owl sought to reassure Anahareo about Dawn.

> Mrs. W says Dawn grown a lot and says a lot of words. Staying here a while this summer. Try not to be lonesome. She is well taken care of Mrs. Winters feels responsibility kid, happy there. This stage of the thing is trying to all hands but by the time things are squared away and you on your feet and things going ahead she will only just begin to be of an age to know what is going on to[,] as to putting any time here it not be safe here for her here with the animals, the steps the lake, in any case. Later on this will all work out when she is neither helpless or too wise…5

Grey Owl also reported the addition of new kittens to Jelly Roll and Rawhide's family and expressed his gladness that the spring threat of poachers was past. He mentioned the return of Charlie the moose and the two squirrels that regularly visited them in Ajawaan. There was also advice included in his letter. He told her that on her travels she should visit one of his friends who wrote him, Flys Straight. Above all, he cautioned her, avoid risks:

Don't take any chances in big rapids. Always look all rapids before going down. Keep as much as possible to the side channels[,] never run too stern heavy[,] don't fool around in unknown waters, listen to the advice of people who know the country and remember it takes strength as well as skill to handle a canoe in heavy water. Never take a chance especially loaded. Use the portage if there is any doubt at all. IT is not so glorious, but it is better than a post-mortem, or putting a lot of good fellows to the trouble of hauling you out.....Good bye and good luck.6

Financial worries and advice were also themes of his next letter. Though still pleading little money he assured her that the bill for her equipment was not so great and he was concerned she had no cash. This assurance might have come from the fact that he had distinctly heard her calling him once when he was asleep. It had awakened him and he felt sure she was in trouble. Despite his concerns, Grey Owl could not help but let some tone of reproach seep in and told her not to ditch everything and return because she missed Dawn:

You have undertaken a responsibility, to me, to make proper use of your opportunities, so the trip will not be a loss, and to her, Dawn, who whilst not utterly dependent on the outcome, will be benefited by your success. Look at it in a business way, and don't let irresponsible thoughts govern your actions. That is something I have had to fight against here and the thought of my responsibility to others, not only animals, but humans too, has had a very steadying effect.7

In addition to missing Anahareo recent events had also laid Grey Owl low. Mink had killed at least three of the new kits under cover of a storm and high winds. To prevent further casualties he had found and killed four of the mink. Besides the catastrophe with the kits, two groundhogs hiding in the cellar had starved to death, the radio was on the blink and he had few visitors. But he had another book in the offing, which would soon leave him little time to dwell on things. Writing, he told her, "is like a disease, it creeps up on you all the time."8

Archie was clearly feeling Anahareo's absence and the loneliness of his work. Though he understood her love of the wilderness and her need to experience its challenge, he could not help but express the feeling that she sometimes took these journeys and abandoned them without thinking about their financial cost. He realized such feelings would upset her and just as soon as he wrote the criticisms he contradicted them, almost as if he was explaining it to himself as well as reassuring her.

Now that Grey Owl knew about her plans and she had faced his reprimands, Anahareo moved on from Lac La Ronge, paddling to the next trading post at Fort Stanley some 128 kilometres north,on the Churchill River. There she met a First Nations couple who offered to take her to a spot where they had once found "shiny stones." Hoping for gold, Anahareo agreed. The site was north of Wollaston Lake, on the edge of the Barren Lands, a five-day river journey, even with an outboard motor. When Anahareo finally arrived there and was able to examine the stones she saw to her dismay they were only iron pyrite. After spending a few days exploring the surrounding area she concluded there was little worth staking.

Anahareo, courtesy of Katherine Swartile

Some time later, when she was camping at a much used campsite she met two Cree families from Fort Stanley who were bound for Lac du Brochet, a trading post and summer camping site for Cree north of Reindeer Lake. Word of the lone woman traveler had reached them and they welcomed her warmly. When she told them she planned to go to God's Lake, still some distance away, they asked her why she wanted to go there. She answered that she "just wanted to see a whole bunch of country." Obviously concerned about her, a woman traveling alone, they invited her to go with them instead to their summer campsite.

Anahareo eyed the outboard motor that would easily take her a little closer to her destination and accepted their offer, certain that a brief visit would do no harm. Before they set off the men hoisted her gear into an ancient cache, a specially constructed storage platform designed to keep supplies safe from bears, porcupines and other animals. When they secured her canoe to a rack instead of towing it behind their own, she realized they meant for her to spend the whole summer with them. They only relented and hitched her canoe to one of their own when she agreed that when she left them, she would go directly home, rather than to God's Lake.

After an enjoyable journey they arrived at Reindeer Lake, a huge body of water over 240 kilometres long and far too big for Anahareo to navigate in her small six-foot canoe. So she bade her new friends farewell and made her way back down the river she had just traveled, a fast and furious journey in the swift waters. Alone again, she began to miss Dawn, a feeling that perhaps weighed in against making the rest of the journey to God's Lake at this point in the season. At Pelican Narrows she sent word to Archie she was returning to Prince Albert, then paddled her way for ten days, heading for the nearest railroad station at the small mining town of Flin Flon. She came ashore first at Amisk Lake, some thirty kilometres from Flin Flon, and found herself in the middle of a claim-staking spree at Amisk Island, a few miles to the southwest side of the lake. She met the man who made the discovery and he encouraged her to stake her own claims, but she was too intent on returning to her daughter. She made her way on to Flin Flon instead where she hoped there would be a letter from Grey Owl with money enclosed for her return fare.

The letter was there, but its content was not what she expected. Grey Owl had had enough. All his anger, frustration and loneliness came pouring out as he chided her for writing only twice since she had left, labelled her irresponsible to think she could just come and go as she chose, behaviour he compared to a friend married to an actress who visited her husband occasionally, when she needed a break from New York. This man Grey Owl always regarded as a "sucker." In this light, and in view of his lack of money, he told her she must look after herself, at least until he could "catch up on his bills."9

Hurt and angry, Anahareo tore up the letter, bought a prospector's license, returned to Amisk and prepared to stake out the area her friend had recommended. She made camp on a wide flat rock, a difficult place to erect a tent, but it had a wonderful view of the lake and surrounding country. She wrote to Grey Owl and told him how upset his letter made her. She also wrote to James Wood, the Prince Albert National Park administrator and made a plea for a loan to tide her over while she staked. She explained that she had staked three claims and hoped to make a strike and then "square away my numerous debts." He sent her some money and explained that Grey Owl's finances were really in bad shape. When she replied she told Wood she had not realized the money situation was that extreme and that she would do her best to return his loan soon.10

Grey Owl also wrote to Anahareo and said he was ashamed of his previous letter. He protested that he did trust her, but, as he explained, "all alone, with no one to talk to, things tended to get out of perspective."

> Well kid, I feel bad about that letter, so pessimistic and speaking as though I didn't trust you or something. And really Gertie I do.

Only, up there, no one to talk to see? And an idea gets into a person's mind and starts to grow and develop[sic] and becomes an obsession. Say it's a damn good thing I'm no longer jealous—I would be the devil himself, I guess. It is you cured me of jealousy. I did not know before I met you, that a woman could be true and faithful. 'My proud and gallant Anahareo' as I tag you in the book.11

Later on in the letter Archie returned to his apology:

Look kid, don't be upset by that fool letter. I should have known better. You up there alone in a strange country, trying hard to make the grade. You know, kid, we quarrelled once in a while but who doesn't? And what does it amount to? Just words. And they and the few blows etc. are kind of fading in a person's memory. I have a murderous nature at times, but the old common sense prevails even if "Scotch Basta" sometimes. Life is too short; some people say, but I say life is too big, to allow any temporary foolishness to cloud the sun and shadow of our trail. I think the bond between us all, Jelly, Rawhide, Dawn and you and I is indissoluable [sic]. We have seen hard times together, and nothing can ever wipe out the memory of it.12

Grey Owl blamed his reaction on the general despair and loneliness he felt and also the worry over "poor patient tireless faithful Rawhide," who had boils and carbuncles on his back, lost his sight in one eye and was now in danger of losing the sight in the other. Rawhide's health issues he felt were due to the "artificial feeding," something he realized was problematical, but he was doing his best.13

Grey Owl also gave her news of Dawn. He had seen her on a recent visit to Prince Albert where it took a few hours for her to become accustomed to him. They went for a walk, Dawn dressed in a "Red Riding Hood outfit" that all admired. Before he closed the letter, he wrote that she should be good to herself and not to worry about Dawn. He added that he was thrilled about her offer to take over the cabin while he went back to Ontario and Quebec, to the "house of McGuinness" to take photos.14

Grey Owl & Anahareo beside Beaver Lodge, Ajawaan Lake, courtesy of Katherine Swartile

Anahareo found it difficult to accept Grey Owl's apology. With stubborn determination she continued to work on her claims and earn her own money to prove to Grey Owl she was able to fend for herself and not rely on his support, just as he had instructed her in that hurtful letter. A few weeks later Grey Owl wrote again to say he had received two of her letters in which she had reinforced how upset and hurtful she found his words. Though he expressed another apology, it was not as fulsome as the previous letter, and stated that perhaps he should not have written as he did, but had done so because if he was there at the cabin alone, day and night, with only his thoughts for company. In such circumstances it was to be expected he would get "streaks of discouragement." He tried to make further amends by explaining again how he paid her great tribute in *Pilgrims of the Wild*, especially her courage, though he added that he made her "a little more womanly" than she actually was. When all was said and done, he told her, they "must not allow the shadow of past mistakes to shadow our lives all the time."15

As for the state of his finances Grey Owl explained that his debts were beginning to clear, though he still had to break into his November check to pay for winter provisions, his "alone Christmas" and also to ensure a good Christmas for Dawn and one or two others that he thought "deserved it and would be glad of it."

> So we will all 3 spend Xmas apart. I wish it could be otherwise. Well I am the guy that has the cash (ha! A sense of power overwhelms me a glass of Johnny Dwar[sic], Perkins and make it snappy) and if it is going to be a lonely time here I will get my Christmas spirit (I mean feeling not what you think) by trying to make 2 or 3 others happy and bore a hole in Jelly's side wall in the pantry and feed them apples. No rats this year the mink killed them... drink up my bottle of scotch and talk back to the announcers which is after all perhaps a better Xmas than you will have so far away from your so-loved daughter.16

At the end of October Grey Owl wrote her again, anxious about her preparations for winter since she had told him nothing definite. He wrote: "hope you know what you're doing and won't be caught in a jam." He was worried because there was only one mail delivery left until December and he wanted to know how she fared. Recounting bits of news in a chatty, almost overly casual manner, he told her the moose had come back to visit after an absence that had made him think the moose was dead. He also mentioned that the beaver were undermining the cabin footage. They had created streets, compartments and annexes that required thirty-four bags of sawdust to make it safe and noted that Beaver Lodge would slide into the lake if he did not take precautions in the summer. He closed with the news that the publishers had read the book manuscript of *Pilgrims of the Wild* and were thrilled. Such news should have made him happy, but he could feel himself irritable and knew he needed a vacation.17

He wrote his last letter for the year in mid-November, wishing her a merry Christmas and sending her a gift. He also told her that Dawn had a "touch of grip" and that he had asked Mrs. Winters to have a tree for Dawn, lamenting that he could not be there to watch her open her presents. But on Christmas Eve he would think of Anahareo and hope she would find some happiness "on that day we used to celebrate so sincerely all alone." He closed by instructing her to "cheer up kid and remember there are many years to come after this difficult time when you will have Dawn for always." He signed it with humour, "Archie—bald (not yet.)"18

It was clear from Grey Owl's correspondence that Anahareo's attitude toward his harsh words had not softened. Stubborn and proud, she was still determined to make her own way. By late October Anahareo had finished her staking, cutting large swathes of brush and marking out the area. She made a rushed trip to the mining town to record her three claims and then went looking for work. With the Depression on, her only hope was to travel ninety-six kilometres east of Amisk Lake, down the Sturgeon River to The Pas to look for a job, otherwise she would have to sell her canoe for a ticket to Prince Albert. She still had plenty of food—dehydrated fruit and vegetables, sowbelly, beans and other goods, as well as the fish she caught and the pemmican she had obtained at Fort Stanley and Pelican Narrows and from the odd Indian family that she had met. There were no jobs in The Pas so she was forced to sell her rifle to buy the supplies she needed and prepared to head back to Amisk.

With the best of intentions Anahareo tried to set off in the canoe, but high winds and wet weather delayed her ten days. When she was finally able to launch her canoe she was feeling ill. After about thirty-five kilometres of paddling, she came to the head of the Sturgeon River and sighted a group of log buildings and a man with dogs barking all around him. He waved her in and as she drew closer she recognized him as an old woodsman, Angus MacDonald, she had met once before. She explained her intention to paddle on, but MacDonald could see she was ill and made her come ashore. Once inside his rough and messy cabin she collapsed unconscious.

MacDonald nursed her the best he was able to in his ramshackle home. In the days before the railroad his place at one time had served as the halfway point for shipping machinery and supplies for the mining community. Once the railroad was built his services were no longer required, so much of his place had fallen into disrepair while MacDonald scraped by with a bit of trapping. As Anahareo recovered she tried to tidy up the place and instil some sense of cleanliness in the kind hearted man who had cared for her.

Grey Owl had no idea she had fallen ill and that she was staying with MacDonald. She was reluctant to write to him, still hurt and angry over his words and still determined to manage on her own. MacDonald eventually convinced her to write to him and the two walked the forty-six kilometres through the bush to the nearest post office to send the letter.

The size of Amisk Lake meant that it did not freeze until the first week of December, and MacDonald used that time before the freeze to hunt mink while Anahareo smoked and cured moose, Canadian geese and ducks that he shot, and tended the fishnet and fed the dogs. Once freeze up finished and Christmas week arrived, MacDonald harnessed the dogs to a sled, filled it with his furs, and he and Anahareo traveled up to Flin Flon. She had sold her canoe to MacDonald and was now intent on using the money to purchase a ticket to Prince Albert. Once in Flin Flon Anahareo found a parcel and three letters, one from Grey Owl and two from Mrs. Winters, filled with news of Dawn. Inside Archie's letter to Anahareo was another for MacDonald that contained five dollars and thanked him for his kindness to Anahareo. The letter to Anahareo was sad and reminiscent of their times together and included a gift of twenty-five dollars, but no invitation to return home. His previous hurtful words still rankling, the omission of the invitation to return only made her more determined that she would not go back until he invited her.

Distressed and full of self pity, Anahareo spent most of her money on alcohol to console herself, drinking her way through the Christmas period. MacDonald kept an eye on her, ensuring that she did nothing to harm herself and tried to counsel her with tales of his own experience. He persuaded her to return to his home, and no sooner had they arrived, a woman called and asked Anahareo to be her companion for the winter. Anahareo would keep her company while her husband, who only came home every other weekend, worked at the mines. The timing could not have been better for Anahareo.

Anahareo passed a reasonable winter with the woman, visiting and playing cribbage; on the weekends, when the woman's husband was home, Anahareo used their dog team to visit MacDonald. Over the winter she wrote to Grey Owl and thanked him for his Christmas present, the only person, he later told her, who had expressed gratitude. She still remained firm in her resolve to return only by invitation. When Mother's Day approached Grey Owl wired Anahareo a bouquet of red roses. June finally arrived, and with it the end of Anahareo's job as a companion, so she sold her claims from the previous autumn and went prospecting.[19]

Archie, meanwhile, wrote to her expressing once again his pride at her ability in "conquering the Churchill," the long river she paddled up north the previous summer. He told her he had written a children's book and was overwhelmed with demands for his writing. The previous book, *Pilgrims of the Wild*, now in its third edition, was already deemed a classic and making Anahareo beloved by all though they still persisted in calling her an "Ojibway." Such was his success that he was offered a book tour in England and wished for her to come and take his place at the cabin, something he felt she would like, while earning a few dollars. She could have Dawn and Margaret Winters as companions. In this situation she would not feel as though she was taking. He closed the letter by encouraging her to look after herself and the money she earned.[20]

Busy prospecting, Anahareo did not receive the letter until her anxiety over news about Dawn prompted her to take a trip to Amisk Lake late in the summer. Her invitation to come home had finally been issued. After collecting her gear and saying her goodbyes, Anahareo boarded the train for Prince Albert. Mrs. Winters and Dawn greeted her at the station.21

Chapter Thirteen

The Weight of Pilgrims of the Wild

P*ilgrims of the Wild* became a critical success in Canada, the United States, and most especially Britain. While the beaver's decline was so often reported in dry and factual terms by conservationists or government employees that gained little public attention, Grey Owl had come along and created an engaging and lyrical work that caught the public's imagination. The book's London publisher, Lovat Dickson, drew up a masterful promotion campaign that included a lecture tour of Britain, a strategy that eventually put the total sales of the book in Britain at 50,000.[1]

Grey Owl was enthusiastic about the book tour. He recognized it as an important opportunity to promote his message. "It will surely be a great medium of getting my ideas before the public & would inevitably lead to a similar campaign in Canada, when we might get direct action on this home wild-life of ours that so badly needs it."[2] Under the weight of such ambitious plans Grey Owl put much thought into his attire and programme to make an impact that would support the book's message and meet audience expectations. In a high state of nerves, he assembled Bill Oliver's films of the beaver and began to prepare his lectures. He was afraid he would not be able to handle lecturing on such a scale and would let everyone down. Anahareo found him anxious and restless when she arrived to help him prepare for his tour.3

Just after her arrival Grey Owl flew up to Lac La Ronge to get materials for Anahareo to make his hunting shirt and leggings. He bought five moose hides and about two pounds of beads. His plan was to create an outfit of full Indian regalia to wear on the tour because he felt that such an outfit was what they expected of him. He was anxious about it though. Despite the fact that in interview s he had long described himself as half-Apache, and emphasized the time he had spent with Anishnabe on Bear Island and other places among his friends and acquaintances, a very public display of Aboriginal heritage during a tour in the land of his birth was something very different.

Though it might be argued that Grey Owl was already caught up in an image created earlier that had now taken on a life of its own, he also knew the psyche of the land where his childhood. This was a country whose only idea of a North American Aboriginal were derived from books, paintings, films or encounters with Buffalo Bill's Wild West Show that had actual Lakota and Cheyenne fighting in full regalia on stage, or, after the show, sitting beside teepees behind stage, their hair hanging loose or braided with feathers. Film, art and literature were no different. These images reinforced the idea that Indians were linked with nature and the disappearing wilderness and that they were disappearing too, an idea that Grey Owl himself also held.4

Taking the idea that Aboriginals had an innate understanding of the wilderness as well as a strong connection to it, Grey Owl fashioned an elaborate full regalia costume to reinforce the truth of his message to his British audience—the wilderness was in peril. "The difference between civilised man and the savage is just this," he wrote, "civilised people try to impose themselves on their surroundings, to dominate everything. The Indians is part of the background. He lets himself—not just drift—but go with nature." Later he scribbled in his notebook, "remember you belong to Nature, not it to you," a phrase that eventually became Grey Owl's slogan.5

Under Anahareo's skillful needle and Grey Owl's instructions the outfit took shape. She beaded his shirt and leggings elaborately, creating patterns reminiscent of her own Algonquin and Mohawk background. When the outfit was completed Grey Owl packed it along with his pipe, moccasins, gun case, vests, blanket and jacket and any other accessory he thought would be needed. He told Lovat Dickson, his publisher and tour manager, about his portrayal in any publicity. "I think the truest definition of my status (though I don't of course estimate myself his equal) is that of a modern Hiawatha and perhaps an interpreter of the spirit of the wild."6 In cultured Britain Grey Owl would be the spokesman for the wilderness.

During the course of his journey to the Atlantic to embark on the ship for Britain Grey Owl stopped in Mattawa and called in to see Anahareo's father, Matt. He brought news of Anahareo, who had not seen her family since she had boarded the train for that week-long visit those many years before. The family and neighbours had a square dance with Matt playing the fiddle and everyone, including Grey Owl, dancing up a storm.7

While Grey Owl embarked on his lengthy book tour, addressing over two hundred audiences, back in Canada Anahareo also had some public attention. In December an article appeared in the newspapers entitled, "Mrs. Grey Owl Aids Husband; Has Ambition." Though the reporter noted her prospecting exploits, he described her in an understated and dignified language and presented her as a woman who, with her husband, had "made a study of the animal adopted as Canada's national emblem and now threatened with extinction." He also described her as a woman with personal ambitions that included a hope to write and direct a play about herself and Grey Owl. In addition to her own dreams she had ambitions for "the rehabilitation of her own people north of '54," something she might accomplish by "striking it rich" and so able to "provide her people with civilization's best offerings."8

Despite the emphasis of her interests, experiences and ambitions, the article devoted nearly half of its space to her connection with Grey Owl and the campaign to protect the beaver. Calling her "Annah-An-Eo" it described her as the key to Grey Owl's transformation from "a hunter of the beaver, the natural prey of his trapping forebears, to their greatest champion."9 Though Anahareo had defined herself in modern terms— ambitious, independent, skilled and courageous—her name and her image was inextricably linked to Grey Owl and the beaver. In the past such links had allowed her to present herself in such a unique light and push her ideas of an Aboriginal woman's capabilities, but as the fame of Grey Owl's work with the beavers and her own part in it grew with the popularity of his books and films, so her image became attached to the public's expectations of her, as much as it did their expectations of Grey Owl. These expectations were grounded in Grey Owl's own depiction of her in the book, an image that was perceived as someone at home in the wilderness, passionate and knowledgeable about beavers, and devoted to Grey Owl and his work with conservation. It was a situation that increasingly, as time progressed, had its own problems.

That she became so adored by the British who asked questions about her and gave Grey Owl gifts for her as he toured the country shows that the British were more open to an unconventional image of an Aboriginal than Grey Owl anticipated. Or perhaps it was because she was a woman that they had no problem with her modern outlook. Whatever it was, there was no denying the British loved her for her feistiness, strength and bush skills. Her striking beauty, modern with European overtones, only added to her attraction.

Grey Owl's British tour was an overwhelming success. His lectures and films, showing the lithe and beautiful Anahareo in her buckskin jacket and trousers, paddling a canoe alongside Grey Owl or playing with the beavers, won the hearts of the British people. Grey Owl accumulated a trunk and eight large suitcases stuffed with gifts for Anahareo and Dawn from booksellers and other admirers. An Iroquois singer from eastern Canada who had performed at the

Royal Albert Hall, along with two English friends, made Grey Owl a Plains headdress. Grey Owl's presentation style, with its dramatic lighting, staging and delivery, created an appealing and entertaining atmosphere. He worked tirelessly, giving interviews, signing books and appearing on radio, in addition to his many lectures.10 More often than not, in the course of his appearances, Grey Owl made use of any opportunity to plea for better conditions for Aboriginals as well as for wildlife. One reporter stated, "Since Gray Owl [sic] came to Britain on a lecture tour he has made hundreds of speeches, and the people who have heard him no longer think of Red Indians as savages." In the face of such praise Grey Owl only tried to emphasize to the reporter the superiority of the Aboriginals' experience and that of the Canadian wilderness. When asked about his impressions of London he replied that it felt like a jungle and he knew what it felt to be a trapped animal. "There seemed no escape for me from this maelstrom of haggard people and roaring machines; I was caught. Mankind I thought has become a stampeding herd. I thought of the wilderness, cold and clean."11

The huge success of Grey Owl's British tour had not gone unnoticed in Canada or the United States. Newspapers ran articles and pictures of his tour and invitations to lecture mounted, awaiting his return. By the time he arrived back in Canada in the February of 1936, a contract for a North American tour was drawn up and ready for him. But before that, on his voyage back to Canada, Grey Owl finally succumbed to the stress of the last four months and drank heavily. His companion, Betty Somervell, an avid supporter who befriended him on the tour and had hosted him and his entourage at her home in the Lake District, tried to watch over him to ensure he would not "get absent-minded and fall overboard, or give all his money away, which he loved doing." After she scolded him thoroughly when she found bottles of drink under the bed, he promised to stop drinking and for the remainder of the voyage occupied himself by dictating to her his next book, *Tales of an Empty Cabin*.12

Landing at Halifax, he journeyed first to Montreal where the pair relaxed for a day, taking a sleigh ride and then attending the cinema to watch Charlie Chaplin in *Modern Times*. From Montreal they went on to Ottawa to meet for several days with Parks Branch officials, including James Harkin. Grey Owl also saw a doctor who diagnosed him with bronchitis and a very bad nervous condition. Moving on from Ottawa to Toronto, Grey Owl's physical and mental health deteriorated further.13

In Toronto Grey Owl stayed with the Rotenbergs, a couple related to one of his contacts in Britain. There he encountered Arthur Stevens, the Justice of the Peace who had issued his license to marry Angele Egwune and had informed Ivy Holmes of his previous marriage. Stevens had recognized him as the same Archie Belaney and had previously written to Grey Owl after reading one of his early articles but said only that he admired and supported Belaney's work in wilderness preservation. On this occasion the two had a pleasant conversation and Stevens reiterated his admiration and support.14 The remaining time in Toronto Grey Owl filled with luncheons, phone calls and interviews. During one such interview Grey Owl expressed his view that Aboriginals "should not be christianized at the expense of their ancient code of justice and morality." He continued:

> I should like to see the aborigine retain his attitude to the world and life. Why should he be asked to accept the youngest religion? The Old Indian faith, even sun worship, teaches honesty, integrity, reverence, love of nature and love of his fellow man as much as Christianity does.15

Grey Owl's statements caused an uproar when the article appeared in the Toronto *Mail*, a city of strong Protestant faith. The Rotenbergs' house was barraged with prank calls and reporters anxious for a story. One obnoxious reporter forced his way into the Rotenberg's home and up to Grey Owl's room, firing off incendiary and insulting remarks that so enraged Grey Owl he lodged a complaint with the newspaper and the reporter was forced to apologize to the Rotenbergs and Grey Owl.16

There was some part of Grey Owl that rose to the challenge of the battle of words and he continued his round of interviews and luncheons for several more days, his head filled new ideas about books, tours and films. Betty Somervell left for England and Grey Owl went on to Ottawa to meet with the well-known author and Governor General, Lord Tweedsmuir (John Buchan) and Mackenzie King, the prime minister, to ask for their support and funding for his next film documenting the Mississagi River country. On his arrival he met the prominent Cree leader, John Tootoosis, who had come to Ottawa to present petitions to the government pleading for a more humane policy toward Aboriginals. Grey Owl offered Tootoosis the use of his room, assisted him with introductions at the Department of Indian Affairs and enjoyed long conversations with him. Though Grey Owl pressed him for details about life during the days of the buffalo hunt and war parties, which the elders on his reserve still remembered, Tootoosis insisted on explaining about the current problems his people faced. These problems Grey Owl knew something about from his experiences with the Lac Simon and the Bear Island Anishnabe. The two discussed these issues in a detailed, friendly exchange that led Tootoosis, nevertheless, to conclude Grey Owl was not Aboriginal.17

Besides the conversations with Tootoosis, Grey Owl worked on gaining support for his film project. He visited Lord and Lady Tweedsmuir at Rideau Hall again and later dined with the prime minister at his home. Grey Owl also called in to the head of the Department of the Interior who, as the prime minister informed him, would make the final decision about his funding.18

As Grey Owl's visit in Ottawa drew to a close, the stress became too much for him and he finally broke down and began to drink. By the time he arrived in Toronto he was in such a state that the Rotenbergs, who welcomed him once again, put him to bed for thirty-six hours. It was only then that his hosts and his publisher, Hugh Eayrs, broke the news that his daughter Dawn was in hospital with life-threatening pneumonia. Grey Owl immediately left for Prince Albert.19

Anahareo & Dawn, courtesy of Katherine Swartile

Anahareo was already at Dawn's side when he arrived, wild with worry. Pneumonia was a serious illness in this time before antibiotics, and the possibility of Dawn's death was very real. Anahareo could easily imagine the worst and with her recurring fears and worries over Dawn's health she found it difficult to be hopeful. Eventually Dawn recovered, but the strain on Anahareo, after months of isolation at the cabin with the beavers, proved too much. She went to pieces and embarked on a drinking bout that coincided with Grey Owl's own stress-induced spree. The two had a terrible argument, as all the pent-up emotions and suppressed thoughts rose to the surface and exploded in a torrent of wild accusations and statements. Anahareo became so upset with Grey Owl she tried to choke him, her anger and frustration feeding her actions. Their arguments continued over some days, and in the end they agreed to part, at least for the present, though Grey Owl decided to put Anahareo on an allowance of $50 month, nearly half his wage.20

Grey Owl returned to Beaver Lodge under a cloud after reports of his behaviour had reached the Parks Department and beyond, up to the Ministry of the Interior. Grey Owl had never been popular with the wardens and park staff because of his introverted and loner habits and the stand-offish attitude he took with them. He felt they were coarse, ignorant and unappreciative of wilderness preservation. But the higher officials of the Parks Department recognized Grey Owl's value and he still received a steady stream of letters from people asking for directions to his beaver sanctuary. The Parks officials forgave his actions this time since they had occurred all on his own time, but they wrote him a strong letter warning him he would be dismissed if he misbehaved again.21

Despite his painful parting with Anahareo, Grey Owl tried to focus on finishing *Tales of an Empty Cabin*. He brought in Ettie Winters' daughter and son, Margaret and Stan, to help him with the beavers and type up the manuscript. Stan was cook and carer for the beavers while Margaret typed, enabling Grey Owl to finish as close as possible to the publisher's June deadline. Anahareo, meanwhile, took Dawn to Waskesiu for the summer and stayed at the shack tent. It was a simple space, with wooden walls and a tarp on the roof, divided into a bedroom and a living area.22

By this time Waskesiu was the size of a town in the summer, boasting nearly 5,000 people at the height of the season, with its own water works system, electricity plant to serve the over 250 summer homes, dance pavilions and myriad other buildings along the lake shore.23 Amid the bustling community Anahareo was able to secure a job as a lake guide for a University of Colorado professor emeritus of zoology, Theodore Cockerell, and his wife. Cockerell's brother, Sir Sidney, was the director of the Fitzwilliam Museum at Cambridge and had heard Grey Owl speak twice on the book tour and had invited him to his home for tea. So impressed was he with Grey Owl that he wrote to his brother Theodore about him. Theodore Cockerell was an eminent professor whose interest encompassed many areas, including geology and palaeontology. He was also a well-known naturalist and collector. He had traveled extensively to remote parts of the world and, whether working on wild bees or the genetics of the red sunflower, he did it with passion and zeal. It was no surprise he was attracted to Grey Owl's work and Anahareo's interest in the wilderness.24

During one of Anahareo's trips with Cockerell around the lakes, on the first of September, Art Howard, a park warden, accompanied them. While the professor and his wife prepared a picnic on shore, Howard and Anahareo took the canoe on the lake to catch some fish. When they were paddling back across the lake Howard lost his balance and fell overboard, capsizing the canoe. After several attempts to climb on top of the sinking canoe the two of them decided to swim to shore. Howard quickly tired, became disoriented and started thrashing around in the water. Anahareo tried to push him toward the shore but she had difficulty keeping him above water and eventually, after about three quarters of an hour, had to head for the shore alone. When she arrived she ran along the beach, swam across a channel to the warden's cabin and phoned for help. Superintendent Wood, Warden Les Holden and two other boats of volunteers arrived one-and-a-half hours later and Anahareo took them to the spot where Howard had disappeared. The boats dragged the lake for the body and around sundown they located it, in about seven foot of water.25

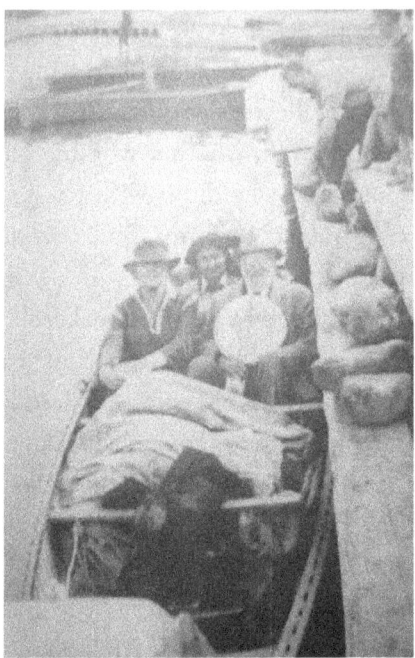

Anahareo, Professor Cockrell & his wife, courtesy of Katherine Swartile

Anahareo was so distraught over the incident her first thought was to seek her former source of comfort and support and so she phoned Grey Owl. In an effort to take her mind off the incident he immediately told her to bring Dawn to the cabin and the both of them could entertain Betty Somervell, who would arrive in a few weeks time. Anahareo would be welcome assistance in showing Betty the different sights around Prince Albert National Park while he ploughed on with his writing and looked after the beaver.26

The previous month Grey Owl, Dawn and Mr. and Mrs. Winters had attended the commemoration of the sixtieth anniversary of the signing of Treaty Six, at Fort Carlton, eighty kilometres southwest of Prince Albert. Grey Owl returned from the experience invigorated and committed to finding ways to assist Aboriginals. Though various tribal representatives attending the ceremony were for the most part certain he was not Indian, they chose to remain silent and allow him to be their spokesman at this time since no other Aboriginal had such access to government officials, the media and the public sympathy. Grey Owl thought their silence meant they accepted him in their community and it lifted his spirits enormously after his gruelling tour. When Anahareo and Dawn arrived they found him cheerful. A few days later Betty Somervell arrived.27

Betty Somervell, or "Summy" as her friends called her, had traveled from England with her husband to America for business. At Grey Owl's invitation she decided to visit him at his home at Beaver Lodge and meet the famous beavers and Anahareo. She left her husband in New York and took the four-day train journey to Saskatchewan, changing trains at Regina and then journeying overnight to Prince Albert. After a night's stay with the Winters Summy hitched a lift on a truck, riding north into the forest until she came to Waskesiu. The weather had turned cold and by this time all the summer residents had left, leaving the rows of summer cabins empty. The little wooden store was still open, run by a local man called "Doc" and Summy took a room there for the night. Plain but clean, it smelled of newly cut pine. She waited there for the next few days until the lake was calm enough for a small boat to take her to Ajawaan Lake. During that time she ate her meals at the little table in the store and even minded the counter while Doc was out. The customers fascinated her, and she noted particularly the Aboriginals and bush men who came in to purchase items like tobacco and snuff.28

At last, early one morning, boatmen took her across the lake to the other side. There they paused to make a fire and brewed some tea. After the short break the group walked up a streambed to the next lake while around Summy chipmunks scurried along, whiskey jacks flew overhead and she recognized signs of moose, deer, and bear. She was truly in the wilderness now. The group paddled across another lake and reached shore just as it was growing dark. Grey Owl was waiting there, clad in his red flannel shirt and buckskins, ready to take her on the remainder of the journey. When he saw her bags he commented, "Gosh what a lot of luggage you women take around." He heaved up her large suitcase and bag onto his back and led her through the portage path to the final lake, Ajawaan. At the end of the portage he retrieved his paddle out of a tree, stowed away from any hungry beaver, and helped her into the canoe.29

Summy sat in the canoe, very still, not daring even to let her elbows rest on the gunwales, almost afraid to breathe, lest she tip over the canoe. As they paddled along the water she became conscious of a little ripple behind them. It was Jelly Roll, following Grey Owl home. When they were in sight of the cabin, Grey Owl gave his special owl hoot, and the door of the cabin burst open and Anahareo came running to the landing stage. She gave Summy a friendly welcome and took her straight to the cabin to warm up by the stove. Summy's first impression of Anahareo was that she looked like Peter Pan, "a wiry little boy in her buckskins, high jack boots with a knife tucked into the top; with her black short hair and black twinkling eyes in her lovely face." The two of them hit it off immediately, getting on "like a forest fire," Summy soon calling Anahareo, "Pony," the name her father gave her those years before and that close friends and Grey Owl sometimes used.30

Summy found the cabin warm and cozy, with the big stove going and oil lamps to provide the light. Grey Owl's bunk was along one wall, with bookshelves over it containing two radios (one for Grey Owl who preferred classical music and the other for Anahareo who liked jazz). On top of one of the radios Grey Owl's precious war bonnet sat on a wood block painted with a face. Over by the window stood the table and some stools. The beaver house still took up half the cabin and contributed some pretty rich smells of its own. Packing cases filled with food were in the middle of the cabin, supplies enough to last a month. Any concerns she might have had about sleeping there were soon alleviated. She was to bunk with Anahareo and Dawn in the upper cabin, up a flight of log steps, behind Beaver Lodge. Later she found the storage tent, which the beaver occasionally cut down, and the toilet in the little house called the "bear den," a name that no doubt harked back to one of Grey Owl's first pranks on Anahareo and one Anahareo could not resist playing a variation of it on Summy. When Summy mentioned that the hut seemed a long way from the cabin, especially at night, Anahareo told her she had once met a bear on the way there and "they had quite a job to squeeze past each other on the narrow trail."31

That first evening when Dawn was tucked up, the three sat around the stove and talked, Summy relaxing into the profound quiet of the Canadian wilderness. Suddenly the door burst open and "Jelly Roll came marching in on her hind legs, dropped down and turned quickly round so her big flat tail wouldn't catch in the door, and came to see what was going on." Summy curled her legs under her on the bed, cautious after the tale of Jelly Roll taking a bite out of a warden's leg, but Jelly Roll eventually got used to Summy and even allowed her to stroke her.32

Anahareo, Grey Owl & visitors, courtesy of Katherine Swartile

Over the course of her visit Summy observed Grey Owl's close relationship with Jelly Roll. She watched the two talk to each other often, exchanging little grunts. Grey Owl would get down on his knees, with Jelly Roll lying with her head on his knee and her little fist holding tight on to his buckskin fringes for hours. At dusk he would go out in the canoe with a little ramp on the side and Jelly Roll would heave herself out of the water and sit opposite him while he paddled her round the lake.33

The bad weather confined Summy close to the cabin in the first days of her visit. Grey Owl, anxious to share his new work, read her *Tales of an Empty Cabin,* keeping her awake until 4am. By the third day the weather had cleared enough and Summy, Anahareo and Dawn, now four years old, paddled to Little Trout Lake to show her around. In the days that followed Summy was enchanted by everything she saw and the people she met. And at night she came to know Anahareo better, sharing confidences and discussing dreams and plans with Anahareo.

Anahareo valued these talks with Summy. She knew the visit to Beaver Lodge was only a brief respite and she needed to decide what to do next. Summy had a sympathetic ear and Anahareo poured out her thoughts to her. The wild popularity of her character in *Pilgrims of the Wild* and the films led her to consider attempting a career in filmmaking in Hollywood. She was photogenic and enjoyed the filming experience with the beavers, so it seemed an inspired idea. It was also an adventure that had echoes of glamour and excitement, though she realized she needed money to pursue it. To accumulate the necessary funds to try Hollywood Anahareo considered resuming her claim staking up north.34

By the end of Summy's first week at the cabin Anahareo felt she needed to go back to her shack tent at Waskesiu, but the newly formed bond with Summy made her delay her departure. She shared tales of her experiences in the park with Summy and took her around to locations that had appeared on the Parks Department films and visited Anahareo's friends in a lumber camp.35

Summy also heard about Grey Owl's pet moose, Charlie, who often slept against the cabin door. They had to be careful of the male moose on the trails since September was the breeding season and a rutting moose could be dangerous. On one occasion Grey Owl blew into his birch bark moose caller and summoned Charlie with its bellow. The moose was so disappointed there was no female he jumped up and down on Grey Owl's best canoe. At some point early in the visit Margaret Winters joined them and toured around with Summy, Anahareo and Dawn.36

Eventually everyone but Grey Owl went to Anahareo's shack tent in Waskesiu and visited again with Doc and some of Anahareo's friends. Following that they all traveled on to Prince Albert, Dawn and Margaret by car and Anahareo and Summy following in a truck. In town they shopped and visited various friends. To Summy the comparative hustle and bustle of Prince Albert seemed such a marked contrast to the silence and beauty she had enjoyed at Beaver Lodge. A few days later Summy and Anahareo returned to Waskesiu, Summy staying this time in a room at Doc's. There Anahareo showed her more of the area, taking her to Montreal Lake and Love Lake, viewing the majestic beauty, the wonder of the wildlife, and meeting various Indian and Euro-Canadian friends of Anahareo in and around the park.37

Towards the end of her visit, Summy made her way back to Beaver Lodge to say her final goodbyes to Grey Owl, escorted by some of her new friends who stayed a few days entertaining her and Grey Owl. They played the gramophone, made films and Grey Owl, full of exuberance, decided to throw knives, a common form of entertainment in the bush and one he had practiced many times with Anahareo. This time, unfortunately he cut himself. It was one of a number of signs of his poor health that Summy had observed during her visit. His weakness was so pronounced sometimes that he often fell down when he went to get a drink of water, a fact she wrote in a letter to his London publisher, Lovat Dickson. Her concerns overshadowed her parting the next day as she returned to Waskesiu, to Anahareo, who took her on to the Winters and Prince Albert where she boarded the train for her journey back east.38

When Anahareo left Beaver Lodge, taking Summy to her shack

tent in Waskesiu, it was the last time she saw Grey Owl. Though she had gone to him for comfort in the face of the drowning tragedy she knew there was no permanent place at Beaver Lodge for her anymore. As she confided in Summy, she had hopes and dreams that extended beyond Beaver Lodge. She was still very young, just thirty, full of determination and a naïve optimism that she could make her dreams happen.

Chapter Fourteen

Difficult Choices

Anahareo was a well-known figure in Waskesiu and the Prince Albert National Park. Over the years she and Grey Owl had made many acquaintances among the various permanent residents of the park headquarters, the lumberjacks who worked in the outlying areas, and the miners who came in from the gold field. In such a fluid and unusual community Anahareo could, for the most part, be accepted for the independent and strong-minded person she was. As her fame as Grey Owl's heroine in *Pilgrims of the Wild* spread and admiring, interested people wrote or visited Grey Owl, Anahareo and the beavers, the park officials became increasingly concerned about the image both she and Grey Owl presented to the public. In 1936, an estimated 600 people made the trek to Ajawaan Lake. Under such pressure to maintain a scenario that attracted this paying public to the park, the park officials were naturally keen to keep the news of Anahareo's split with Grey Owl as quiet as possible, as were Grey Owl's publishers whose sales depended on the idea of the two as a couple.1

Anahareo's increased fame had not lessened journalistic interest, either. She was a celebrity who was beautiful, photogenic and interesting to interview. In early October, shortly after bidding Summy goodbye, a reporter published an interview with Anahareo in the Vancouver *Sun*. Entitled "Mrs. Grey Owl's Amazing Life Story," the article emphasized her beauty and distinct appearance, describing her as "petite, pretty, weighs about 120 pounds, has soft lustrous skin [Anahareo] prefers to be called 'Pony'...she has coal-black hair, parted in the middle with small curls over her brow... her cheek-bones are high, naturally, and her chin is rounded ... dressed in riding breeches...high boots, ...over a trapper shirt she wore a deerskin jacket made in 1929." No mention was made of her split with Grey Owl, and her absence from his side was explained by the impossibility of keeping him company when he was working. "He needs to be alone when he is writing," she explained. "If someone is around him it affects his work."2

Grey Owl, courtesy of Glenbow Museum Archives (now in U. Of Calgary)

Despite the public's continued perception that Anahareo and Grey Owl's relationship was still close, Anahareo knew her future lay somewhere else. She had mentioned her hope to pursue a film career in Hollywood to others besides Summy. Several people had noticed and remarked on her photogenic qualities so evident in the beaver films. A Hollywood producer approached Professor Cockerell, the entomologist from the previous summer, and asked him to help arrange a screen test for Anahareo, but Cockerell, who had his own idea about Anahareo and was not aware of her dream, or at least did not give it serious consideration, declined the opportunity on her behalf, because he felt Anahareo, as a "child of nature" would not be interested.3

Perhaps his refusal saved her a heartbreaking experience so often endured by Aboriginal actors in Hollywood during this time period when film companies had dropped ethnic actors from their payrolls to save money. For these companies taping eyelids back to create a seemingly Chinese person or donning a black braided wig and dark makeup did just as well.4 Cockerell however, clearly had not fully appreciated or accepted Anahareo's modern character and appearance but had instead viewed her as an Aboriginal linked to the pristine wilderness and unsullied by modernization.

As her growing celebrity created differing and distorted views of her Anahareo became more aware of both the negative and positive side of living in the public eye. The days of October passed and the pressure of discovery about her split with Grey Owl mounted as did her worries about her future. The Depression still held its grip and jobs were difficult to find, especially for someone whose skills were all centred around surviving in the bush, mushing a dog team or prospecting. Pursuing her hope of working in films in Hollywood required money and the best hope of accumulating it was to resume her prospecting in the north. But that venture also required an outlay of money. Funds became so desperate that she wrote for help to her good friend Summy now back in Cumbria. When Summy sent some money she was full of gratitude:

> Gosh, Summy, I just don't know what I would have done had you not come sailing through. I have never been quite so down as I have been the last month, as I hated like the dickens to have to write you

for cash. But you are the only person in this world to whom I could ask.5

As she mulled over her options for employment events made the decision for her. She found she was pregnant. There were tough choices in front of her. She made her way instead to the busy town of Calgary, after telling everyone that she was on her way to Hollywood to pursue a film career. In Calgary she took a room, giving the name Mrs. Gertrude Bernard and awaited the child's birth. June arrived and her daughter Ann was born at the General Hospital in Calgary. On the certificate Anahareo gave her own name as Gertrude Philomen Bernard, put the parent's status as unmarried, and gave Manauan, Quebec as her regular residence.6

Anahareo never publicly stated the name of Ann's father. By the time she discovered her pregnancy her relationship with Grey Owl was finished. He was already in Toronto at a convention of Canadian authors and quietly scouting around for another companion to feature in his upcoming film and to help him prepare for his second tour the following summer. In view of this, proud and stubborn Anahareo might not have wanted to involve him, if he was the father.7 She was also aware that if she remained in the Wakesiu or Prince Albert area, pregnant and alone, it would generate a great storm of media attention the park officials and Grey Owl's publishers would hate in their desire to maintain the myth of the continued romance. Though she might care little for their views, she would not want their wrath along with the negative media attention.8

It is also possible that Grey Owl was not the father. Their initial split in 1936 had been very acrimonious and had occurred after a period of a growing distance between them. She was still young and beautiful and looking for the kind of support and reassurance she was no longer getting from Grey Owl who was consumed with his writing. She had described herself as "lonely" on more than one occasion. In the summers Wakesui came alive with dances and parties and she had many opportunities to there to meet other men the summer before. Whatever was the truth her pride and stubbornness would concede nothing. She would face this alone.

Once Anahareo was released from the hospital after Ann's birth she was desperate for money to pay the debts she had accumulated for back rent and food. To meet those debts, she took Ann to Banff to try to get a job as an experienced canoe guide, scarcely a week after the birth. Unfortunately the terrain was largely unsuitable for canoes and guiding jobs were scarce. She knew little of the guiding work of an area required horses, packing and mountain climbing, rather than canoeing and portaging and she was unable and unwilling to capitalize on her name as Anahareo. Just as she found work with one American party, she became ill. After she recovered, she eventually managed to find other work paddling canoes along the small stretch of the Bow River, which ended after a short season.9

With all the guiding options finished at the summer's close Anahareo searched around for another way to earn some money. She still owed rent and she knew the colder weather would soon come. Inspired, she approached Canadian Pacific Railway's film department and offered to shoot the rapids of the Bow River on film for $50. The Bow River was under the authority of the Parks Branch, which meant the film company needed Parks Branch permission for the stunt. The Parks Branch knew Gertrude Bernard and Anahareo were one and the same and refused permission, citing safety concerns. There is little doubt, though, that the Parks Branch were influenced by an underlying fear that the expected media attention for such a stunt would reveal the split between Grey Owl and Anahareo. In the hope of discouraging any such event the Parks Branch sent her back to Calgary.10

Back in Calgary Anahareo could only think to write again to Summy again and explain her situation. Prior to this Summy had the occasion to meet Rev. J.M. Roe from Calgary and concerned that she had not heard from Anahareo she asked Roe to check on her, giving him the name Gertrude Bernard. Reverend Roe, the rector of St. Barnabas Anglican Church in Calgary, was a former priest of the

Indian Mission at Wabasca, north of Athabasca, and had arrived in England as part of an escort for a group of Canadian children attending the coronation of the new king. His companion escort was a Miss Wilna Moore, a high school teacher and former mission worker from Saskatoon. Two of the Canadian children in their party were Aboriginals and Summy and her husband requested they spend some time in Cumbria with them. On their visit, one of them contracted appendicitis and when he recovered Summy escorted him back to Rev. Roe where she discussed her concerns about Anahareo's situation. She asked him to try and locate Anahareo and tell her that she would cable any money Anahareo needed.11

Back in Calgary Roe began his search. The Department of Indian Affairs had no record of a Gertrude Bernard since her family had never lived on a reserve and were not classed as status Indians. Any mail sent to the address Summy had given him was returned unclaimed. Finally, through the assistance of the Royal Canadian Mounted Police, he located Anahareo. They had recently been made aware of her thwarted attempts to get permission to shoot the rapids and her subsequent move to Calgary. A meeting was arranged between Anahareo and Roe, and as soon as Roe saw her he immediately recognized her from the many photographs he had seen of her and Grey Owl.12

In the course of her discussion with Roe she acknowledged her identity and admitted to her estrangement from Grey Owl, but would not give the reason. She did say that when they had split she had requested that her daughter Dawn remain with the Winters until she could support her daughter herself when she would have sole custody. She also explained the reasons for keeping her identity secret: the fears of the Parks Branch and the promoters of Grey Owl's lecture tours that their separation would become public.

Roe, enchanted by this petite beauty, was completely won over by her, a situation coloured by his familiarity with the romantic idea of Anahareo's role in turning Grey Owl "from a bloody trapper to the Brother of the Beaver People." He was convinced of her power over animals and her "wonderful fund of Indian lore," later recalling one evening when he and his two young sons lit a small campfire in their garden and Anahareo joined them there. There she remained "squatting before the blaze...telling them animal legends. For nearly two hours, the lads sat in rapt attention. The fire dwindled to a pile of grey ashes, but still the soft voice of Anahareo, speaking perfect English, carried on the tale of birds and beasts and her little brethren of the wilds."13 Yet again Anahareo was seen as "a child of nature." Like Professor Cockerell, Roe viewed Anahareo through his own romantic stereotypes influenced by *Pilgrims of the Wild*, but also by older images derived from the art, film and literary depictions.

Anahareo and Ann remained under Roe's watchful eye until the public heard the news of Grey Owl's marriage to his new partner, Yvonne Perrier, whom he dubbed "Silver Moon." Though he had tried to conceal that his new partner was not Anahareo, it inevitably leaked out, and all concerned tried to put it in as positive light as possible. Publisher Lovat Dickson had written to Hugh Eayrs when he heard of the marriage in December 1936, "we shall not announce a fresh marriage, if there is one, in England, for Anahareo is just as much a hero to the English public as Grey Owl.14 With the news common knowledge Anahareo was no longer compelled to keep her estrangement with Grey Owl secret, and could use her name freely wherever she was.15

With such a view, Roe encouraged her to move to Saskatoon because he thought she would have better job opportunities in an area closer to the wilderness. But Saskatoon, situated in the dust-ridden prairie, felt the Depression severely. All around the soil was dry and barren from years of drought. Many had emigrated north for better prospects.16 Ignorant of Saskatoon's poverty, Anahareo took Roe's advice and moved there with Ann. Given its impoverished state it was no surprise that she had little success in finding a job and her money soon ran out. Desperate, she sat on a bridge with Ann by her side and contemplated suicide until, looking down at her poor helpless baby, she changed her mind. Gathering her courage she decided to appeal to the local authorities for help. The mayor contacted Wilna Moore, a minister's daughter and Roe's fellow escort on the coronation trip in England. Moore had spent some time teaching at a mission school and still busied herself with various benevolent projects. Presumably Anahareo cited Reverend Roe as a person who could most recently vouch for her, because after the mayor referred Anahareo to Wilna Moore, Moore wrote to Roe asking about Anahareo. Roe's reply, which he described in a newspaper article a year later, was to vouch for her, but also to explain "the difficulties and temptations to which a woman of Indian birth may succumb more easily than her sheltered white sisters," and added that he was sure that Anahareo, "back in her native environment, among the creatures of the wilds, with whom she had such affinity, could become an even greater national figure than her more publicized mate."17

Though Anahareo clearly had won him over, it was not as a modern woman skilled in bushcraft on par with any man, but because he saw her as an Aboriginal woman who had failed to overcome the base sexual instincts of her race, but nonetheless still possessed her "noble savage" characteristics that made her, as Roe put it, "one of the creatures of the wild." This blended image, grounded in paternalism and condescension, could not in the long run work to Anahareo's benefit, since she would not be regarded as an equal, a person who could make her own choices while receiving assistance. She would instead be regarded as a dependent Aboriginal woman, adrift in the modern world, incapable of making sound decisions on her own. This dependent role was one that had been long established between Aboriginals and government agencies in cooperation with religious institutions. It was a role both Roe and Moore would most naturally assume in their experience in religious based mission and benevolence work.

Anahareo was in a new situation, without Grey Owl's support and encouragement, and as much as she tried to use the bush skills that gave her such confidence it produced little result. All her modern ideas, her determination and hopes to fend for herself were undermined by her inability to find work because of the poor economic climate and her need to look after her young baby. Any single mother in need of employment during this time period faced great challenges and problems, in addition to possible legal penalties. As far back as the late nineteenth century Euro-Canadians had long since tried to pressure Aboriginals, women in particular, to conform to Euro-Canadian behaviour standards and set a clear racial hierarchy between Euro-Canadian women and Aboriginal women. Once the settlements were established, the twentieth century government officials wanted to build a nation that reflected middle-class, Western (mainly Anglo) values of behaviour. These included ideas of female purity and monogamy in marriage where women were homemakers and moral guides and men the breadwinners. In the minds of the middle-class Euro-Canadian bureaucrats these behaviour codes and moral values were best achieved through laws and the church and school institutions.[18] With such strong ideas it was easy to suggest Aboriginal culture was at odds with the kind of model citizen the authorities chose to emulate, and while their aim was to shape the behaviour and morals of the poorer classes as well as the Aboriginals, it was the Aboriginals that most often came under scrutiny.[19]

In newly settled western Canada the model behaviour seemed most at risk, so the authorities, the schools and religious institutions were more likely to step in. When they did step in they were armed with Aboriginal stereotypes that labelled the women as "wild," possessed of weaker morals, given to drunkenness and prostitution. The women could also potentially lead Euro-Canadian men astray to commit the ultimate sin of interracial sex—miscegenation. As late as the 1940s an agent stated, "Indians, [though they were] like the Irish in the way they make a living... lacked moral fibre and religious conviction the white races had developed.[20]

These perceptions and views served as a basis for justifying arrests, and even occasionally imprisoning Aboriginal women for such actions as living in common law with a man, or bearing children out of wedlock. Though it was Aboriginal women on the reserve who were most often imprisoned, Indian women in urban areas were occasionally arrested. One Aboriginal woman in Ontario during the 1920s, for example, was arrested and imprisoned after she was found sleeping on a railway platform with "a man not her husband," and was reputed to have been traveling around the country with him.21

Roe, Moore and the Saskatoon mayor viewed Anahareo's situation with a seemingly sympathetic light, but all three were inevitably influenced by the prevailing attitudes of the day, most especially Moore and Roe. Their mission experience meant they approached any solution to Anahareo's dilemma coloured by views that she was morally and racially inferior. Given these attitudes it was no surprise that Wilna Moore helped to arrange to place Anahareo's daughter, Ann, in Bethany Home, a Salvation Army residence for unwed mothers. One of the Salvation Army women working in the home, Major White, was distantly related by marriage to Grey Owl. This relationship possibly was the reason they placed Ann in a home for unwed mothers rather than another institution designated specifically for children needing care.22

Major White & other nurses at Bethany Home, courtesy of Anne Gaskell

That this was an improvised situation and not part of Bethany Home's usual procedure was clear. Ann was admitted without her mother and was no longer a newborn. Wilna Moore had also agreed to pay them a monthly sum for her care. Despite the lack of support Moore promised, Ann remained at the home, a situation that sometimes caused problems during inspections. Ann later recalled that during one visit from a Salvation Army inspector the staff hid her in a closet. Finally, when Ann was three, a young childless Ango-Canadian couple, Mary and William Eagle, with Anahareo's agreement, took Ann to live with them in Calgary, permanently relieving the home of the need for further subterfuge.23

Anne as a young child, courtesy of Anne Gaskell

Anahareo was still living in Saskatoon during this time under the paternalistic eye and guidance of Wilna Moore and others and visited Ann at the home. Such visits left Ann with a vague impression of a woman wearing breeches and high-topped boots that clicked noisily along the wooden boards, but no sense that she was her mother. Any idea of a mother began when she entered the Eagles home at the age of three, added an "e" on her name to become Anne, and vanished out of Anahareo's life for many years.24

After Anne's placement in Bethany house Anahareo turned towards her other daughter. Established now in an apartment in Saskatoon she contacted the Winters about Dawn's situation and they brought Dawn to live there. They had relations living in Saskatoon who could look out for the pair. Though she had Grey Owl's allowance to help her with Dawn, and the assistance of the Winter's family relations, it still proved too much for Anahareo to manage and ultimately Dawn returned to live with the Winters.25

Though one part of Anahareo wanted to have her daughters with her and felt that she should have them, the reality was different. As a single mother, she did not feel capable of rearing them. Her confidence was slipping, she was unable to find work and only had what little money Grey Owl still sent her to support herself. That she could no longer go off to prospect or follow any of her dreams she fully realized now and it depressed her and for a time she took solace in drinking. But she was still young.

Chapter Fifteen

The Backlash After Grey Owl's Death

Anahareo was still living in an apartment in Saskatoon in April of the following year when she turned on the radio and heard Mrs. Winters appealing for her to make contact. Grey Owl was dying. Anahareo rushed to Prince Albert, but Grey Owl died the morning after her arrival, before she could see him.

Grey Owl's health had not improved after Anahareo left Beaver Lodge that September in 1936. *Tales of an Empty Cabin* had been published in October, and after attending the convention of authors and marrying Yvonne Perrier in Toronto in November, he spent the winter preparing and filming new footage in Abitibi, Ontario and more later in the summer. During this time he had several bad coughing spells and was noticeably weaker, a condition made worse by bouts of drinking. To compound these difficulties Charlie the tame moose died, as did his former mentor and father figure, Alex Espaniel. These losses took a great emotional toll on Grey Owl.[1]

After he had made several appearances at events involving various First Nations organization over the summer he returned to Beaver Lodge with Yvonne to prepare his regalia for his second British tour. He was not left in peace though. A thousand visitors came to Beaver Lodge that summer, including Viscount Clarendon, and English aviator, Major Blacker.2

In September Grey Owl began the tour, accompanied by Yvonne and a young Canadian Rhodes scholar and novelist, Kenneth Conibear, whose western Canadian background and experience made him well acquainted with the wilderness. This tour of Britain was even more successful than the first. Grey Owl worked hard to give his best performance, despite the strain, his extreme fatigue and bouts of drinking. On his travels Grey Owl also briefly met his mother in Oxford when she attended one of his lectures, a meeting that no doubt added to his strain, not just for the awkwardness from their estrangement, but from the fear she might reveal his true identity. His worries were groundless and he left her reassured she would remain silent about his lack of Indian ancestry and he continued on with his tour and to his biggest success—a Royal Command Performance for the whole royal family. It was a huge triumph for Grey Owl. Then, before sailing back to North America at the end of December, he met his aunts once again when he gave a lecture in Hastings, as he had done on his earlier tour. They too had kept silent about his true ancestry.3

Grey Owl landed in New York and spent the next three months on another gruelling tour, this time through the United States and Canada, traveling nearly 10,000 kilometres in overheated trains. Grey Owl's health steadily deteriorated but he was consumed by his cause—the need for conservation and the desire to get that message out as much as possible. By March 1938, he had given nearly 200 lectures in the six months since he had started. His success in Britain and then the United States reinforced his image and contributed to the success of his Canadian tour. After his final lecture at the end of March, Yvonne and Grey Owl returned to Prince Albert and Yvonne was hospitalized, exhausted after enduring months of touring and looking after Grey Owl. Grey Owl was desperate to return to Beaver Lodge, so park staff arranged for his transport there, only to collect him three days later after he phoned to say he was very ill. A week later he was dead after succumbing to pneumonia, an illness his weakened lungs and constitution could not fight. Before he died the staff and his friends told Anahareo that he had asked for her.4

Upon hearing of his death the day after her arrival Anahareo took Dawn, who was not yet six years old, to the funeral home to see her father so that she could understand that her father was dead. Though Dawn later attended the funeral, Anahareo stayed away because she felt it inappropriate to be there, given that Yvonne Perrier was still in hospital and unable to attend herself.5

As soon as word of Grey Owl's death was released, North Bay, Ontario's newspaper, *The Nugget,* published an article they had held on to for three years that revealed Grey Owl to be "a full-blooded white man, probably of English descent." They had received the information about Grey Owl's background from Angele, Grey Owl's Anishnabe wife. She explained his real name was Archie Belaney and they had a daughter, Agnes. The article set off a frenzy of reporting, with journalists digging wildly for information and creating massive speculation. Everyone—Summy, Lovat Dickson, Grey Owl's employer Major Wood—was taken by surprise and denied the statements outright. Anahareo was dumbfounded. She was sitting with Dawn on her knee when someone brought in a newspaper that claimed Grey Owl had been born in Hastings. Initially she scoffed at the reports. Who else would have known him as well? But time and tenacious investigation uncovered Grey Owl's two aunts in Hastings who confirmed that he was their nephew. Eventually reporters located his mother, Kittie Scott-Brown in Oxford. The various articles and many commentaries cast Grey Owl in a very bad light, portraying him as a fraud. In Canada, however, of the eight dailies that commented on his exposure, not one condemned him. One mentioned that he would not have been as effective under his own name, another said that his identity would not jeopardize his attainments as a writer and naturalist. Sadly, that was not to be the case, his message and achievements became lost to the idea that he was a fraud.6

There are many possible reasons for the strong black lash following the revelations of Grey Owl's background that failed to separate out the importance of his message from the manner of its presentation. Some undoubtedly felt a sense of betrayal that a person in whom they had placed great faith and support would have not been truthful about their background. At the deepest level the success of his deception inferred to some who had believed him that they had poor judgment skills. That they would have been less likely to accept such a strong conservationist message or give it as much attention had it been presented by an Englishman in a suit and tie, or even in buckskin, no matter how dynamic the performance, was not an argument that the public would accept, since it cast them in an uncomfortably negative light. Others have suggested that another undercurrent of the strong backlash might have come from people who disliked the idea that an Englishman would have wanted to be a race other than European, in a time when Europeans were seen as the superior race.7 Some felt that Grey Owl's just wanted to gain money and fame, but in fact Grey Owl put much of his income back into his work to bring his message to as many people as possible.

Amid the uproar that filled the newspapers with speculative rumours and interviews with people associated with Grey Owl, Anahareo and Yvonne Perrier came under scrutiny. Because of her association with Grey Owl Anahareo's public credibility became suspect and her image began to deteriorate. One article entitled, "Grey Owl's Deserted Wife is Found in Poverty," appeared in the *Daily Express* and suggested that while Grey Owl "was triumphantly touring England with a French woman," Anahareo was forced to earn a living in a "gambling and drinking hall," statement that carried with it the insinuation that she had engaged in prostitution.8 Though appearing to cast Anahareo in a sympathetic light by insinuating that Grey Owl had abandoned her, he did her no favours by suggesting that the manner in which she chose to support herself was to engage in prostitution.

Such allegations concerned Grey Owl's publishers, Hugh Eayrs and Lovat Dickson, who were frantically trying to salvage Grey Owl's reputation and future sales of his books. Dickson intended to sue the papers that reported libellous accounts of Anahareo and Perrier and requested statements from them both. He received no word from Anahareo, leaving him to wonder what means of income she had. Eventually Yvonne sent in her statement and continued corresponding with the publishers because she had her own agenda about Grey Owl's future works. Determined that Anahareo should have no part in any publications whatsoever, she requested the publishers delete any photographs or references to Anahareo in a forthcoming anthology and Lovat Dickson's tribute, *The Greenleaf*.9

Dickson thought it a great pity to delete her name from the anthology, an act he was certain would be even more noticeable in England where "Anahareo is even more thought of than Grey Owl." He asked Perrier that she reconsider, because he knew "it will hurt the sales of the book," not so much that "fine passages of Grey Owl's work will therefore be excluded... but that it will matter that Anahareo, of whom he spoke so warmly on his first lecture tour and about whom everybody has read in *Pilgrims of the Wild*, should be obviously ignored." He refused to delete her from any other works, since it was impossible to "disentangle her personality from the *Pilgrims of the Wild* story."10

In the light of Grey Owl's deception questions hung over Anahareo about her own ancestry. Hugh Eayrs managed to locate Isabel LeDuc, Anahareo's former Wabikon mentor and ask her what she knew of Anahareo's background. LeDuc replied that as far as she knew, "Anahareo, as I shall call Gertrude Bernard...she usually disclaimed any white and was proud of her Iroquois blood."11

The publishers were not the only ones scrambling to deal with fallout from the revelations about Grey Owl's background. The staff at Prince Albert National Park, headed by Major Woods, stung by the controversy, decided to play down their seven-year association with Grey Owl. The presence of the beavers still reminded people about Grey Owl, though, and as such posed a problem. A government official in Ottawa wrote to the superintendent asking, "would Jelly Roll and Rawhide revert to the wild if left," and suggesting they employ an Indian boy to look after them if they were still a tourist attraction. Woods replied that it would generate bad publicity if the beavers were left to go wild and Grey Owl had requested the Parks Department look after them. Yvonne asked the Parks Department to appoint her as the beavers' caretaker, but it was deemed inadvisable. Her presence would only reinforce the connection to Grey Owl.12

Despite the promises to Grey Owl the beavers did not fare well. In the summer following Grey Owl's death an Aboriginal boy, Billy Clare, was duly appointed to look after the beavers but by 1939 Rawhide was dead and Jelly Roll was seen only occasionally and her children had disappeared. They had indeed, as the park official put it, become "a dead issue."13

Grey Owl's will had made provision for five-and-a-half-year-old Dawn, and in the immediate aftermath of Grey Owl's death, she remained with the Winters in familiar surroundings. Anahareo, meanwhile, spent time between her shack tent and the Winters' place in Prince Albert, attempting to make sense of the series of revelations about Grey Owl's background and its effects on her own life. She, like Dickson, Eayrs and Summy, initially felt that there was little if any truth to the allegations about his background. Dickson still was convinced Grey Owl was Indian. When Summy offered to fund a trip for Anahareo to visit her in Cumbria, Lovat Dickson supported the idea with the notion that Anahareo could meet Grey Owl's mother, Kittie Scott-Brown and determine if she possessed any Aboriginal blood.14

The arrangements were made for July and at the end of the month Anahareo set off from Prince Albert. Traveling east, still distinctively dressed in her buckskin jacket, red neckerchief, breeches and prospecting boots, Anahareo was easily spotted by journalists eager to find out more bits of the unfolding story of Grey Owl. In Winnipeg, as she strolled through the station of the Canadian Pacific Railroad, one journalist talked to her. Anahareo used the opportunity to speak up in support of Grey Owl. She stated that while she "felt no personal resentment against the people who have started a controversy against Archie," she added she could see "no reason why it should have become a controversy in the first place....[N]o matter what people thought he was, he did give the world some wonderful writings. The fact that he was a white man and an Englishman made him all the more remarkable." When pressed about why she was going to England she only said that she had been invited, refusing to disclose who invited her, but she did admit they had funded her travel.15

Though the journalist described Anahareo's clothing, the focus of his interview was her relationship to Grey Owl. There was little else discussed except Anahareo's declaration of her Mohawk heritage and the name *Paharomen Nahareo* which she most likely made to affirm her authenticity to the interviewer. There was no comment, negative or positive, about her clothes and no recitation of her many exploits and skills. And neither was there mention of the conservation work with the beaver. The public's animosity and backlash over Grey Owl's deception was still too fresh.

Though Anahareo was willing to travel to England to meet Grey Owl's mother she had more or less come to accept that Grey Owl was indeed an Englishman from Hastings. When the journalist's story appeared in Toronto's *Daily Star* they ran the headline, "Wife of Grey Owl Admits He Was English, Not Indian," and added her emphasis that she was Mohawk and her Indian name was *Paharomen Nahareo*, or Flaming Leaf, in English. Though she publicly defended Grey Owl, accepting his deception towards her was personally difficult. Somehow he seemed a different person than she imagined or understood. Later, she described the sense of bewilderment and loss she felt, as well as the feeling that over all those years she had lived with a ghost:

> When, finally I was convinced that Archie was English, I had the awful feeling for all those years I had been married to a ghost, that

the man who now lay buried in Ajawaan was someone I had never known, and that Archie never really existed.16

Near the end of her life Anahareo when she reflected on his deception she stated, "To me he was an Indian, and one of the best men I ever met."17

When Anahareo arrived in England Summy spent a month with her exploring Britain. They stopped in Oxford and Anahareo met Grey Owl's mother one afternoon and asked her many questions about Grey Owl, but she refused to answer them. They parted amicably and Anahareo continued to correspond with her, though she never learned anything more about Grey Owl from her. Despite Kittie Scott-Brown's refusal to answer questions, Anahareo was convinced there was not a drop of Indian blood in her. With most avenues of possibilities now closed, Dickson and Summy finally had to accept that, no matter what Grey Owl might have given as his background, there was no doubt he was English.18

Summy continued taking Anahareo to different places. Scotland was one Anahareo's favourite spots, perhaps because of the rugged untamed countryside. The two also spent some time at Summy's home in Westmoreland, Cumbria where Anahareo drew a beaver on the oak beam in one of the bedrooms, opposite the beam that Grey Owl had drawn one. She gave Summy one of her buckskin jackets and admired Summy's beaded gifts from Grey Owl. The two also had long discussions about the past as well as possibilities for the future. Summy told Anahareo that the best she could do for Grey Owl was to write a book about their life together. Anahareo, lacking confidence in her ability to write, was initially reluctant, but she agreed it was one way to defend Grey Owl's image. She and Summy discussed the possibility of writing a book with Grey Owl's publishers. They went along with the idea but they instructed Anahareo to refrain from mentioning Grey Owl's background in the manuscript.19

Anahareo

Anahareo posing for book promotion, courtesy of Katherine Swartile

Anahareo returned to Canada in mid-September and began to write, though she felt the restrictions concerning Grey Owl's background made it difficult to defend his character. Using pencil she recorded her memories in exercise books and made notations for Summy in the margins like, "Hi Summy. How the heck do you spell that?"20 Though her diligent work creating a positive image of Grey Owl might have given Anahareo a focus and purpose, it did not immediately give her money for food and lodging. She wrote to Summy in October and said that she had to show the grocer some of the articles in order to get food on credit. In January she was up at Christopher Lake, where the Winters and other friends had cabins, still trying to make ends meet. There she heard that Jelly Roll was in very poor shape, so she wrote to the park staff full of concern and asked permission to go to Beaver Lodge and keep a fire going and to check on the beavers. One of the park staff wrote back that it was not possible for her to make the trip into Ajawaan Lake. The beaver were frozen in for the winter and did not require any attention.21

Anahareo might have been writing about Grey Owl and the beavers in her book, but as far as the Parks Department was concerned, that part of her life was closed. In the time she had initiated the separation from Grey Owl Anahareo had experienced the most difficult hardships of her life and no amount of pride and determination had enabled her to fight the economic and social forces that challenged her. She realized now the full cost of her parting with Grey Owl. It was a hard-won lesson and one that she was not going to forget.

Chapter Sixteen

A New Life With Old Problems

In the winter of 1939, when Anahareo traveled to see her friends the Wards in Christopher Lake, just outside the southeastern border of the park, she rode along in a truck with another person hitching a ride to Waskesiu, Eric Moltke. He sat in the back, in the open air. It was a cold ride so Anahareo offered him her gloves. A good-looking man, he was six foot with a slim build and a courtly manner that women found attractive. And he could "dance like hot damn." Moltke remembered Anahareo's own charm and beauty from the time he first saw her some eight years previously at a bootlegger's party, just after he had arrived in Prince Albert. Dressed in her usual breeches and prospector's boots she was with Grey Owl who had played the piano. Even then Moltke felt someday he would marry Anahareo. By the end of 1939 it would become truth.

Kristin Gleeson

Eric with first wife, Helga, courtesy of Katherine Swartile Papers

Born Count Eric Moltke Huitfeld the same year as Anahareo in Skona, Sweden, Eric's upbringing could not have been more different from Anahareo's. His father was connected to a noble family whose origins were German. During his childhood he, his brother and two sisters spent more time under the strict eye of a nanny than with their parents. The times Eric was able to escape her eagle eye he spent with the gardener, who nurtured Eric's passion for working the soil. His cold and distant father scorned Eric's interests. Under such a stifling upbringing Eric grew to despise the rigid rules of the class system and all that he felt his family represented. When he reached his twenties he left Sweden for Canada and eventually settled in Prince Albert, where he knew the sheriff. There he supported himself with casual work in construction and occasional sums of money from his family in Sweden. After a time in Prince Albert he married the sheriff's daughter, Helga, and they had two daughters; but by the time Eric met Anahareo again on that truck ride in 1939 his marriage was over.2

In the months following the trip to Christopher Lake, Eric courted Anahareo, visiting her at the Winters or at her shack tent in Waskesiu in the summer months. On December 2, they got married in Winnipeg, where they hoped they might find better job prospects. It mattered little to Eric that Anahareo was poor and not a noblewoman and even less that she was an Aboriginal. Back in Sweden, where various classes and races mixed little, his family would certainly not approve. And though Winnipeg might be more inclined to forgive a nobleman marrying someone from the lower classes, racial mixing was a different situation altogether.

Many in North America and Europe at this time believed in the science-based idea of a racial hierarchy. The idea was formed in the nineteenth century and placed Aboriginals very low in the racial ranks. Regarded as "primitive" they were down near the animals in ranking, while the Europeans and their descendants were placed at the top. The idea of racial purity and eugenics gained much ground in 1920s and 1930s in Germany and other parts of Europe and North America.3 In such a context, especially in an urban area of western Canada such as Winnipeg, where social conformity was important to maintain their "civilised" image, many would view Eric and Anahareo's marriage as a serious and even criminal act.

Though Eric was raised with such codes and standards he held them in contempt. Anahareo was beautiful, vibrant and intelligent. She shared his interest in world events and they could talk for hours about their views. That was enough for him. Anahareo found Eric handsome, charming and interesting, and he shared her delight in dancing and music. She also valued his regard for her as an equal and the easy manner in which he dismissed race and class. He knew of her past experiences and it made no difference to him. And it could not have escaped her thoughts that with Eric as her husband she would have the extra security that assured that her experience in Saskatoon would not be repeated. In such difficult times Anahareo could no longer look to the wilderness and her bush skills to support herself. Her days in the wilderness were over, at least for the present.

Eric and Anahareo celebrated their newly married state through the Christmas, using the money they had saved and hoping that funds from Sweden would arrive to tide them over until they could find work. They tried to generate some income by pooling their remaining money with a drunken lawyer they had met and set up a bootlegging business. Though they made the alcohol it proved too much of a temptation for the three of them and they ended up with little to sell. Eric, like Grey Owl, was no stranger to drink and by this time it was a familiar part of Anahareo's life. For Anahareo alcohol was an integral part of any celebration, good time, relaxation or party that enabled her to overcome her shyness and become outgoing, but for Eric it was a daily necessity. The party could not go on, though. With no money and little prospects the two finally found work in a packing company, cleaning hides. It was gruelling work, but at least it gave them an income.4

When she could find time Anahareo still worked on the book, jotting down her memories and description in the notebooks. After she eventually completed the narrative she sent the notebooks off to Summy who typed them up for her and handled the arrangements for the manuscript's publication. Anahareo had hopes that the book might give her reasonable income to help her straightened circumstances. She wrote and urged Summy in 1940 that "if [Lovat] Dickson is taking it, tell him that I must eat and tell him that I'm not kidding."5

By 1940 Lovat Dickson had returned to Canada to join Grey Owl's Canadian publishers, MacMillan, and Peter Davies took over his list in England, including the rights to Anahareo's manuscript. Though Davies was satisfied enough with Anahareo's efforts and published her book that year, Anahareo was not happy with the book. She felt that the restrictions on writing about Grey Owl's ancestry had hampered her efforts to provide a true and compelling story that defended his image. The opening, where she had "thrown things in for atmosphere" to fill in the space that might have been given over to

Grey Owl's background, she especially despised, feeling that it was "all wrong." As she later wrote to an agent:

> There were a few people in hot water over Grey Owl being a Britisher and I was asked not to mention his ancestry or his marriages. I had quite a time dodging between what Grey Owl had written, and at the same time refraining from what the public wanted to know and still come out with a story.6

The quality of the book bothered her so much that in the years to come, if she ever came across the book in a library or anywhere else, she would rip out the first chapter.7

The royalties, when they did arrive were small, a mere £20. The advent of the Second World War focus had shifted away from such concerns as wilderness preservation. Years later Margaret Winters recalled that the boat carrying the shipment of the Canadian print run had been torpedoed and all the books lost.8 Such events were disastrous for the book's success. When the £20 in royalties eventually did arrive Anahareo gave them away to a person begging on the street. It might be that she acted in such an impulsive manner because of her mixed feelings about the book and how little it earned, as well as her personal experience of destitution.9

Two years before Anahareo's book was released and just after Grey Owl's death, Lovat Dickson had published *The Green Leaf, A Memorial to Grey Owl*, which contained press commentary on Grey Owl, excerpts of his writings, pictures, as well as testimonies about him by Lovat Dickson and Superintendent Wood that helped to some degree to restore his reputation as a conservationist. The following year Lovat Dickson brought out his own biography of Grey Owl, *Half Breed, The Story of Grey Owl,* in which he passionately defended Grey Owl against the charges of fraud and impostor.10 It might have been his work on this biography and the feeling that his efforts to restore Grey Owl's reputation should not be put at risk that prompted him to instruct Anahareo to refrain from mentioning anything about Grey Owl's background.

Regardless of any success Lovat Dickson might have enjoyed from his book, Anahareo found no financial support from her own. After a year of struggle tanning hides in the packing factory, Eric and Anahareo spent the Christmas of 1940 at God's Lake. Eric later recalled its wild nature in a letter to Anahareo:

> Came home with Jack O'Brien, Kasha and two other bohunks. Kasha tried to kiss you and as usual I swung missing and hit you in the eye. That was very very rash and you were very very angry with me for a long long time.11

Eric's rash behaviour at the party was part of his impulsive nature and was not unlike behaviour that Grey Owl exhibited in his younger days. In some ways Anahareo had chosen a partner that possessed characteristics that had drawn her to Grey Owl. His charm, wit and an alcohol-fuelled love of a good time were all qualities she had enjoyed with Grey Owl. And with both Grey Owl and Eric she was happy to drink along with them and have fun. With her days in the bush behind her and still raw from the memories from her experiences in Calgary, Saskatoon and Banff, Anahareo's confidence had diminished. She no longer had trips to the bush to reinforce her sense of capability and strength that marked her for an exceptional woman. She could only get menial jobs that did little to challenge her inquiring mind. With Eric beside Anahareo, alcohol became a way to escape or find confidence.

The Christmas they celebrated in 1941 was all the more important because shortly afterwards Eric enlisted in the army and left to serve as a tank driver overseas. The war had finally caught up to them. The parting between Anahareo and Eric was doubly difficult because she was pregnant. With Eric away Anahareo decided to move to Saskatoon, possibly at the encouragement of Wilna Moore who had remained in contact with Anahareo. Wilna also discussed with Anahareo the proposal to put her daughter Ann into the care of a young couple from Calgary. Whether Eric was unaware of Ann's existence and Anahareo therefore felt she could not bring her daughter to live with her in Saskatoon is not clear. She did however agree that the Calgary couple, the Eagles, could have Ann in their care and raise her as one of their family. It was a private agreement that was not pursued through the courts.12

Anne with uncle, Norman Eagle, courtesy of Anne Gaskell

It was not long after Anahareo arrived back in Saskatoon that she gave birth to her third daughter, Katherine, in early March. Wilna Moore became Katherine's godmother. On Wilna Moore's advice Anahareo eventually rented a small house, living on her small army wife's pension. Though she was known only as Gertrude Moltke and lived an ordinary homemaker's life Anahareo still had not shed her breeches, shirt and bobbed hair, a look that was still viewed as unusual, especially in this small town. But with the luxury of a guaranteed income she allowed herself to dream that she could bring nine-year-old Dawn to live with her and the new baby.13

When Eric heard that she had rented a house he was unhappy and wrote to her that Wilna Moore was "a silly old goose," and that "she gives bum advice. Any fool knows that taking rooms is cheaper than a house," he said. But later Eric realized what it meant to her to have the house for her two daughters and wrote her:

> "we both had had trying times but we seem to come out of it with flying colors and now you are living in Saskatoon in a nice little house surrounded by your children and I hope having a pretty fair time."14

Since her entrance into Anahareo's life Wilna Moore had set herself up Anahareo's mentor and guide. Wilna's brother was a minister and she was still single, finding intermittent employment through her Presbyterian connections. Like other missionaries and religious workers such as the Reverend Roe, Wilna thought Aboriginals had a poor moral compass and needed constant help and guidance on making the right choices. Anahareo became her own special project, someone she could help and advise on to a better life (a life Wilna approved of). She encouraged Anahareo to modify her behaviour and advised her how to manage her house, and her family. Though Wilna became a familiar figure to Katherine who would learn to call her "Aunty Moore," Anahareo eventually chose to follow Wilna's advice only when it suited her.15

Eric wrote to her as his unit moved around Europe and North Africa. During one of his leaves he managed to visit Anahareo's good friend Summy at her home in Cumbria. Perhaps because he felt enlisting in the army might redeem him he sent a letter to his parents and finally told them of his divorce and his new marriage to Anahareo. He wrote Anahareo that his parents were pleased with the news and thought he was a hero for becoming a soldier, writing to him in the expectation that he would return to Sweden with his family as soon as the war was over. Though Eric had no intention of returning to Sweden he did feel encouraged enough by their response to visit them in Sweden on leave after the war.16

Anahareo, meanwhile, gave her attention to raising Dawn and Katherine and approached parenting in the manner her grandmother had raised her. She never scolded or punished but taught them proper behaviour through direct experience of consequences, telling stories that contained lessons and other traditional Indian methods. She recounted family stories and tales of their Aboriginal heritage to make them proud of their roots. When Katherine had trouble sleeping, Anahareo, understanding the power of the mind, invented a Mohawk ritual that she told Katherine came from Big Grandma and soothed Katherine so that she slept. Though Anahareo no longer spoke publicly about wildlife preservation she still believed in an animal's right to existence and passed that belief onto her daughters. When a mouse decided to move in, for example, rather than set traps or put out poison, Anahareo put out a saucer of food for it so it would not raid her cupboards.17

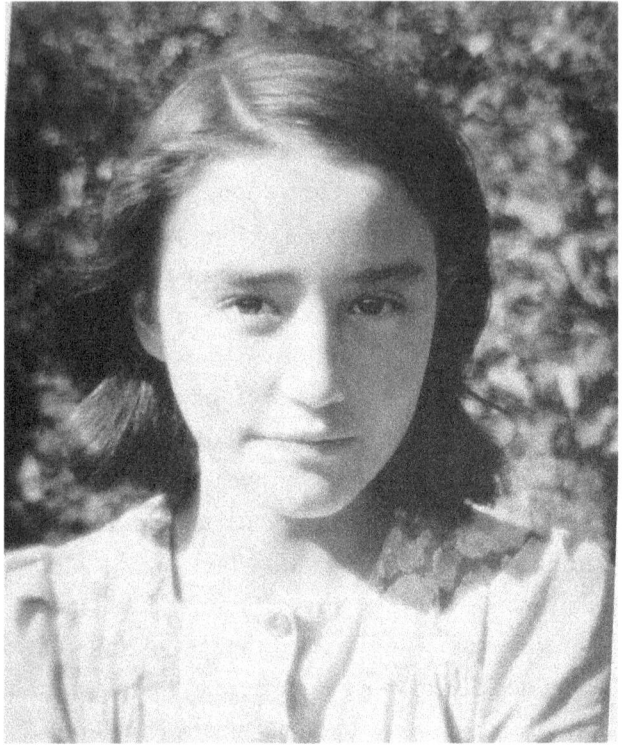
Dawn c. 12 years old, courtesy of Katherine Swartile

Finally, when Katherine was four years old and Dawn nearly fourteen, Eric returned from the war. Katherine opened the door to him and saw only a strange soldier. Later, after he sat down, she set about exploring the intriguing backpack he had brought and had a terrible shock when this same man shouted at her to stop, not only because he was a stranger, but also because no one had ever shouted at her before. Anahareo defended Katherine, but it only made matters worse. Everyone needed time to get used to the new situation.18

In the months that followed it became clear that Eric was having trouble adjusting to life after the war. He suffered from nightmares, was unable to find employment and drank heavily. His own approach to parenting came from his Victorian childhood experience that believed children should be seen and not heard. Such a view directly opposed Anahareo's philosophy and created a deepening tension in the home. Money became tight and the occasional funds sent from Sweden soon disappeared to purchase drink. To make matters worse Dawn developed diabetes, required hospitalization, and afterwards, in the light of the smallness of the house and the difficulties there, Dawn decided to return to Prince Albert to the Winters family.[19]

It was difficult for Anahareo to part with her daughter and she tried to make up for it by writing often to exchange news and maintain some kind of connection with her. Dawn had also formed a close bond with her sister in the time she had lived in Saskatoon and was particularly glad to hear news of her. Not long after Dawn left, in December 1947, at the time of the Princess Elizabeth's marriage in England, Anahareo wrote Dawn: "Got up at 4am to listen to the Royal Wedding and Katherine too. Took Katherine to a show—western. Katherine sobbed through it. Said it was because it was so sad."[20]

Dawn was not the only one who had left Saskatoon. Wilna Moore had moved away as well, pursuing her own project setting up a radio station on the Alaska Highway. She wrote to Anahareo that same year full of her breezy advice, instructions and moral monitoring:

> Just how do you like this. I have been wondering what has happened to you! You had better write at once to put my mind at ease. I am hoping that you and Eric are still turning your back on liquor. Anyway write and let me know the best or worst. When I am returning I scarcely know. It has been one very hard and trying time to put it very mildly. More of the gruesome details when I see you. I have been going night and day so far haven't dared to leave the place. It is just possible that I shall be back about the end of July, but only for a short space. Did you ever try to pull off a Big Thing without any money? Well that is my predicament and there-

fore the worry, but I think it is all going to turn out. I have bought a very fine property for the station.21

Though Anahareo and Eric might have turned their back on drinking for a time, Eric's abstention was short lived. Eric had a job tending the university grounds, but his alcohol intake increased to such a point that Anahareo decided to take action. She left with Katherine and accepted a job as a cook and housekeeper at a place called Hills Farm. She wrote to Dawn and explained:

> Here we are at last. Guess what? Katherine and I are on a farm. I'm cooking for 2 men. It's a beautiful house with electric lights and washer. I do no outside work and the people are very nice. Katherine is in her glory. I am sure glad to get away from that Herman Ave. and everything in it. We may not go back there either as Miss Moore has a job for me at $125 a month [,] that won't be until July of course[,] no we will surely get a week or so together. I mean you, Katherine and I. I didn't ask you to come for Easter because Eric wasn't working. He is still at the house in Saskatoon and working at the university. Miss Moore is coming by the end of June and I was thinking how lovely it would be if we could all have a week together up at the lake[,] however time will tell[,] but these are my plans.22

It was clear that Anahareo missed Dawn and had wished for a visit at Easter but knowing the circumstances at home wisely deferred it. Further on in her letter Anahareo asked Dawn to write her at the farm and send her a photo if she had one and finally, she closed the letter, "Well sweetheart I think that I see the day ahead when I can see more of you and under happier circumstances so bye bye for now with all our love ad plenty of kisses from Mudder."23

Anahareo tried to be as positive as she could about her own situation on the farm in her letter to Dawn. Though she told her about the luxury of the washer, years later she wrote that the flies in the farmhouse soared around "like balls of lightning" because one of her employers did not like fly killer. She also recounted the time she had quite a scare when Katherine and some other children played in a bin of weed killing chemicals. Anahareo rinsed their mouths with water and managed to get them to vomit. To her relief there seemed no other ill effects.24

Anahareo & Katherine, courtesy of Katherine Swartile

Though she told Dawn she was glad to "get away from that Herman Ave. and everything in it" it was a difficult decision. To leave meant facing a world as a single mother, a situation that could only recall the bitter experiences from before. And these bitter experiences only made her more cautious, so that it could only be the promise of a job with some security that would entice her to leave Herman Avenue, no matter how bad it was there. Job security also gave her some degree of confidence again. Besides increased confidence, Wilna Moore's promise of a job made Anahareo hope that she could manage on her own and even dare to dream that she might be able to have Dawn by her side as well.

Wilna's promised job did not materialize in the end and Anahareo's hope of even spending at least some weeks with Dawn up at Christopher Lake remained unfulfilled. She did manage to take Katherine there for a short time, staying once again with the Wards. The Wards made her feel welcome as one of their own; they doted on Katherine like a grandchild and called Anahareo "Pony," which no doubt gave her some reassurance and comfort.25

Before the end of the year Eric had obtained a job at Canmore, a small town near Banff in British Columbia. Perhaps because it was the promise of a fresh start or that the housekeeping job ended but Anahareo decided to return to Eric with Katherine and make the move to Canmore. Located near the base of the Three Sister Mountains, 108 kilometres west of Calgary, Canmore was a working-class town originally established as a stopping place and depot on the Canadian Pacific Railway in 1883. The Bow River and a tributary, The Policeman's Creek, provided the town boundaries. A short while after its establishment it became the thriving base for the coal mining industry of the Bow Valley. A quarry five miles east and a cement plant brought further prosperity early in the twentieth century but by the 1940s Canmore was a sleepy town, well past its peak. There were a few shops, a grocery store and drug store in the main part of town and a general store, called The Mine Store, on the other side of the river. The Canmore Hotel was the hub of the town's social life and frequented by coal miners and railway workers through the years. A Chinese family owned a café on the main street across from the hotel. Such industries tended to attract immigrants from eastern Canada and European countries, and a few from Asia.26

Despite its diversity, like many western Canadian areas, the town was not immune to the negative perceptions and images of Aboriginal people. The nearest reserve was forty kilometres east at Morley, where the Nakota speaking Stoney People lived. The government gave them the reserve in 1877 under Treaty Seven and in 1947 the Stoney People acquired a small additional reserve at Big Horn. Many of the Stoney People continued to try to live a traditional nomadic lifestyle by blending seasonal hunting and trapping and meagre government rations, and taking any available carpentry, logging, ranching or other odd jobs. The families lived in one-room cabins with no amenities other than a wood-burning stove and the children attended the residential school at Morley.27 Living such a lifestyle on a reserve meant that few of them, if any, ever visited Canmore; but if they did, Canmore residents, rather than admire the value these people placed on their traditional culture, no doubt thought they were backwards and typical of any stereotype of their imagining.

Anahareo was not from a reserve; she grew up in a town, had modern sensibilities and learned bush skills as an adult. The Algonkian and Iroquoian based languages and woodland culture of her ancestors was very different from the plains language and culture of the Stoney People. But these differences mattered little to the people in towns like Canmore. In their eyes she was an Aboriginal just like any other and, under their close scrutiny, was subject to the same sort of stereotyping as any First Nations that might come in from Morley or elsewhere. She was not permitted in the hotel bar with her husband, no matter whether her drinking habits were more controlled or not. Eric's choice to marry someone classed racially lower than he would make him suspect to some people, but it would not bar him from the hotel.

In such an atmosphere Anahareo felt isolated. Never at her best in towns, she was at heart a shy person who was not good at small talk and aimless chat with a neighbour. Like Eric, she took a keen interest in world affairs and had strong views about them, something that would not have been the centre of concern for any of her neighbours.

Upon their arrival in Canmore, Eric, Anahareo and Katherine

had moved into a two-room cabin, called "the Doll's House." It was a very basic home at the edge of the town, near the bush, with no electricity. They carried their water either from a neighbour's stream or caught it in a rain barrel. Eventually a water truck made rounds which eased the daily chore of hauling water. They heated the house with a wood-burning stove and stuffed it with wood Anahareo had chopped from dead trees she dragged from the bush that bordered the town.28 Though Anahareo would have enjoyed fewer amenities when she was living in the wilderness, her current situation lacked all the adventurous promise of the bush.

Using the ingenuity and skill fostered under Grey Owl Anahareo did her best to create more comfortable surroundings for her family. She fixed up the outhouse, made a table, created a cupboard out of a long box, and used the case of the hand sewing machine for another cupboard. With her sewing machine and knitting needles she made clothes for Katherine. She continued to try to make Katherine feel connected to the wilderness and her own heritage. She told her stories about Jelly Roll, Rawhide, and living in the bush, as well as stories about Big Grandma and their Mohawk ancestors, all the while stressing the importance of wilderness conservation. In an effort to interest her daughter about the thrill and wonder of the wilderness, Anahareo sometimes took Katherine out to the bush where she would make a fire, cook things like bacon and eggs and demonstrate different bush skills. Eventually it was clear that what was exciting and interesting to the mother was not necessarily so for the daughter so the lessons stopped.29

Though Anahareo may not have been able to pass on her love of the bush to her daughter she had more success in creating an empathy and understanding for animals. Anahareo frequently used expressions like, "she's her own cat," to convey the idea that the cat had a mind and a viewpoint that was independent of humans and as such had their own place on the earth. She always attracted stray dogs or cats and never hesitated when she found an animal injured. Once when Anahareo discovered a nest of young magpies she took down the nest to prevent boys from discovering it and killing the young birds. She hoped that the parent birds would follow, but they did not so she raised them at her home. Eric, though verbally claiming he would have nothing to do with these rescue missions, still could not resist feeding the birds. In a desire to involve Katherine in the care of the birds Anahareo told her to wash one that was muddied from a puddle. Katherine used her initiative and put the bird in a bucket and gave it a good scrubbing. To Katherine's great distress the bird went into shock and seemed dead, but Anahareo picked up the bird, wrapped it in a towel then put it in the crook of Katherine's arm and told her to be quiet for an hour. Katherine watched breathlessly while the bird slowly recovered.30

By the time Anahareo and her family moved to Canmore Katherine was old enough to attend school. The school in Canmore was a fair size, with an average class size, taking in pupils from the town and the area surrounding it. With the children of the nearest reserve attending the residential school in Morley, Katherine would have been one of few, if any, Aboriginal or mixed-race children in the school. She was curly haired and not noticeably Indian in appearance. Though Anahareo's own clothes and hairstyle reflected her modern but eccentric sensibilities and she taught her daughter to be proud of her Aboriginal heritage, Anahareo recognized it was to Katherine's advantage to appear as Euro-Canadian as possible for her to succeed in school. When Katherine asked to have her hair put into braids, Anahareo adamantly refused because she thought Katherine would look like a stereotypical Indian. And while it was true Anahareo had no talent for baking and no interest in activities like the PTA, fundraisers or coffee klatches, she avoided going to Katherine's school so the staff would not connect her with Katherine.31 Anahareo's own experiences in school and her hometown as well as those later in life were strong enough to compel her to compromise her attitudes for her daughter's sake.

Katherine herself recalled no single racist experience in her years at Canmore school. A pair of fur mitts her mother had tanned, fashioned and beaded were stolen from Katherine one of the times she wore them to school. Katherine was upset but knew they were taken more from envy at their quality and beauty and not because of any racist feelings. Katherine's fourth grade teacher seemed to assume Katherine was fully Euro-Canadian. Once when the teacher was discussing Grey Owl she mentioned that he was Indian. Katherine raised her hand and said that he was actually English, from Hastings. "How do you know?" the teacher asked. Katherine explained that her mother was Anahareo. The teacher was sceptical.32 Ironically it seemed impossible to reconcile the known image of Anahareo with the woman who was Katherine's mother. Grey Owl was still out of favour and Anahareo's life was such a long way from her former public image, no matter that she still wore breeches and shirts.

It was incidents such as the teacher's comments, in which Grey Owl and his message were badly or inaccurately depicted, that kept Anahareo formulating ideas and plans to promote him in a positive way. It was a project that caught Wilna Moore's attention for a time and a crusade that Dawn eventually took on. Though Dawn was back living with the Winters, she was always in touch with her mother and from the time she was seventeen was actively engaged in trying to rehabilitate Grey Owl's reputation.33

Wilna Moore, in contrast, found Grey Owl's story fascinating and exciting, like something from a dime store novel. She was convinced she could create an exciting narrative of his life into a book and she enlisted Anahareo to help her with this project. During her intervals from teaching Indian children Wilna visited regularly and swept Anahareo off to a motel where the two would spend days discussing their various ideas as well as events in Grey Owl's life that Anahareo could recall.34 With the war well past and economic recovery sustained it seemed to Wilna that a book would be successful this time, unlike Anahareo's 1940 publication.35

Anahareo was less certain about writing a book. She felt a film about Grey Owl was the better project, but went along with the idea. At the very least recounting memories would bring her closer to the wilderness and happier times. Beginning about 1950, with the help of her sister, Wilna compiled into a manuscript the stories gleaned from Anahareo, Grey Owl's books, his letters, and interviews with his former friends back east. Once completed, in December 1952, she sent the manuscript, along with Grey Owl's letters and other attachments, to Macmillan Publishers, Grey Owl's old firm. Wilna included a note stating:

> My sister and I have been working for two years on a story of the Life of Grey Owl.... I might say that we have Grey Owl's original notes for all his books, a sheaf of most interesting letters during the Prince Albert Park period which reveal the man himself. These were not incorporated in our original but we plan to delete a good deal and instead focus on this period of his existence. We can also have the detailed letters written by Anahareo, by Archie's mother, Mrs. Scott Brown after Grey Owl's death. They tell a good deal about his early childhood in England.
>
> We have been friends of Grey Owl and also Anahareo for a long time, and it has been our desire to clear his record in the eyes of the world and set him forth as the great man he actually was."36

Wilna met with the editor in December and was brimming full ideas about the biography. She explained she planned to approach Rank to make a film of her book and added that she might consider Anahareo to act her own role. She also told him that Anahareo had studied Hollywood actors for some time and knew of no one that could successfully portray Grey Owl. Already though Wilna was aware of the weaknesses in her own book and explained to the editor how she would rectify them.37

That same month Wilna wrote again to the editor after meeting with Anahareo and discussing changes she wanted to make to the manuscript:

I am enroute C.P.R. back to Prince Albert after a most interesting and worthwhile visit with Anahareo...Most of all we spent five days overhauling (from memory) what has been written, and also giving the thing heavy concentrated thought into late nights.... I have about fifty pages deleted fairly early in the writing of the story, which included a succession of episodes in and around Bisco —Archie's pranks, etc... the man we are exalting.38

Though Macmillan had given Wilna no response by February she was still busily reworking the manuscript and generating ideas for its use. She wrote to them in early February to share her progress:

I have spent considerable time in the Mississauga country and Mr. Bates had arranged the camp, also people whom I wanted to meet (the old Grey Owl cronies)....we did a lot of research—I have done considerably more since I was in Toronto and have several lists of amendments and minor changes to make. I am presently also re-writing the first four chapters, but first want to have your news as is (making them not so fictional—although truth to tell that man's life as was, was even more exciting than fiction. The telling, therefore was bound to be in fictional style....39

A short while later Wilna was back writing again to the editor with a few more corrections:

Since you still have the Mss under consideration it has occurred to me to send to you a short correction of event sequences at one of the difficult periods in his life. There are other changes of course, but these are rather important as you will agree and I thought they might interest you.
    A. <u>Episodes re Archies' flight from Bisco</u>
    (a) Affair with the knives at 'Joe's Place' (name fictituous [sic] real name "Sam Gerien")
    (b)Assisted by Aleck Spaniel gets off into a few days hiding.

(c)School Board & Town officials to his aid—clear up affair and Belaney back to town to attend Banquet & dance in his honor.....40

The letter continued with more listings and corrections and additional explanations. It was clearly still a work in progress. All her extra efforts to modify the manuscript could not detract from its problems and in some ways contributed to it.

At the end of February the editor received a thorough assessment of the book from one of his staff who had been assigned to read it. He reported that the manuscript itself was "bulky, untidily put together and poorly typed," and that "the spelling and punctuation leave much to be desired and the authors frequently use words in their wrong context." These were defects that could be remedied by a competent editor but there were other problems. Though the authors, in the reviewer's opinion, had "got closer to their subject than Lovat Dickson managed in *Half Breed, the Story of Grey Owl*, and they do succeed in conveying to the reader something of the extraordinarily complex nature of the strange man who came to be known as Grey Owl," the assessor stated that:

> [He found himself] wondering whether certain episodes recorded were really fact or fiction. So many legends have grown up around Grey Owl's entire life and so many pitfalls lie in wait for the most sincere biographer that it must be a baffling job attempting to shake loose the clinkers of hard facts from the ash piles of legend and hearsay.41

To alleviate some of his doubts the reviewer contacted a man from the Temagami-Biscotasing area who was "something of an expert on the Grey Owl story" about a knifing incident and the man stated he had no recollection of the knifing incident in Bisco. "This very lack of documentation," the reviewer wrote, "makes me uneasy and dampens my enthusiasm for the biography."42 Ultimately they declined to publish the manuscript.

Though Macmillan was receptive to the idea of publishing Grey Owl's biography Anahareo realized any attempts to set forth the image of the Grey Owl she knew were not going to happen through Wilna Moore's book. Already legends and conflicting images, many of them negative, were attaching themselves to his name. Trent Frayne's article, "Grey Owl, the Magnificent Fraud," had been published in *Maclean's* in August 1951 and was read by a large Canadian readership, as was Kathleen Strange's article, "The Story of Grey Owl—Canadian Legend," published in July of the same year in *Family Herald and Weekly Star*.43 Anahareo's own name carried little credibility, especially when attached to a poorly executed manuscript and an advocate, no matter how well meaning, like Wilna Moore. It was a setback, but Anahareo still had hopes that one of her projects might one day come to fruition.

Chapter Seventeen

A Stubborn Vision

The move to Canmore had not solved Anahareo's difficulties with Eric. He now had a job driving heavy machinery on construction sites, but his drinking and reckless spending had not stopped. He was by nature someone who enjoyed the moment, and while he was not bothered by differences of class, race or religion, he also had little motivation to try and improve his family's situation. Anahareo dreamed of building a house, but Eric had no interest in that idea. Any money he received from Sweden he generally splashed out on impromptu parties or an all-night open bar at the hotel a place Anahareo could not drink because of the law that banned First Nations from public drinking places. Eric's generosity meant that he attracted many people who were eager to socialize with him. Anahareo drank to excess on various occasions and she would join in at any of the private parties. Eric, in contrast, drank daily, as a matter of habit and addiction, and Anahareo found that his constant drinking and partying meant there was little left to spend on essentials like food, clothing, heating and a car.1

A few years after their move to Canmore, her frustration reached such a level that she left Eric again. This time she took Katherine to the outskirts of Banff where she found work at a Chinese garden.2 Anahareo's decision to leave each time must have been extremely difficult for her. She was caught between her deep feelings for Eric, her fear of destitution and her consideration of Katherine's well being. Katherine was older now, but she still needed a secure home and the home Anahareo had established with Eric grew more unstable under his careless disregard for the practical necessities. Anahareo was used to living frugally with bare necessities but the financial worries were so extreme that her prospects at the time appeared better without Eric than with him.

After a while she and Katherine returned home, only to leave again later and go to Calgary where she worked as a cook. Each time she returned to Canmore after Eric promised to reform. Some of the reforms lasted only a short while or never materialized. That she returned each time was not surprising, for if the promises were kept, there was no doubt that she and Katherine would fare much better with Eric.3

All through these events Dawn was in close touch with her mother, keeping up with the news and writing her supportive letters. Dawn was a grown woman now. She had attended business college in Prince Albert but had visited when she could, practicing her shorthand while Anahareo read things out to her and now, having finished college, she was about to start a job as a secretary.4

In the summer of 1953 Dawn had big news to share.5 Anahareo's daughter Anne (she now had an "e" to her name) had sought her out in Prince Albert while Anne was visiting there with a girlfriend. Anne had grown up assuming she was the daughter of the Anglo-Canadian couple, the Eagles, and that the two younger daughters, Rosemary and Maureen, were her sisters. She had spent her childhood in a middle-class area just outside Calgary. Mary Eagle worked as a nurse, first as matron of Fearnie Hospital and then later in a doctor's practice, while Mr. Eagle worked in sales, initially for an insurance company, and then for a biscuit and sweet manufacturer. Anne had birthday parties, violin lessons, dressed up for Halloween, went to the zoo, played with her bicycle or her little driving car and, along with her family, attended the Calgary Stampede, dressing up in cowgirl outfits.6 Such a life was markedly different from Anahareo's youth, or even Katherine's life in a little two-room shack at the fringes of a small working-class town.

When Anne was sixteen she made a startling discovery. She came across the papers that discussed the arrangements Bethany Home had made with the Eagles. Such a discovery came as a great shock and challenged her whole understanding of herself.7 Up to this point she had assumed she was from an Anglo-Canadian family, with all the future expectations of an Anglo-Canadian woman. She had experienced no racism directed at her family or herself. Now she discovered that not only was she adopted, but she was also a different race to the people she had regarded as her family and that race experienced many disadvantages and prejudice.

Though Calgary was a city, it still harboured negative images and views of Aboriginals. In most people's eyes it would be much better for a person's future prospects to be regarded as Euro-Canadian rather than an Aboriginal. Anne's dilemma was difficult. Should she now think of herself as Aboriginal, an identity that would subject her to different treatment and perhaps even a different legal status? Many would feel shame by such a background and be inclined to ignore or hide it. To complicate matters further her Aboriginal mother was Anahareo, the common law wife of Grey Owl, a man many of the public regarded as a charlatan and fraud. Such connections would hold little appeal to most teenagers with middle-class Euro-Canadian sensibilities, conscious of others' opinions. But Anne was curious and wanted to know more about this unknown mother. With the support of her girlfriend Anne went to Prince Albert, to the Winters, the last publicly known place of residence of Anahareo's daughter, Dawn, Anne's best link with her biological mother.8

Dawn's shock was nearly equal to Anne's, but she was wary too. She wanted to protect her mother and she was concerned about the effect Anne's appearance might have on Anahareo at a time when her home situation was so precarious. She wrote to her mother, and cautioned Anahareo that it might not be best for Anne to come see her since Anahareo would probably not appear to Anne at her best advantage in her current environment. But Anahareo would not have it. Throwing all caution aside Anahareo wrote she was thrilled that Anne had been found and wanted to meet her, regardless of the situation:

> Right now I am the happiest person alive and dear girl how I will love seeing her again. Never mind about my feelings when she finds me in this environment it will only show her how necessary it was for she and I to be apart. As with you the only time I ever had a [decent] place in which to live I worked hard to have you with me. …The Eagles knew where I was and I trusted that they [would] have told me if she was sick or etc., but after I moved and when going through Calgary I looked up the Eagles in the directory and found that they weren't listed, well from then and since then I've had to fight every thought of her because I was afraid something [might have happened].9

Not long after Anahareo wrote to Dawn, Anne traveled to Canmore to meet her mother. Just as she arrived in town with the Eagle family Anne walked down the street and noticed a woman cycling along in breeches and shirt and she mistook her for Chinese. It was later that she discovered that the woman she saw riding was in fact her mother, Anahareo.10 Her misunderstanding was more a reflection of Anne's own experiences in Calgary and assumptions that a Chinese woman would more likely ride a bicycle than an Aboriginal woman. That she would imagine that woman to be her mother was perhaps even more remote in her anxious and confused mind. Even as a private figure, riding a bicycle in her usual eccentric breeches and shirt, Anahareo was now someone who, in a small western Canadian town, could be mistaken for Chinese rather than a modern Aboriginal woman.

When Anne arrived at the house a range of emotions swirled around the group. Surrounded by the makeshift chairs, tables and cupboards in the tiny rough house at the edge of town and experiencing Anahareo's "how ya doin' kiddo" approach Anne could easily feel overwhelmed, especially given her upbringing. Building a relationship on such diverse circumstances, especially after years of separation was difficult. Anne had no real memory of her mother and had never met her sisters. Katherine, not yet eleven, was thrilled at the idea of another older sister and threw her arms around her in uncomplicated joy. The day-long visit ended with enough positive feelings that both Anne and Anahareo agreed she would return later and stay for a few days.[11] After that second visit Anahareo arranged for Katherine to spend time with Anne at the Eagles. Katherine was eager for the visit and carefully put on the new velvet dress her mother bought for the occasion. When Katherine arrived she could not help but be aware that the dress, though new, did not match the level of affluence she saw around her.[12] It was a difficult situation for them all, with such differing backgrounds and experiences, yet so closely related by blood.

It was only a short while later that Anne married and began her own life as a wife and eventually, as a mother. Though she kept in touch with her mother and sisters, the communication was sporadic, as her own immediate family became her primary concern and focus. Over the course of time Anahareo explained to her the sequence of events that brought her to be placed in the Bethany Home and then into the care of the Eagles. She came to understand these decisions, but for Anne the Eagles, who raised her for all those years, would always be "Mom and Dad" to her.[13]

Just after the meeting between Anne and Anahareo circumstances at the Doll's House deteriorated further. The situation was so bad she decided to leave, but not before discussing employment possibilities with Wilna Moore back east. She wrote of her decision to Dawn:

> Things are pretty bad here....Eric got $500 from Sweden and all that meant was a big drunk, the loss of his job and the car went for $55. We are still in the same place owing to the shortage of water again. I am so depressed to put it mildly. I wish I could wire you to come at once. But the situation is such that it is impossible. I am going to leave Eric because ... he can't help himself. You see Miss Moore tells me she has a spot for me in a winter/summer resort in E. Canada which included the souvenir angle, etc.14

Anahareo waited impatiently for Wilna Moore to tell her the job details and finalize the arrangements. After some weeks with no word, she took matters into her own hand and decided to head for Mattawa with Katherine. The pair hitchhiked east, building fires by the roadside to keep warm and to cook bits of food that Anahareo scrounged. It was a rough and desperate strategy to make the journey east, especially with an eleven-year-old child in tow. By the time they reached Timmins, Ontario, Katherine was ill. Anahareo had no money and she was unable to secure a lift for either of them. A kind farmer offered them his place to stay and Anahareo accepted gratefully. There she managed to contact a priest who helped contact her family in Mattawa. Her sister Johanna sent through what money she could and Anahareo used it to pay for Katherine's train fare to Mattawa, while she hitchhiked the rest of the way by herself. She arrived there three days after Katherine.15

Some time after Anahareo's arrival Dawn wrote to express relief she was there safe and explained the mishap with Wilna:

> I am very happy that you managed to get down to Mattawa without mishap and I am happy too that you are not mangled by the ball and chain....I would like to got to Toronto to be with you both....
>
> I was talking to Miss Moore on Sat. and the reason you didn't hear from her was because she didn't pick up her mail for a few

weeks therefore she did not get your letter until after you were on the road so don't be hard on her.

Say hello to grandpa, know we never met but blood is thick.16

Though Anahareo had corresponded with her family over the years she had not seen them or Mattawa since she had boarded the train for the week visit to Grey Owl, nearly thirty years before. Sometime in the 1940s, the family had moved to Squaw Valley and Johanna and her remaining daughter now lived there with her eighty-nine year-old father and bachelor brother, Eddie. Though Anahareo had not compromised on her appearance and still wore her breeches, shirt, neckerchief and prospecting boots, and she dressed Katherine in blue jeans and cowboy boots, the family welcomed them warmly.17

Hannah, Johanna, Dawn & Anahareo, courtesy of Louise Montreuil

Home among her relatives, Anahareo enthusiastically visited up and down the extended family houses, socializing and becoming reacquainted with her relatives and getting used to being among her family. Would they still regard her in the same way as they had all the years before? Her father was still hearty enough, chopping wood daily and playing the fiddle at the family square dances. Eddie and

Johanna and some of the cousins played cards with her. She and Eddie stayed up many nights talking, drinking, and occasionally arguing, and catching up on past experiences. Eddie had become a bush guide and cook and the two had plenty of stories to share about their beloved wilderness.18

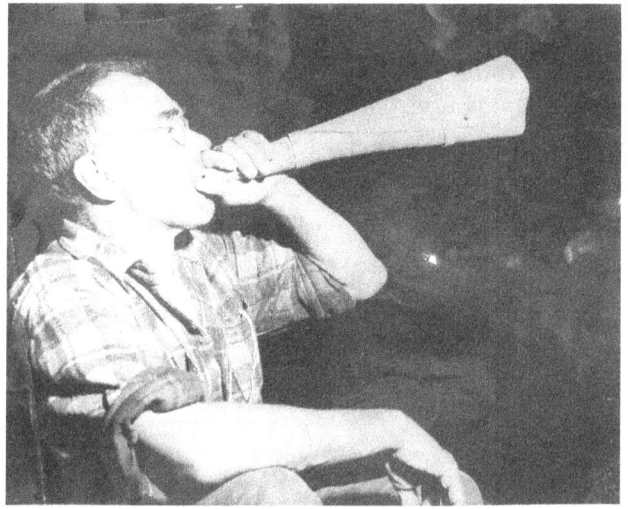

Eddie with moose caller, courtesy of Katherine Swartile

Wilna Moore's resort job never materialized. Determined not to return to Canmore Anahareo decided to remain in Mattawa and find work there. She eventually took a job assisting a local undertaker dressing and putting the makeup on those people being prepared for burial. She enrolled Katherine in the public school across the bridge, forgoing St. Anne's, which all the Aboriginal children, including Katherine's cousins, attended. Anahareo still firmly rejected the Catholic Church with the same energy that she had those many years at the disastrous Easter confession in Senneterre. The autumn after her arrival in Mattawa the priest refused her father communion because he had inquired about the possibility of his daughter Johanna being released from her marriage to a man who had deserted her thirty years before. Such an action only strengthened Anahareo's rejection of Catholicism.19

Crossing the bridge from Squaw Valley to attend the Mattawa public school Katherine encountered no perceptible racial discrimination among her classmates. They pressured and questioned her more about her faith which, given her location and background, they assumed was Catholic. For the most part though, Katherine found playmates among her cousins and other children in Squaw Valley. She went sledding with her friend Mitzi and called at her house many times after dinner, whistling a tune on her way there. When her mother was working at the undertakers, though, Katherine would sometimes go across the bridge with her and play with Euro-Canadian children while her mother worked.20

Though the distance was much greater than before, Anahareo continued to keep in close touch with Dawn. Dawn still hoped she might visit them in Mattawa and meet her mother's family. She was due to start work soon, so she wanted to spend time with Eddie, Johanna and her grandfather before that. She especially wanted to meet her grandfather because he had told Anahareo he felt he would die soon. Eventually, in the spring of 1954, Dawn, now twenty-one years old, arrived in Mattawa and met her grandfather, aunt and uncle. It was a special opportunity for her since her father's family were not in touch with her or were unreachable. Now she was able to meet and find connections beyond just her mother and sister. It was an event she relished. Her grandfather, the only grandparent still alive, had many more years to share with his granddaughter. He was still was still playing the fiddle at the family square dances and chopping wood daily for the fire in 1960, at the age of ninety-seven.21

Though Wilna Moore was not able to arrange a job for Anahareo in a resort she was not short of energy to manage other aspects of Anahareo's life. Worried about Katherine's prospects Wilna decided that Katherine would benefit from going to boarding school and encouraged Anahareo to consider the idea. Wilna then wrote to Eric's family in Sweden on Anahareo's behalf and asked if they would fund Katherine's education. In April she wrote in great excitement to Anahareo when she received a reply:

> Got a letter from Sweden in reply to [the query?] asking help for Katherine's education. It was from Eric's brother in law who does business for the family, etc. He thought my idea for a girl's school is excellent and is willing to send money out directly (month by month I presume) to the school and submit its accounts.22

It was great news as far as Wilna was concerned. The brother-in-law wanted some assurances that at least Anahareo consented fully to the idea:

> However he said before they could consider it you would have to write your willingness that Katherine attend the school and that I send it on to him. (He said you or Eric, but in the last paragraph asked that you send the written willingness.) Now that is excellent, isn't it?23

That the brother-in-law was willing to accept only Anahareo's written consent showed that Wilna had more than likely explained the separation between Anahareo and Eric and he understood that Eric might not necessarily want Katherine to attend a boarding school. As far as Wilna was concerned Anahareo's consent was a given. She continued her letter with suggestions about possible schools:

> Now I've been looking around. The Bishop told me of an excellent one, in Regina. That's a very good one, I understand as I was informed of it from another source altogether. I told the Moltkes I would find an Anglican which I stated was the nearest to Lutheran. Can be the thin edge to get more for Katherine as time goes on, I was awfully happy that he asked for your willingness showing that they are prepared to acknowledge your rights, etc. I

wrote nicely about you and Eric both—tried to paint the need yet not hurt any feelings. I find I did it.24

Wilna hoped her strategy involving Eric's wealthy family might lay some groundwork for future assistance for Katherine and Anahareo. Funding Katherine's education could also establish stronger ties with the family as well as direct financial benefits. Wilna was certain this was a good plan and wrote to Dawn explaining it and assuring her that Anahareo was enthusiastic. In an effort to support the plan and be near Katherine's school Dawn made some dramatic decisions:

I saw Dawn and told her. She is all for marrying this boy she's going with and having him move to Regina so she will be near Katherine. A place for Katherine to go. Well I feel that will help all round.25

Anahareo in the mean time was following her own course. By the spring, after some discussion with Eric and hopeful assurances, she was considering returning to Eric, a move that Wilma endorsed. In the same letter about the boarding school she wrote:

Then I do hope you come west as soon as you can your suggestion in your letter that you might return to Eric is good I think. It is his responsibility and he'll likely be more considerate about letting you handle ½ his money.26

In the eyes of Wilna and most members of the Anglo-Canadian middle classes in that time period, divorce was unacceptable and separation was a step to be avoided if at all possible. Such actions violated the sanctity of marriage and held terrible social and economic consequences for the family and wife in middle-class society. If Eric was behaving, in Wilna's mind, it was best Anahareo return to him, but there was no need to change the plans for Katherine.

Besides missing Eric, Anahareo's decision to go back to him was doubtless based once again on his promises to reform and to allow Anahareo to handle half the money. Life in Mattawa, the small town that stifled her when she was young, had not changed that dramatically and Squaw Valley held little promise beyond her current situation. Though she and her sister shared the same burden of a broken marriage Johanna had roots embedded in Mattawa. She was deeply religious and very active in the community. Anahareo's independent spirit and vigorous approach to life in reality gave her a closer affinity to her brother Eddie than Johanna. Ultimately she knew, despite his faults, it was Eric who understood her best and accepted her.

The path towards reunion between the two was not smooth. Eric got wind of Wilna's plans and wrote an angry letter to Anahareo. He was furious that Wilna had presumed to contact his family in Sweden and insinuated he had taken money meant for Katherine a fact that he only discovered when he wrote to the family lawyer after he had received no money. He was also angry with Anahareo because she had known about the plan for months and had not told him. "I would never take money from Katherine," he wrote. He was adamant about boarding school, though. "I don't want her to go to boarding school," he said without any further deliberation. His own experience had been too horrendous to allow him to consider such a proposal for Katherine. By the end of the letter his anger had dissipated enough for him to close with the words: "I hope you are still wearing pants and not dresses. Pants suit you better."[27]

Anahareo with woman, presumably Mrs Ward, at Christopher Lake, courtesy of Katherine Swartile

By August Anahareo and Katherine had left Mattawa and Anahareo had returned to Canmore. Katherine went to stay with friends, the Wards, at Christopher Lake for the summer while plans for Katherine to attend the boarding school moved forward, despite Eric's objections. Dawn meanwhile arranged her wedding for August and hoped for Katherine to attend. The Wards put Katherine on the train to go to Prince Albert but she arrived after it had taken place. Though she missed the wedding Katherine stayed on with her sister for a while, then returned to Christopher Lake, this time staying with the Wards' daughter, Maida, until it was time for her to leave for the boarding school.28

Maida Switzer wrote in late August to Anahareo to assure her that Katherine was doing well:

Well I've been making friends with small Katherine and she is a lovely child. We will be glad to have her as our little borrowed daughter next term if plans go through for her.29

Mar tells me Eric doesn't like you called Pony but I don't like hearing you called either Gertie or Gertrude because it doesn't seem like you at all. Anybody can be Gertrude or Mary or Sally but to me there is only one Pony. She is pretty swell.30

Maida had addressed the letter "My Dearest Gertrude," and explained the reason:

Mar tells me Eric doesn't like you called Pony but I don't like hearing you called either Gertie or Gertrude because it doesn't seem like you at all. Anybody can be Gertrude or Mary or Sally but to me there is only one Pony. She is pretty swell.30

Eric would have known that the name Pony was special to her because her father called her that. But Eric's dislike of Anahareo's long-held nickname may have been more to do with his own idea of what name suited her best. He might have thought "Pony" conjured up old, traditional Aboriginal images that did not suit Anahareo's modern image. Or it might have been that Pony was a name that was used most in a life and times in which he had no connection and he wanted no reminders of it. For Anahareo, though, it was still an integral part of her and many continued to call her Pony throughout her life.31

In September Anahareo took a job working as a cook at Spray Lakes, a camping resort just outside of Canmore while Katherine remained with the Switzers. She wrote Dawn about her plans:

.... I am leaving for Spray Lake to cook in a few minutes. Katherine is staying with the Switers if you should want to send a hurried message to her... I shall have to work 14 hours a day.32

Katherine left the Switzers and returned to Canmore. Eric continued to refuse to let Katherine attend boarding school. That Wilna Moore had gone behind his back to set up the plan had only ensured that Eric would not budge on the matter. Katherine, now twelve years old, resumed her schooling at the public school in Canmore.33

When Anahareo had returned to Canmore earlier she found that her absence could not have been more ill timed. It was during that year Hollywood producers had come to the area to film *The River of No Return* with Marilyn Monroe and needed someone to stand in for the star to shoot the rapids. Anahareo, the natural choice, was still in Mattawa. After all her hopes and ideas to work in Hollywood and bring Grey Owl's story to film, a golden opportunity to make important contacts had occurred at the very time she was away in Mattawa.34

Anahareo and Katherine took up the threads of their existence in Canmore once again. Eric continued to work in construction and their life was a little more secure, but money and drinking remained problems. Eric had trouble controlling his drinking and with Anahareo sharing the addiction she found it hard to hard to help. A few years after their return, a work accident crushed Eric's leg and left him permanently disabled. The family moved to Calgary so Eric could be near the hospital for his treatment. Unable to work, and depressed about his situation, he drank even more. Anahareo's own health was poor too. She suffered from depression and tiredness. Though the situation worsened she still could not bring herself to leave Eric in such a state despite Dawn's encouragement. It was not until seventeen-year-old Katherine left for beauty school in 1959 that Dawn convinced Anahareo to live with her in Dawson Creek to help look after her children while she went through a divorce and went back to work. Once Anahareo decided to leave, Eric made arrangements to go back to live with his first wife, Helga, who said she was willing to look after him. It was a relief to Anahareo that he would not be alone. They parted on good terms and Anahareo continued to write and phone Eric and Helga until his death a few years later, in 1963.35

About the time Eric had his accident, in 1956, Summy visited Canada and briefly met Anahareo. Anahareo must have explained about Eric's injury and needed medical treatment. In any event Summy left £40 in a bank for Anahareo, in Huntsville, and then wrote several letters to try and find her address but had no success. Eventually, the money was returned. She tried to trace her when the agent wanted to buy the rights to her book, in 1959. Since that time another film agent had asked after Anahareo.36 Was it possible that her dream of a film about Grey Owl might become reality?

Chapter Eighteen

The Public View Again

A few years after Anahareo moved in with Dawn, she discovered that a malfunctioning thyroid had caused the depression and ill health that had lasted for nearly fifteen years. She wrote and told Eric about her illness and said how much better she felt once it was diagnosed and treated.1

Anahareo's improved health gave her a renewed outlook on life and enabled her to generate new ideas about the future. Despite her disappointment over her missed Hollywood opportunity, Anahareo still hoped to make a film about Grey Owl. Dawn shared her enthusiasm for promoting Grey Owl's story and had quietly waged her own campaign through the years, writing to magazines and publishers to urge them to reprint Grey Owl's works, or to correct diplomatically any inaccurate information printed or broadcast about him that she came across.2

In November 1959, before departing Calgary, Anahareo received a letter from an English agent representing an American film producer asking if she held the motion picture rights to her book and would she like to explore the option to sell them. She wrote back eagerly:

Indeed I would. I realize that film companies fictionalize and it is good when it succeeds in heightening the interest and color of the story. If, in this case, they come within a mile of Grey Owl's personality, they will have themselves a good strong story. There is dash, daring and beauty and adventure, and, of course, romance.3

Anahareo was certain that Grey Owl's story contained the vital elements of a Hollywood film, without any need to embroider or change it. She felt the same about Grey Owl himself and was afraid a scriptwriter would be tempted to follow the awful past portrayals of Grey Owl that included her own:

So far he has been put forth as either a 'panty waist' or an absolute scoundrel. Actually he was a many-sided person and forcible on all sides. I fear, so much, that the script writer will fall by the wayside and turn out the usual low level of Northern pictures, and, therefore, spoiling a story—a true story—for all time. How can the script writer escape when all he has to go by is what he can glean from certain or uncertain biographies: The book "My Life With Grey Owl" being the worst.4

To avoid such a risk she asked if she could spend time with the script writer. She felt that it would make it easier for her to explain Grey Owl and also he would get to know her better as well, because she had no better opinion of past efforts portraying her:

The usual portrayal of myself has been that of a sweet, gentle Indian maiden—whispering to the leaves—swaying with the breeze, tra la—. No, no, I'm a rebel really.5

Anahareo could not accept inaccurate presentations of Grey Owl or her. She was not asking for Grey Owl to be depicted as a flawless hero, she wanted him shown as the complex figure he was, good and bad. She was also definitely not willing to approve any script that showed her as a clichéd stereotype, the Indian maiden, the image she felt others had employed for her in the past. It was an image Anahareo recognized as false, at least as far as she was concerned, and was far as possible from the real "rebel" that she was.

Anahareo patiently awaited the agent's reply. After a year, in January 1961, she finally broke down and wrote to clarify the film's status. A month later the agency replied that the company unfortunately were not able to arrange the sale of the film rights. Any hope of this particular film project coming to fruition was dead.6

Since the consolidation of the studios and the demise of silent films the industry relied on the versatility of wigs and makeup rather than authentic Indians to play Aboriginal roles. Perhaps because of this Hollywood Indians continued to be depicted either as violent, noble victims or shuffling "redskin" primitives more at home in a tent than a house. The men stood rigidly scowling, spoke ponderously, angrily or in a dim-witted manner with broken English and many "ughs." Native women usually wore heavily beaded, fringed buckskin dresses and looked longingly at the white hero. Jay Silverheels, the Mohawk actor who played Tonto in the *Lone Ranger* television series, and for years the only Indian actor working in Hollywood, was acutely aware of the negative and harmful portrayals of Indians in film. The enormous energy he and fellow actor John War Eagle put into questioning the validity of Hollywood's portrayals in the 1950s had only minimal success. Hollywood showed a brief period of superficial acceptance following Second World War but the onset of the Cold War and the hysteria of the McCarthy trials ensured any display or sympathy for "Indianness" in Hollywood was politically risky.7

Television expanded rapidly in the 1950s and became the perfect home for B grade Westerns. Their popularity inspired TV studios to create series like Roy Rogers and the Lone Ranger that acquired hoards of fans. Soon Hollywood was making full-length feature films based on the series' heroes. In each case the old Indian stereotypes left from the nineteenth century still dominated the format. Vicious or noble savages appeared just as they had done in the silent films and in the dime novels at the turn of the century. The same old themes appeared that showed Indians for and against settlers, soldiers, miners or ranchers or helpless Euro-American women. There were Indian princesses, friendly chiefs, noble savages and violent warriors. Football heroes or modern soldier heroes modelled on Jim Thorpe occasionally supplanted these caricatures. Despite the new heroes the dialogue was still the same, full of the "ughs" and "how" sentiments of the past. The costumes had not improved either, with many characters still dressed in phoney or mixed tribal dress. In Hollywood and the minds of the TV studio staff any Aboriginal or be-wigged Euro-American hired to play an Indian tended to serve for any tribe because, to the filmmakers, they all looked alike.8

Among such attitudes it is no surprise that Anahareo had difficulty gaining support for a film project featuring the story of Grey Owl. She had insisted that she be portrayed accurately, despite the Indian maiden depictions others had foisted upon her in the past. But the strong image she presented countered all the long-held stereotypes that Hollywood used to portray Aboriginal women. Though she had a deep affinity for the wilderness and was skilled in the bush, she was too modern in attitude and appearance. She would not be wearing heavily beaded and fringed buckskin dresses. Her hair was not in braids hanging down to her waist. She could wield a hatchet, portage heavy loads with a tump line and paddle hours in a canoe. She had no need to look longingly up at her hero, whatever his race. She was no Donna Reed playing Sacajawea, pining for Charlton Heston in the 1955 film, *The Far Horizons*. Even more to the point was the problem of Grey Owl. At a time when policies encouraged Aboriginal assimilation into the Euro-North American society how would Hollywood deal with an Englishman who rejected this society and took on the culture and later the identity of an Aboriginal?

Despite the producer's lack of interest in her film idea Anahareo was certain the film project was worthwhile. In pursuit of this goal Anahareo traveled to Toronto and stayed with Wilna Moore to search for a potential producer while she supported herself as housekeeper. She contacted Macmillan Publishing Company and asked them how to get an agent to help her with attracting interest in her film. They recommended Mr. Kingsley Wing in New York. In July 1961 she wrote to him and laid out her hopes for a film that would portray him neither as a "near saint" or "an absolute scoundrel." In her view Grey Owl was "a many-sided person and tolerated no half measures on either side."9

> Grey Owl has been called "The Imposter of the century," by one, "The greatest Hoax", by another, and by others, "The magnificent fake"—this all, because he happened to be an Englishman instead of the Indian that he said he was.
>
> ...It will be difficult to dove-tail the above with his writings, his lectures and his sincere drive for conservation of the beaver, the forest and an attempt to bring about a better understanding of the Indian....It won't be an easy picture to produce. It will require a man of great good taste to do it, or water the story down, which I say, heaven forbid!10

She found no success with Mr. Wing and eventually she decided to travel to Vancouver. It was a fruitless journey but it put her on the same coast as Hollywood. She was certain that Hollywood would see the great potential of a film about Grey Owl. With that hope in mind she traveled to Los Angeles still convinced she would get someone to take on this project. She wrote to Dawn in November of 1962 and told her she would stay for a few days to find a producer interested in the film. Her efforts brought no results and so she took a job as a maid to support herself while she knocked on a few more doors. She received some mild interest from Jack Douglas Productions but it came to nothing. Eventually she returned to Canada and went to live with Katherine, who was now married and living in Whitecourt, about 160 kilometres west of Edmonton.11

Dawn waged her own campaign for a film as well and wrote to

Disney in 1964, but they explained they did not accept any outside proposals. She also continued to write persuasively to editors and publishers to try and keep her father's works in print and she spoke at schools or appeared at various events with exhibitions booths that contained information about Grey Owl. Through her and others' efforts a plaque was erected in his honour in Temagami Provincial Park, in 1959, and in 1963, the American magazine *Sports Illustrated* published an article that positively emphasized Grey Owl's conservation message, as did a 1967 article in *The Canadian Outdoorsman*.12

The author of the article in the *Outdoorsman*, M.U. Bateman, claimed to have met Grey Owl. He discussed Grey Owl's origins fully and somewhat inaccurately in the first section of the article and wrote about all of Grey Owl's relationships with women. In Bateman's view, however, the most important moment in Grey Owl's life was when he met Anahareo, "an attractive daughter of a Mohawk family." After she accompanied him into the bush and they discovered the beaver kits, he decided to cease trapping. Anahareo approved his change of mind, "but being a practical girl she knew they must eat. And so it was she who first encouraged Grey Owl to write. Thus heartened, Grey Owl began the task that would change his life..."13 The article continued to describe his efforts to raise awareness of the decline in beaver and the disappearing wilderness. Bateman closed the article in praise of Grey Owl:

> In spite of his human failings, the pure white light of his literary art shines forth, bright and clear. His work in the field of wildlife conservation is perhaps best expressed in his own words.
>
> He said... "I have cast a stone into a pool, and the ripples will be reaching the shores long after I am gone.14

In 1967 Dawn appeared at Prince Albert's Winter Festival as their special guest to visit schools and give lectures on animals and tell stories about her father. "It's just wonderful the way they are treating me," Dawn said in an interview, "and the children are so interested in the animals and Grey Owl." One of the people involved with the festival was John Diefenbaker. With his support Dawn almost succeeded in installing a small display on Grey Owl that year at the Indian pavilion at Montreal's World Fair, Expo 67. She had designed the exhibit to show a wax representation of Archie in Beaver Lodge sitting by the table as Rawhide minded his house, while a voice narrated extracts of his lectures.15

Anahareo, c. 1971, courtesy of Katherine Swartile

Once more wilderness conservation became an important issue. This time, however, there was an urgency that stemmed not from a wish to restock disappearing game for food, sport or profit, but as a holistic approach to preserve the health of the planet. Rachel Carson's 1962 book *Silent Spring* prompted an awakening awareness of the manufacturing industry's wanton pollution of the earth in pursuit of its own profits. The revelations contained in the book and the description of its direct impact on people in their everyday lives motivated them to demand greater accountability from industry and other groups that provided pesticide products used outdoors, on food, or released as pollutants into the air and water.

As the public became more aware of the negative impact of pollution and the importance of the wilderness to the health of the planet, more Canadians began to view Grey Owl through his role in pioneering wilderness preservation and felt he should be recognized for these achievements. There were others, scholars and journalists among them, who still emphasized the sensational side of Grey Owl's life. One such article published in the magazine *True Life* in the mid-1960s described Grey Owl paddling madly down a creek while a group of Anishnabe armed with rifles chased after him to force him to marry Angele. As Dawn later recounted, Anahareo threw the magazine across the room in disgust and said, "that's enough of that bull-shit! I'm going to write a book and tell the truth about Archie." In 1966 she corresponded with Lovat Dickson about her decision. She told him she sent three excerpts she had written to a publisher: one about Aunt Ada, one about Angele and the other excerpt describing the time she first got drunk. With these three excerpts under her belt she decided to begin the book.16

Dawn bought her a stack of brand new legal pads to fill with her writing, but Anahareo left them untouched and chose to use carefully steamed and flattened used envelopes instead. After years of living in the bush she was unable to shed her frugal nature. Eventually Dawn bought a Dictaphone, which delighted Anahareo, because the tapes could be erased and reused after Dawn typed them up. Dawn later regretted erasing them when she realized many of the numerous recorded incidents did not make it into the book. For Anahareo, writing the book allowed her once again to immerse herself in the period she felt most happy and most at home, and fall in love again with her "Jesse James."17 And through this exploration she could depict herself as she wanted, rather than one filtered through Anglo or Euro-Canadian eyes. The image that finally emerged was not a stereotype, but a real individual who was feisty, intelligent, determined and strong willed, and whose bush skills set her apart from most men and as well as most women.

After shaping Grey Owl's image with words, while the book was going through publication in 1970, Anahareo created a physical model of Grey Owl and Jelly Roll out of twigs and toothpicks. Later it served as a basis for a sculpture that she cast into a mould. It showed Grey Owl sitting on the ground with Jelly Roll climbing onto his lap. It was not completely new territory for her. Years before when she was with Grey Owl and wind bound in camp she had fashioned heads of her father out of clay.18 In the summer of 1971 Dawn took the sculpture and showed it to Shirley Popham, Chief of Conservation Group of the Department of Indian Affairs. Popham later explained her reaction:

> Mrs. [Dawn] Bruce had with her [a] sculpture of Grey Owl done by her mother who was Grey Owl's wife. As I said earlier I thought that the sculpture was exceptionally well done.
>
> We agreed to assist Mrs. Moltke in the promotion of this sculpture and any subsequent pieces she might do of Grey Owl (she is considering doing a series).
>
> We have agreed to purchase an unspecified number of castings for sale in Prince Albert National Park and it was suggested that we might be able to further assist in the sale by preparing newspaper – magazine articles concerning Mrs. Moltke and her sculpture of Grey Owl.19

The attention Anahareo's sculpture generated and its potential for positive publicity also created a renewed interest in Grey Owl's cabin at Ajawaan Lake. After many years of neglect the park finally began to restore it.20

Back in 1939, Dr. van der Sleen, an internationally known natural history lecturer from the Netherlands, had written to Ottawa and urged them to maintain the Beaver Lodge, but when the Canadian writer Kathleen Strange visited the cabin in the late 1940s the poor situation was evident. She later wrote:

> [It was in] a sad state of decay and disrepair. The cabin...was dirty and neglected; his snowshoes propped against the wall, were rotting away; and his canoe, in which he spent so many happy hours, was lying on the ground broken in half.21

For seventeen years Dawn had urged the Parks Department to keep Beaver Lodge in repair and finally, during the time that Anahareo was writing her book and creating the sculpture, they decided to rebuild it. They replaced the bottom three sets of logs and kept the remaining ones and eventually fully restored it.22

The Parks Department decision to restore the cabin was part of their recognition that some park visitors would have a keen interest in Grey Owl and Anahareo and want to visit the site. A nicely presented cabin would obviously attract more visitors. As Anahareo later wrote to a enthusiastic fan, "I am sure you would fell much better to see it now. Dawn says there is a loneliness there, but the spirits still abid[e]."23

As part of the sightseeing experience for cabin visitors the Parks Branch planned to have an interpretation program and decided to commission Georgeann Short from the University of Saskatchewan to write the story of Grey Owl. As part of her project Short interviewed a number of people connected with Grey Owl. She visited Beaver Lodge with Stan Winters, son of the woman who cared for Dawn in Prince Albert years before. Stan had visited the cabin one summer with his sister, Margaret, and helped Grey Owl look after the beavers while Margaret typed up the manuscript. Besides explaining the logistics of feeding the beavers and the layout around the cabin, he recounted stories about the whiskey jacks that visited the site regularly as well as the exploits of Jelly Roll and Rawhide. He remembered that the whiskey jacks were very tame. They came down and sat on his shoulder or hand as Stan explained:

I'd be cooking out here on the open fire and if I didn't put a lid over the frying pan and go in the cabin or something and come out and absolutely everything would be gone. Then the first wind that would come along and down would come the potatoes and the bacon and the whole work from the trees. They didn't eat it. It was just such an adventure for them to be packing stuff and be hiding it.... Toothpaste. I'd come out to clean my teeth and I've seen a Whiskey Jack clean the toothpaste off your brush, just like that.24

Besides the whiskey jacks Stan made friends with the squirrels and even the beaver mice that were in the beaver house. The beavers were also his great friends and took much of his attention. As he explained, he was "general choreboy" to twelve or thirteen beavers and for five months it was his responsibility to go back in the woods and cut trees for them to eat and cook their rice. But Jelly Roll was, without a doubt, the "queen bee":

But Margaret, my sister spoiled her. She (Jelly Roll) used to sit like a squirrel and shell her own peanuts and one night Margaret was sitting here not doing anything so she shelled a bunch of peanuts. The next day I went to give Jelly some peanuts and no way, she wanted these shelled. Another time Margaret took all that brown skin off the peanuts, and low and behold that was the only way Jelly would take them after that!25

Rawhide, in Stan's view, was a diffcrent temperament to Jelly Roll. Nothing bothered him:

He was just one of the workers workers around here. The tourists didn't bother him, people didn't bother him, he'd crawl right over people if they were in the road. He didn't share any of the luxuries that Jelly had. ...Bread, he used to get a loaf of bread. It used to be funny...Raw Hide would come out a loaf of bread in his arms like this and he'd go out and he'd dive, and his back feet would be out like this kicking because he couldn't get down with his loaf of bread. Until it got soaked up and then he'd go down.26

If Stan went to Wakesiu for a few days and came back he said it was "just like coming home to a bunch of little kids. They'd wiggle around and jump and old Jelly Roll, she'd just got into a fit when you came back—like 'what did you buy me down town?'"27

But it was his description of Grey Owl that was most poignant. Once, when Grey Owl returned after a lengthy absence during which Stan cared for the beaver, he was dismayed to see they came to Stan before him. "It shook him up pretty badly," Stan recounted, "he thought he was losing his touch with the beaver." Then Stan adopted a wild beaver and petted it before he did. "Again he thought, oh my gawd, I'm losing it, the beavers aren't going to be with me anymore." But as soon as Stan departed they went back to Grey Owl.28

Despite the beavers' temporary transfer of their affections Grey Owl regarded Stan as a good friend. And in the few years before his death Grey Owl showed him the place he wanted to buried:

> He used to lay down and say see "it just fits." Just about 6 or 7 feet from tree to tree and he used to lay there every once in awhile [sic] and when he died the Park Superintendent and I had quite an argument. I said he wanted to be buried here and they wanted him up there, but I think up there is a much nicer spot.29

Short's study on Grey Owl included an interview with Anahareo. During it Short asked a range of questions about the beaver, Grey Owl's personal life and how he got started writing. She also asked how Anahareo felt when it was revealed that Grey Owl was not Aboriginal. "Of course I was surprised," answered Anahareo, "especially since we were together for eleven years, I think I was more surprised than anyone else, after all." Anahareo also talked about the meeting Grey Owl's mother:

Yes, I met his mother in England one afternoon and I asked her an awful lot of questions, but she didn't answer and she refused to answer even through letters she wrote, we wrote back and forth, but she'd never tell me anything at all, except about the price of coal in England.30

One of the other people interviewed was one of Grey Owl and Anahareo's visitors, Eva Pease, who recalled the visit:

We walked to the portage and he came over the lake [to the warden's cabin] and got us in the canoe. So spent a most interesting evening with the two of them. In the evening he didn't want to paddle us back, so she, with a flashlight walked around the lake with us, took us to the portage.31

She also mentioned Anahareo specifically:

She was a fairly well educated girl you know and I think when I got back to Regina...I must have sent her a box of goodies... She wrote and thanked me for it. I saw her once

in Winnipeg when I was working down there, on Main Street, early one morning when I was going to work but she wasn't in very good condition so I didn't stop her....They just seem[ed] to go from bad to worse. It's too bad but I guess she's alright now. It's just too bad her life was wasted.32

The study revealed Grey Owl for what he was—a complex and sometimes lonely figure who cared about the beavers and believed in what he was doing. Anahareo, his companion and first supporter emphasized these aspects in her interview. The brief view of Anahareo when she was with Grey Owl, recounted many years later, also revealed a thoughtful but also complex person who could come across as "educated," with the implication that it was not something expected in an Aboriginal. Yet she was also a person who "wasn't in very good condition," one morning in Winnipeg. A person whose life was "wasted."

The tide against Grey Owl was indeed beginning to turn. In 1972 the CBC broadcast a sixty-minute television show and six-part radio documentary on Grey Owl, each emphasizing his positive role as a conservationist. Mrs. Winters, Lovat Dickson and others were interviewed for these programs. His books were republished in paperback and several articles appeared casting him in a positive light, including Vera Fidler's beautifully illustrated article in the May 1972 issue of *Canadian Geographical Journal*, "Grey Owl: A Man Ahead of his Time."33

The view of Grey Owl and his contributions was undergoing a transformation, though Anahareo's role in raising McGinnis and McGinty and convincing Grey Owl to stop trapping that he had described in his book had faded into the background. Anahareo was no longer the beautiful and charming woman by his side talking about her most recent adventures. She was in her sixties, lived with her daughter and on the surface appeared to be an average grandmother. Society had caught up with her in some ways. Short hair was not unusual for women, including Aboriginal women. Nor were pants a unique fashion statement anymore. An Aboriginal grandmother was not subject to the same sort of restrictions and expectations present for a young woman in the 1930s. Even her views on wilderness conservation were becoming popular among certain sectors of the public. It would take something more to get Anahareo back in the limelight and this time it would be on her own terms.

Chapter Nineteen

A Life Recognized

While renewed interest and support of Grey Owl's conservation efforts grew and to some degree shifting focus away from the more sensational aspects of his life Anahareo continued to work on the book of her life with him. In 1972 her efforts were finally published under the title, *Devil in Deerskins*. She had gleaned the title from one of her conversations with him in their final years together. He told her it was going to be his last book:

> When I asked him why it was going to be his last book he said that after they read that book they wouldn't read another line from him. And I asked him why and he said Oh, there are things about me that even you don't know. So, I asked him what he was going to call the book and he was going to call it 'Devil in Deerskins' ... and I figured that was what he was going to come out with, to tell all, so, but he didn't get around to it.[1]

The title's strong legacy and connection to Grey Owl only served to contribute to the book's success. Besides a revealing and intimate portrait of Grey Owl, Anahareo also created a striking image of herself. With an engaging honesty the book captured the nature of Anahareo's impulsive, enthusiastic, and at times, naïve regard for Grey Owl and the bush. This tone is captured so effectively in the opening when she first sees Grey Owl at Camp Wabikon in 1925:

> ...I saw a man dressed in brown deerskins stepping with the speed and grace of a panther from a canoe. And there he stood, tall, straight and handsome, gazing wistfully across the lake in the direction from which he had come. As he stood there with his paddle in his hand, his attitude seemed to express such yearning and loneliness that my heart quite went out to him. However I was young and scatterbrained, the mental or spiritual attitude of people didn't interest me for long, and, unseen by him, I immediately began to take stock of this most striking man's appearance.2

Anecdotes about the beaver, Grey Owl's exploits and her prospecting experiences painted a vivid picture of the adventurous life she led while she was with Grey Owl. Unlike her previous book, Anahareo was also able to devote time to Grey Owl's background as well as her own.

With a sympathetic eye Anahareo described the stifling atmosphere of Grey Owl's Victorian upbringing under the watchful eyes of his maiden aunts and the love and obsession with wood lore and Indians that eventually led him to leave England for Canada. When she wrote about her own background Anahareo traced her family's story back to the early 1800s, recounting events that, in all but a brief mention in a 1937 article by Leslie Sara contradicted previous descriptions of her full Aboriginal heritage. With more than a touch of glamour she related a story of her grandmother's mother, who she named as Mary Robinson. During a Mohawk raid in her Connecticut community a group of warriors had killed her family and captured her but, impressed by her remarkable bravery, the Mohawks let her live. After three years among the Mohawks Mary chose to marry the chief's son and remain there. Eventually she gave birth to a daughter. Not long after her birth the War of 1812 came to a close and the Mohawk band lived in hiding and occasionally raiding settlements. Anahareo described the fatal end:

> Their presence became known, and the soldiers went in and killed them all, except for a few women and children. Mary Robinson, Kanistonou [her husband], and a new-born son were killed, and Grandmother, scarcely a babe-in-arms, was taken to Montreal and given to the nuns. She received her education in a convent there, and then, as a young lady, went to join her people at Oka, the Lake of Two Mountains.3

It is ironic that, at a time when it was just becoming acceptable, and in some ways "fashionable" to be Aboriginal, Anahareo chose to recount the story of Mary Robinson, a Euro-American. Perhaps it was her own sense of sly humour that prompted this revelation, having endured Lovat Dickson's restrictions on writing about Grey Owl's background in her previous book. Or perhaps it was an ironic taunt at the current fashion for being "Indian." Though there were chiefs among her Algonquin ancestors who were involved in a dispute with the government over hunting grounds and the name Marie appears among the names given to her grandmother and great-grandmother there is no other direct evidence to support this story.4 But that it is possible in a more distant past than Anahareo stated that it is true. Anahareo wrote that it was through her grandmother she heard this story and all the evidence that to prove it was among her grandmother's belongings that lost to the family long ago.5

Anahareo at an interview about the book, courtesy of Katherine Swartile

This time Anahareo's book did not fade into the background. Grey Owl's star was in ascendance once again, the cabins were restored and the recent media attention and republished books could only feed the interest in Anahareo's story. Sales of her book climbed, and it eventually reached number four on the Toronto *Star* bestseller list. Once again in the public eye her image was up for scrutiny and some found they still could not set aside old expectations and perceptions of Aboriginal women. Dawn later recounted the reaction in an interview with a journalist: "when the book came out the people made out she was promiscuous. She laughed. She knew it wasn't true. One particular article in Saskatoon was very bad." In other interviews, like the one in the June 9 edition of the *Toronto Star* depicted Anahareo in a more positive light as she posed beside her sculpture of Grey Owl.6

Lovat Dickson, perhaps carried away by the emerging spotlight on Grey Owl and Anahareo, wrote his own book about Grey Owl, *Wilderness Man*, and published it the year following *Devil in Deerskin's* release. Relying heavily on Anahareo's previous publications, work done by the young historian Donald Smith, as well as some personal memories, he presented a lyrical portrait of Grey Owl's life. Romantic and literary in its description of the bush, *Wilderness Man*, created a picture of a heroic man, despite his foibles, who was defending a great cause, but came to a tragic and untimely end. Anahareo was notable in the book as a young nymphlike being who was Grey Owl's undoubted inspiration and love of his life. His description of their initial meeting would not be out of place in a novel:

> She was nineteen—dark, slender, and as beautiful and lithe as a panther. She was sitting reading on the dock one afternoon when he swept in with a swift stroke of his paddle, jumped out, and pulled his canoe up on the shore. His approach had been so silent that she was startled. She lowered her book, took him in, then began reading again while he watched her. She assumed that he was an Indian. He wore deerskin trousers, hitched up and supported by a highly coloured Hudson's Bay belt, and a worn buckskin vest. His long black hair hung to his shoulders. His face was dark and very handsome.7

Dickson's book enjoyed success and contributed to Grey Owl's rising profile, as well as supporting the notion that Anahareo played a key role in Grey Owl's rejection of trapping and involvement in wilderness preservation. Dickson's lyrical writing style and his undoubted publishing connections led him to consider pursuing his own ideas about making a film of Grey Owl's life. In the year of *Wilderness Man's* publication he wrote to Anahareo about his film possibilities and asked her questions about some of the sequences of events in Quebec. He continued to pursue the film possibility during the next few years, and for a while it seemed as if it might bear fruit.8

With Grey Owl's name in the public eye more often, other projects evolved. Nancy Ryley of CBC Television produced a moving portrait of Grey Owl released in December 1972 that included lengthy interviews with Lovat Dickson, Anahareo and some of Grey Owl's friends in Biscotasing.9 Sitting in a woven basket chair that hung from the ceiling Anahareo quietly reminisced about aspects of her life with Grey Owl. Grey Owl's popularity could only improve with such wide television exposure as a new generation of people with environmental concerns became aware of his early efforts. As Anahareo put it in a 1971 interview in the *Globe and Mail*, "He was ahead of his time. Now that the whole world is threatened they understand more and his books are starting to be reprinted."10 On the back of the renewed popularity Anahareo still made efforts to generate attention for her own film project but was unable to find anyone with sustained interest. Other, independent projects occasionally arose though, and she was included in those. In 1973 CBC's *My Country* invited her to present and discuss certain items connected to Grey Owl on one of their programs. Writing to Lovat Dickson for advice she considered showing seven or eight of the letters Grey Owl had written to her that were still in her possession.11

By now Anahareo's desire to promote Grey Owl's message was not confined to film projects. After the publication of *Devil in Deerskins* both Anahareo and Dawn received letters from people who expressed admiration for the work of Grey Owl and Anahareo, some recounting memories of personal encounters. The media also increasingly sought her opinion on broader matters of the environment and the affairs of First Nations. A 1971 *Globe and Mail* article promoting Grey Owl's message included Anahareo's views on the James Bay Development Corporation's plans to develop 130,000 square miles of northern Quebec and the effect the project would have on 6,000 native people. In no uncertain terms she stated:

> any interference with nature is damnable. Not only nature but also the people will suffer. It is ironic in Stockholm right now they're having a conference on an environment for humanity and in Vancouver they're trying to clean up an oil slick.12

Anahareo lived on her own now, in Victoria, and there she began to take a more active role in animal protection that was rekindled while writing *Devil in Deerskins*. The year her book was published she joined the Society for the Protection of Fur Bearing Animals, working with Ken Conibear, the man who many years previously had accompanied Grey Owl on his British book tour. In her capacity as a member of the society and her place as a public figure, Anahareo campaigned for various issues regarding animal protection that included banning leg-hold traps and promoting the use of humane traps. Nearing seventy now, she worked tirelessly for the cause, writing letters, manning exhibits and traveling with a film documentary, *Canada's Shame,* while she lectured and gave media interviews. She was able to speak compellingly from her own extensive experience to accurately convey the horrors of leg-hold traps. In an open letter sent in 1975 to the editor of the Winnipeg *Tribune* and other newspapers, she cited a time when Grey Owl came upon a trap by one of the "get rich quick" part-time trappers who set traps in spring when the females along with their young are most vulnerable. "He saw a mother beaver," she wrote, "moaning with pain while her paw was caught in such a trap, holding in her good hand one of her young and suckling it." She then wrote of her own experience in her second season trapping when she came upon a lynx in one of her traps.

> The weather had not been cold enough to put him out of his misery and judging from his tracks he had been there at least ten days. He had stripped the bark from everything within his reach. The only thing that kept him alive was eating snow. I would have let him go but he was in far too poor condition. He gnawed at his trapped paw until the bones were bare of flesh...This of course, and much worse is quite typical of what every trapper sees on his trap lines all the time.13

Besides her the vivid descriptions of the two trapping incidents

Anahareo also graphically described the spring pole trapping method used for squirrels:

> The trap is set in a tree so that when the steel trap jaws snap shut on the animal's leg it hangs helplessly in the air, often wrenching and twisting its leg from its socket in a desperate effort to free itself."14

At the end of the letter Anahareo urged people "in the name of mercy and decency to not wait another day or minute. Write or send at once to everyone of your MP's and MLA's as well as to Prime Minister Trudeau...demanding that the leg-hold trap be outlawed in Canada immediately."15

Anahareo at an opening ceremony cutting tape, courtesy of Katherine Swartile

Anahareo did not stop at writing letters. She began making appearances around British Columbia to support the leg-hold trap ban. On one occasion, at a lecture hall in Ladysmith, a trapper from the audience came up on stage to view the leg-hold trap they had on display. He put his hand in the trap and eased the teeth down slowly and gently on his hand, then made the comment that the trap would not hurt anyone. The spectators, apparently impressed with this demonstration, muttered among themselves. Anahareo, her timing perfect, waited until the noise had subsided and then walked calmly over to the trap, reset it and stuck a rolled up newspaper into the aperture. Bang! As the trap shut it jumped three or four inches off the table, flattening the roll of paper. The audience sat in shocked silence for a moment then broke into applause. Anahareo had made her point.16 Though the issue was controversial, the media faithfully reported her views, respectfully crediting her with the experience and insight she possessed. Finally, she was appreciated not so much for her curiosity value but for her valid insights.

The degree to which she had the media's ear was, however, a reflection of the changing times. The counterculture movement of the late 1960s and 1970s did much to alter the media and society's perception of Aboriginals as the leaders of the movement called for elimination of racism and imperialism. The idea of the pure, unsullied noble savage of the Indian took on new strength as the other stereotypes faded to some degree, under the pressure and demands for racial equality. If the modern industrialized society was only good for polluting and wasting the earth's resources, then the contrasting Aboriginal traditional lifestyle that respected the land and valued its resources was something to be revered. With these sentiments in play Anahareo's opinions and views found much support.17

Despite Anahareo's growing involvement in conservation issues, she could not prevent the health problems that arose from her increasing years, the most pressing of which were the cataracts that clouded her eyes. As she awaited an operation to resolve the problem she continued her efforts on behalf of animal protection. Her activities did not go unnoticed in the wider media and in 1975 interest in a film project arose once again. In this case, it centred on Lovat Dickson's book, *Wilderness Man*. A Toronto film company, Nielson-Ferns, had bought the rights to it. Confident in the film's success, they announced their desire to see Marlon Brando play Grey Owl in a project that included a feature film and a TV series with a minimum of thirteen episodes. Their hopes to secure Brando were based on Brando's interest in the issues confronting Native people, and his plans to produce a TV series of their history. Nielson-Ferns were in discussion with Brando about producing part of the series with him and hoped to use that opportunity to broach the idea of the role of Grey Owl. Despite these big names and plans, the production company continued to have problems finding a satisfactory script and adequate funding for its production.18

Anahareo and Raven, Katherine's son, courtesy of Katherine Swartile

Though no film emerged that year, a Toronto theatre company staged a play, *Life and Times of Grey Owl*, which drew material from Anahareo's book. Invited to watch a rehearsal, her daughter later recalled, Anahareo watched the woman who played her as she sat, wearing a dress, with her legs apart. Dismayed, Anahareo strode up to the stage and closed the woman's legs. "No lady would sit that way," she explained, "especially if she had on a dress." Anahareo never wore a dress.[19]

The opening night proved no better for Anahareo. As she sat watching she became so offended by the play's unrealistic portrayals of her and Grey Owl and its distortion of her book she left during the intermission. When interviewed later by the Toronto *Native Times*, she expressed her disgust over the play. She said she felt it was "totally unrealistic and the actress bore no resemblance in appearance or mannerisms and definitely not in spirit to her." Grey Owl's character was worse. "It turned out to be a parody," she stated. "Archie must have flipped in his crib."[20]

In addition to Anahareo's views on the play, the reporter gave a brief account of her upbringing and her time with Grey Owl, emphasizing it was she who "converted him" to conservation and encouraged him to write. The reporter described Anahareo as warm, honest, direct and outspoken, a person that, "despite many years living away from native people, ...has remained 'Indian.' Anahareo did not hesitate to express her views about the problems Aboriginal people faced and stated that she felt "very strongly about the negative image which white people have of Indians," she added:

> They took our land, broke our treaties and have developed sophisticated weapons to kill each other off and unfortunately take us with them. We can never win. They do not give a damn for their own people—the way they pollute the land and the air. The soul of Indian culture is religion. We never fought over religion the way you see the Christians, Muslims and Jews doing in the 'civilized world.'[21]

Despite the play's inaccuracy and poor production, a more positive image of Anahareo was emerging, due in part to her recent public activities in wildlife preservation and the revival of interest in Grey Owl's pioneering work in conservation. The year 1973 saw the publication of the book *Wilderness Women* by Jean Johnston that included a chapter covering Anahareo's life. Its publication came at a time of a new awareness of the lack of recognition of the role women played in shaping the events, people and society in the past. Johnston's books sought to tell the stories of a select group of women and show the particular role each one played in shaping Canada. In Anahareo's case Johnston summarized the events from Anahareo's book as well as portraying her as the key person who inspired Grey Owl and who was key in his decision to champion wilderness preservation.22

In 1976, Grant MacEwan, the former Alberta lieutenant governor, also wrote a book celebrating the achievements of several Canadian women, entitled, *And Mighty Women Too*. Intrigued and inspired by Anahareo's story he decided to include a chapter outlining her work with Grey Owl and the beavers, convinced she had made a significant contribution to wilderness conservation. It was a popularly written book that set Anahareo in a positive light and, as part of that collection, emphasized her as a woman of achievement.23

With the release of McEwan's book and the renewed interest in the work of Grey Owl and Anahareo, Dawn decided to present Grey Owl's letters, notebooks and photographs to the National Library and Archives of Canada. For Dawn it was a fitting culmination of many years of work to rehabilitate her parents' images, but most especially that of her father.

Two years after the book's publication, in 1978, Anahareo and Dawn were invited to visit Beaver Lodge. A momentous occasion for both of them, it was the first visit in nearly forty years. Dawn and Anahareo traveled there with Grey Owl's half-brother, Leonard Scott-Brown and Dawn's husband, Bob Richardson. Their reception was a far cry from Anahareo's visit in 1939 when the park staff was reluctant to admit to any connection to Grey Owl. In consideration of her mother's health and age, Dawn had asked that the visit be kept low-key, but the Parks Department were ecstatic and considered it an historical event. A half a dozen park personnel and many photographers met them. Despite such a media gathering and attention Anahareo moaned about the modern canoe and refused point blank to don a life jacket to make the journey across the lake, stating, "I never wore a god-damn thing like this in my life, and on top of that, an aluminium canoe."24

It was a memorable event and one that marked the continuing inspiration the site has given to many people over the years. The following year Beaver Lodge was designated a National Historic Site and eventually, in 1988, its location and significance convinced an American couple, Edwin and Margery Wilder, to give

$750,000 to ensure the preservation of the wilderness canoe routes in the nature sanctuary, as well as to take care of Beaver Lodge.25

More tangible evidence of Anahareo's new positive image emerged in 1979 when Grant MacEwan nominated her for membership to the Order of Nature of the Paris based International League for Animal Rights. An award previously only given to Albert Schweitzer, it recognized the enormous impact Anahareo had made in animal rights when she renounced trapping and eventually persuaded Grey Owl to do the same and use his "superb gifts of righting and oratory" to promote the cause of wilderness preservation. It was not only in recognition for Anahareo's important influence on Grey Owl that the award was given, but also to focus attention on the urgency attached to the need to eliminate the suffering of trapped animals. To the organization Anahareo represented the understanding that "compassion is indivisible," because, in Grant MacEwan's words "a person who makes a pretence of feeling for humans and has no feelings for other creatures in nature's community will have trouble appearing sincere." The medal, presented to Anahareo in a public ceremony, on October 14, 1979 was engraved with Grey Owl's words, "kindness is the hallmark of civilization."26

Kristin Gleeson

Anahareo awarded Order of Nature, courtesy of Katherine Swartile

Early in the year of the award and perhaps in anticipation of it Nancy Ryley, the woman who had produced the moving portrait of Grey Owl in 1972, contacted Dawn about the possibility of putting a program together showing Anahareo's life after Grey Owl. Dawn replied with some regret:

> Well, I've worked all week, trying to get something together about Anahareo's life since my father's death, and have come to the conclusion that her contributions were mainly to her family and would probably be of little interest to anyone else.
>
> ...Having met Anahareo, I know you realize that this lady's interesting character didn't evaporate when Grey Owl died and this certainly isn't what I am trying to say—she could have no doubt become a public figure, but she chose to step back with the exception of school lectures and occasional TV appearances.27

Anahareo

Dawn followed this explanation with several accounts of her mother in Grey Owl's time and a few more recent. She closed with an explanation of how Anahareo came to be called "Pony":

Papa, Anahareo's father, nick-named her 'Pony' because of her free-spirited nature—'Like a pony running into the wind.' And run into the wind she has all her life....Her fear of being corralled has made her life difficult—today at seventy-three she is still bucking the wind.28

Anahareo did not rest on her laurels; rather, as Dawn described it, she continued to "buck the wind." Based back in Kamloops, in a modest trailer home near her daughters, she began to focus her sights on the issue of wolf poisoning. She urged the British Columbia pesticide control appeal board to ban the use of the poison Compound 1080 to kill wolves and coyotes that farmers and cattle ranchers complained slaughtered their stock. A permit was issued to the British Columbia Fish and Wildlife to use the poison for five years to eliminate wolves and coyotes suspected of killing sheep and cattle. Anahareo spoke against the poison, emphasizing that there was no actual record of stock numbers lost to these predators to support such drastic measures. She suggested that farmers and ranchers could protect their stock by applying scent to keep away wolves and coyotes or scaring or killing specific predators. She also suggested the possibility of a bounty because anyone collecting it would need a license. A person applying for a license had to submit specific proof there was a problem before a board that consisted of representatives from two animal protection organizations. In an open letter to newspapers she described her personal experience of animal poisoning when one of her own sled dogs ate it by mistake:

"I watched my lead sleigh dog die from poison intended for wolves....I stood helplessly as she cried, moaned and vomited, her whole body writhing in pain until her last breath 35 minutes later...it is easy to say, 'do it,' but if the decision to poison also demanded that one watch the gruesome demise of a poisoned animal, they would think not twice...but many, many times.29

The media picked up on her campaign and published pieces on the issue. "Walking on the moon and flush toilets are not proof of civilization," she stated in one article. "It is our treatment of other living beings that tells the tale." When accused of being a bleeding heart she defended herself, saying she was not a bleeding heart, she was "just for the beaver, the wildlife, the trees." Despite her efforts and others who expressed concern over the safety of poison bait, the appeal was defeated and the poison was issued.30

While battling for the wolves Anahareo also took on the Kamloops City Council when they gave Fish and Wildlife permission to trap some beaver within the city limits because the beaver had been damaging trees and a wharf along a riverfront property. In an angry letter to the city council and local newspapers she told them:

> Killing the beaver now is [like] closing the barn door after the horse has run off. Beaver do not cut trees in the winter months as they are in a relative state of hibernation. I strongly submit that killing these two beavers now is not the humane answer....Leave the lodge until spring, the beaver will move on their own accord or the Fish and Wildlife can step in and relocate them.31

Thanks to her words, and the support they attracted, the city council decided to withhold permission to trap the beaver. Anahareo had won her point this time, and in recognition of her lifelong devotion to animals, the city council presented her with a plaque inscribed with Grey Owl's words that also marked her medal of the Order of Nature.32

Her efforts also attracted the attention of a journalist, Lynne Schuyler, who published two lengthy profiles in the Vancouver *Weekend Sun* and *BC Outdoors* on Anahareo in 1980 and 1981. The articles, which summarized Anahareo's life and outlook, were both very positive, presenting Anahareo as a complex person, spirited, talented and committed to the cause of wilderness protection. "A tiny woman, Anahareo can be as scrappy as a heavyweight, and issues like the Kamloops beaver send her flying out of her corner punching," wrote Schuyler.33

The articles also succeeded in portraying Anahareo as a living, breathing First Nations woman who could not be easily slotted into any old Aboriginal stereotype. There was no sign of a blanket-clad Indian woman, an Indian Princess. Nor was she a curiosity that could be chuckled about or cause puzzlement in her distinctive clothes and unconventional opinions. She was a determined woman, with miles of experience, who was committed to her views.34

Others voiced their admiration of her positive public image and continued to ask her to promote animal protection causes. A friend and member of the Association for Protection of Fur Bearing Animals, Val Gislason wrote to Dawn in 1980 about a new film the society was going to release soon and hoped that Anahareo would publicize it for them. "She has such a good public image," he wrote, "and people seem to like to associate a name with a cause."35

While Anahareo was waging her campaigns, Dawn tried to generate interest once again in making a film of *Devil in Deerskins*. At the suggestion of CBC's Nancy Ryley, the producer of the programs on Grey Owl years before, Dawn contacted a New York producer, Ellen Burstyn, with the idea that at long last many people were ready to hear about Grey Owl story and Anahareo's contributions and significance to it. After Ryley sent a copy of *Pilgrims of the Wild* and *Devil in Deerskins,* Dawn wrote to Burstyn. She enclosed newspaper clippings that emphasized her mother's role in Grey Owl's story and stated:

> The adage depicting a great woman behind a great man is proof the theory is true when the story of these two unique people is told in its entirety. Because Grey Owl created such a stir while lecturing

as 'the educated Indian' and then, after his death he was dubbed 'The Magnificent Fraud,' his wife's part in this drama was lost.36

Dawn also emphasized caution because "the story is controversial, in fact, so controversial if not handled properly, the contents could easily be sensationalized upon, thereby defeating Anahareo's original intent to squelch this approach to their story."37

While she approached the New York firm, the Toronto production company Neilson-Ferns was still working on generating film projects for Lovat Dickson's Book, *Wilderness Man*. The current possibility under consideration was three one-hour programs. They had made a minimal offer to Anahareo for the rights to her book, *Devil in Deerskins*, in order to take parts from it to enhance the Lovat Dickson program, but she refused their offer in the hopes that her own story might stand by itself in a film production. Unfortunately, as in the past, all the discussions and film possibilities came to nothing.38

Though the film industry still did not feel able to commit enough interest and funding to Anahareo's story, the growing recognition of her work and achievements in wilderness protection earned her Canada's highest honour in 1983. In July of that year Governor General Edward Schreyer presented Anahareo with the Order of Canada, citing her passionate, tireless work as a major force in conservation. Anahareo was too ill with arthritis and recurring thyroid trouble to travel to Ottawa, so the government arranged to have the award presented to her in Kamloops, before seventy relatives, friends and official guests.39 All three of Anahareo's daughters attended, Dawn, Anne and Katherine with their families, sharing in the celebration of her years of campaigning and commitment to wildlife preservation and her achievements as an Aboriginal woman. Years of prejudice, judgment and emotional and personal obstacles had helped shape her and bring her to this point. It was her very nature though that led her on a path that few would choose, a nature that refused to bow to the standards of the time period, a person who flew in the face of the long-held negative stereotypes of Aboriginal women and often suffered because of it.

Katherine, Dawn, Anahareo, Anne at award ceremony for Order of Canada, courtesy of Katherine Swartile

The following year Dawn died suddenly from complications of her long-term battle with diabetes while she was attending a meeting of the Grey Owl Society in Hastings, England. Her remains were shipped back to Canada and buried beside her father above Beaver Lodge. Anahareo's own health had deteriorated meanwhile and she was confined to a nursing home. She died just two years later on 17 June 1986, just one day before her eightieth birthday. They buried her next to her daughter Dawn and Grey Owl, her own "Jesse James."

Epilogue

In 2006 Mattawa celebrated the 100th anniversary of Anahareo's birth. The museum opened a new exhibit on Anahareo, the town officials dedicated a street after her and a well-known artist from the area, Clermont Duval, created a painting of Anahareo which a Toronto lawyer purchased and presented to the Mattawa museum. Dancing, drumming, presentations and various displays featured in the celebration. One of the big highlights was the appearance of Annie Galipeau, the First Nations actress who had played Anahareo opposite Pierce Brosnan's Grey Owl in Richard Attenborough's 1999 film, *Grey Owl*. The film, above all, was a love story, the dramatic and at times fractious relationship between Grey Owl and Anahareo. Anahareo's dream of a film about Grey Owl finally came to pass.

Was the woman celebrated on her 100th birthday and portrayed in the film the woman who captured the hearts of the British public and some of the Canadian press in the 1930s? She was all of these women in some part. She was a pathbreaker, a crusader, a vulnerable woman in love and a feisty, courageous and skilled woman of the bush. She was an Aboriginal. Anahareo began her life as a curious, sensitive and intelligent young girl who felt deeply the loss of her mother and grandmother at an early age. Such loss affected her self-confidence and made her at the same time vulnerable to criticism and racism and reacted by withdrawing from its source in an attempt to reject its power. In this vein she avoided school, her uncle and aunt's home and eventually the town and her religion as she gravitated toward the person who loved her nearly unconditionally, Grey Owl. Under Grey Owl's eye she flourished and developed her confidence, supported by his admiration and her growing skills in the bush. His love of her feisty attitude, her unique manner of dressing and hairstyle allowed her independent nature to surface more but also contributed to their tempestuous relationship and arguments that accelerated after bouts of drinking. Drink was a common part of the life of the wilderness for many trappers and woodsmen and often used to pass the long lonely hours or to celebrate after a long trapping season. It became a familiar part of Anahareo's life with Grey Owl. As Dawn later put it, "She learned many things from her husband—she also learned that when you hit town, you painted it red."1

As events offered Anahareo opportunities for adventure and chances to demonstrate and improve upon her bush skills she seized them with enthusiasm. In the beginning Grey Owl was by her side as they both shared the adventures, he the teacher, she the pupil. Later they both became the students of wildlife when they embarked on the venture to save two little beavers and then as many beavers as possible. It was only after Grey Owl's health and his desire and need to earn money through his writing compelled him to withdraw from adventurous journeys and exploits, and eventually withdraw from any company at all in his nocturnal work habits, that Anahareo sought her adventure and source of support and love elsewhere. But her child and the Winters proved no substitute, and her adventures seemed only to provide temporary respite from her dissatisfaction and loneliness.

Lured by the possibility of Hollywood and the feeling that her relationship with Grey Owl could never return to its earlier state

Anahareo parted from him, a decision that would have long-term repercussions and eventually cause her great regret. Pregnant and alone and away from the wilderness, she could no longer avoid the criticism, judgment and racism that had featured in her childhood in Mattawa. The deepening recession and her lack of skills only heaped more obstacles in Anahareo's path. It was no wonder she contemplated suicide. After ruling it out on the bridge, under such pressure Anahareo had little emotional energy to resist the institutions and legalities that regulated situations like hers, a poor single Aboriginal woman with a child to support. It was only after the Winters contacted her that she was able to withdraw again to some degree from the people and institutions that criticized and judged her through racial stereotypes and make her own choices again, but not before she had lost her daughter. Though she regained some of her confidence with the support of the Winters, Summy and the challenge of defending Grey Owl from the critics, her bitter experiences of the two years after her separation from Grey Owl would affect her permanently.

It seemed her good fortune to meet and marry Eric Moltke, a man who disregarded class, race and money, and who admired her nature as much as Grey Owl. But unlike Grey Owl, his love of alcohol and a good time outweighed his responsibility to his family and Anahareo. It became a false security for Anahareo, but one she could not easily break away from because of her past experiences after she left Grey Owl. That she loved Eric made it all the more difficult the times she did part with him temporarily. Caught in a town that had little regard for her and her race she tenaciously pursued a quest to bring Grey Owl and her story to film. Through the film she could prove Grey Owl's worth and perhaps regain some of her own self worth she had possessed during those years with him.

It was only years later, after much persuasion couched in an appeal for her help that Dawn was able to convince her to leave the illusionary security of Eric's home and go live with her daughter. And this was only agreed after she was satisfied his former wife would look after him. With Dawn supporting and encouraging her Anahareo pursued the film idea with more enthusiasm and then began to write the book. As the book took off and she became involved in wilderness preservation activities she was drawn into public life once again and this time the public were ready to listen to her. With such support Anahareo began to speak out and campaign with more vigour than she ever had as she finally fulfilled the promise of all those years before when she found two little orphan beaver kits. Her resolve to save them initiated a national movement toward conservation.

Endnotes

1. Anahareo, *My Life With Grey Owl,* (London: Peter Davies, 1940), 174-177.
2. Grey Owl, *Pilgrims of the Wild,* (Toronto: Macmillan, 1935), 17.

Chap. 1

1. Author interview with Katherine Moltke Swartile (Anahareo's daughter), Kamloops, BC, June 2007. Unless marked otherwise, the accounts described here of Anahareo's early life come from her autobiographies, *My Life With Grey Owl* and *Devil in Deerskins,* (Toronto: New Press, 1972).
2. Donald Smith interview with Johanna Bernard Murphy, Mattawa, Ontario, 1 January 1971, Donald P.Smith, Grey Owl Collection, Glenbow Archives, Calgary and genealogical records gathered by Anne Gaskell (Anahareo's daughter) and Jim Novak taken from Oka mission records, Anne Gaskell Papers, Kaslo, British

Columbia, Wayne Landen (Bernard cousin), to author, email, 28 April 2011 and Florence B. Murray, ed. *Muskoka and Haliburton, a Collection of Documents 1615-1875,* (Toronto: University of Toronto Press, 1963), 23.

3. M. Jean Black, "Nineteenth Century Algonquin Cultural Change," in *Actes Du Vingtieme Congres des Algonquinistes* ed. By William Cowan, (Ottawa: Carleton University Press, 1989) and G.J.J. Tulchinsky, *River and the Bush: The Timber Trade in the Ottawa Valley, 1800-1900,* (Montreal: McCord Museum and McGill University, 1981); Noreen Kruzich, *The Ancestors Are Arranging Things: A Journey on the Algonkin Trail,* (Ottawa: Borealis Press, 2011); "Petition to the House of Commons-Algonquin and Nipissing, *Fourth Session, Third Parliament, 14 Victoria 1851,*" F 4337-13-0-18, Archives of Ontario.

4. Donald Smith interview with Johanna Bernard Murphy, Mattawa, 1 January 1971, Smith, Grey Owl Collection, Glenbow Archives.

5. Family information from Gaskell Papers. For Mattawa at the turn of the century see Leo Morel, *Mattawa: Meeting of the Waters* (Mattawa: Mattawa Historical Society, 1980), Reverend Joseph C. Legree, *Lift Up Your Hearts: A History of the Roman Catholic Diocese of Pembroke,* (Combermere, Ontario: Brown & Martin Ltd., 1988), the newspaper *La Sentinnelle* (Mattawa, Ontario), 1895, nos. 10-52, Library and Archives Canada (AMICUS catalogue no. 7821012) and Peter Handley, *Anent Michael J: The Life and Times of Michael J. Rodden in Northern Ontario,* (Cobalt, ON: Highway Bookshop, 1995).

6. Information about the timber industry came from Tulchinsky, *River and the Bush*, Handley, *Anent Michael*

Endnotes

J. and the research and experiences of Wayne Landen, former curator of Grey-Owen Sound Museum and a relative of Anahareo's recounted in email to author, 2 Feb 2009.

7. Donald Smith interview with Eddie Bernard, 12 Feb 1973, Smith, Grey Owl Collection, Glenbow Archives.
8. Wayne Landen, email to author, 2 Feb 2009 and 3 March 2009.
9. Donald Smith interview with Johanna Bernard Murphy, Mattawa, 1 Jan 1971, Smith, Grey Owl Collection, Glenbow Archives.
10. Anahareo to E.B. c. 1970s, Katherine Moltke Swartile Papers, Kamloops, BC.
11. Anahareo, *Devil in Deerskins*, 36; Author interview with Katherine Swartile, Kamloops, BC, May 2008; and Anahareo to unknown correspondent c. 1970s, Katherine Swartile Papers, Kamloops, BC.
12. Author interview with Katherine Moltke Swartile, Kamloops, BC, May 2008 and Lynne Schuyler (journalist) interview with Dawn Bruce (Anahareo's daughter), Kamloops, BC, May 1980, Swartile Papers.
13. Wayne Landen to author, email 3 March 2009.
14. Today the area is simply known as "The Valley."
15. Author interview with Katherine Moltke Swartile, Kamloops, BC, May 2008.
16. Lynne Schuyler, "Still Bucking the Wind," *The Weekend Sun*, 24 May 1980.
17. Author interview with Angie Montreuil (Johanna's granddaughter), Mattawa, ON, June 2007 and author interview with Katherine Moltke Swartile, Kamloops, BC, May 2008.
18. Wayne Landen to author, email, 3 March 2009; Handley, ed., *Anent Michael J.*, 26, 50-51.

19. Author interview with Katherine Moltke Swartile, Kamloops, BC, May 2008.
20. For more detailed discussion of expectations and conflicting images of Aboriginal women see for example, Sarah Carter, *Capturing Women, Manipulation of Cultural Imagery in Canadian's Prairie West,* (Montreal: McGill-Queen's U. Press, 1997), Katie Pickles and Myra Rutherdale, ed. *Contact Zones: Aboriginal and Settler Women in Canada's Colonial Past,* (Toronto: U. of British Columbia Press, 2005) and Mary Ellen Kelm and Lorna Townsend, ed. *In the Days of Our Grandmothers: A Reader in Aboriginal Women's History in Canada,* (Toronto: U. of Toronto Press, 2006).
21. "Lake Temagami Provide Employment for Bear Island Native,"11 Sept. 1976[no newspaper cited]; Donald Smith interview with Isobel LeDuc, 15 March 1972, Smith Grey Owl Collection, Glenbow Archives.
22. Donald Smith interview with Isobel LeDuc, Temagami, 15 Mar 1972, Smith, Grey Owl Collection, Glenbow Archives.

Chap. 2

1. For the most comprehensive biography of Grey Owl see Donald B. Smith, *From the Land of the Shadows: The Making of Grey Owl,* (Saskatoon: Western Producer Prairie Books, 1990).
2. Grey Owl, *Pilgrims of the Wild,* (Toronto: MacMillan, 1935), 14.
3. Gertie to Billie n.d. [August 1925], Isobel LeDuc Papers, courtesy of Sherry Guppy, Temagami Library, Temagami, ON.
4. Isobel LeDuc to Hugh Eayrs, 28 April 1938, Macmillan Archives, The William Ready Division of

Endnotes

Archives and Research Collections, McMasters University Library, Mc Masters University, Hamilton Ontario, quoted in Smith, *From the Land of the Shadows,* 78.
5. Doug Mackey, Mattawa (local historian) interview with Johanna Bernard Murphy, Mattawa, 1987, author's research archives.
6. Smith, *From the Land of Shadows,* 77,79.

Chap. 3

1. Ibid, 79.
2. See Sarah Carter, *Capturing Women* or Katie Pickles and Myra Rutherdale, ed. *Contact Zones.*

Chap. 4

1. Anahareo, *My Life With Grey Owl,* 75-77 and Donald Smith interview with Anahareo, Kamloops, BC, 5 July 1971 in Smith, *From the Land of the Shadows,* 80.
2. Smith, *From the Land of the Shadows,*79-80.
3. Ibid, 81.
4. Anahareo, *My Life With Grey Owl,* 149.
5. Ibid, 135.
6. Ibid, 152.
7. Ibid.
8. See Cyndi Smith, *Off the Beaten Track: Women Adventurers and Mountaineers in Western Canada,* (Lake Louise, BC: Coyote Books, 1989); Sally Zanjani, *A Mine of Her Own: Women Prospectors in the American West, 1850-1950* (Lincoln, NB: U. of Nebraska Press, 2002).
9. Anahareo, *My Life With Grey Owl,* 191.

Endnotes

10. Grey Owl, *Men of the Last Frontier*, in *The Collected Works of Grey Owl*, (reprinted from MacMillan 1931 edition, Toronto: Key Porter Books, 2004), 12-13.
11. Ibid.
12. Anahareo, *My Life With Grey Owl*, 178-179.
13. Author phone interview with Katherine Swartile 14 July 2010.
14. Lovat Dickson, *Wilderness Man: The Strange Story of Grey Owl*, (New York: Atheneum, 1973), 153.
15. Smith, *From the Land of Shadows*, 82.
16. Anahareo, *My Life With Grey Owl*, 191.

Chap. 5

1. Jim Cameron, *The Canadian Beaver Book*, (Burnstown, Ontario: General Store Publishing House, 1991), 53.
2. H.A. Innis, *The Fur Trade of Canada*, (Toronto: Oxford U. Press, 1927), 49-51,54.
3. 3. Ibid., 54, 61.
4. Cameron, *The Canadian Beaver Book*, 54.
5. Innis, *The Fur Trade of Canada*, 61, 62,76,92; Milan Novak, *The Beaver in Ontario,* (Ontario: Ministry of Natural Resources, 1972), 15.
6. Cameron, *The Canadian Beaver Book*, 165.
7. Ibid., 55.
8. Smith, *From the Land of The Shadows*, 255 note 20.
9. Novak, *The Beaver in Ontario*, 4.
10. Grey Owl, *Pilgrims of the Wild*, 32.
11. Grey Owl, *Pilgrims of the Wild*, 36-37.
12. Novak, *Beaver in Ontario*, 10-11.
13. Ibid.
14. Grey Owl, *Pilgrims of the Wild*, 38.
15. Anahareo, *My Life With Grey Owl*, 208.
16. Ibid., 208-211.

Endnotes

17. Ibid.
18. Donald Smith interview with Anahareo, Kamloops, 5 July 1971 and Emma Dufond, Dave Whitestone's daughter, Mattawa, May 1973, Smith, Grey Owl Collection.

Chap. 6

1. Novak, *Beaver in Ontario*, 8.
2. Grey Owl, *Men of the Last Frontier, The Collected Works of Grey Owl*, 148.
3. Ibid.
4. Anahareo, *Devil in Deerskins*, (Toronto: New Press, 1972) 94-95.
5. Georgann Short, Ajawaan, "Report on Investigations, Grey Owl Project," U. of Saskatchewan, 1971, Smith *Grey Owl Collection*.
6. Smith, *From the Land of the Shadows*, 84.
7. Grey Owl, *Pilgrims of the Wild*, 116.
8. Ibid., 126-128.
9. Ibid., 117-118.
10. Ibid., 122-124.
11. Ibid., 129-132.
12. Anahareo, *Devil in Deerskins*, 103-104.
13. Smith, *From the Land of the* Shadows, 85; Anahareo, *Devil in Deerksins*, 108.
14. Anahareo, *Devil in Deerskins*, 111; Grey Owl, *Pilgrims of the Wild*, 168-169.
15. Grey Owl, *Pilgrims of the Wild*, 170.
16. Smith, *From the Land of the Shadows*, 85, 87; Anahareo, *Devil in Deerskins*, 111.
17. Wilfred Bovey to G.A. Harcourt, 26 Nov. 1929, in Smith *From the Land of Shadows*, 87.
18. Ibid.

19. Ibid., 88.
20. 20. Ibid.
21. Both Archie and Gertie describe Archie's writing habits in their books. Gertie also mentioned it during newspaper interviews in the 1930s.
22. Smith, *From the Land of the Shadows*, 88.

Chap. 7

1. See Sally Zanjani, *A Mine of Her Own*, (Lincoln: U. of Nebraska Press, 1997); Frances Backhouse, *Women of the Klondike*, (Vancouver: Whitecap Books, 1995) and Clare Rudolph Murphy and Jane G. Haigh, *Gold Rush Women* (Anchorage: Alaska Northwest Books, 1997); Jennifer Duncan, *Frontier Spirit* (Vancouver: Doubleday, 2003).
2. Ibid.
3. Zanjani, *A Mine of Her Own*, 1-2,109,113,116,316.
4. Zanjani, *A Mine of Her Own*, 173-174; Duncan, *Frontier Spirit*, 4; Murphy and Haigh, *Gold Rush Women*; Shaaw Tláa, *Dictionary of Canadian Biography Online* www.biographi.ca, accessed 3 July 2009.
5. Zanjani, *A Mine of Her Own*, 4-5.
6. Ibid., 6.
7. Ibid., 131-137; Author interview with Katherine Swartile, May 2008.
8. Zanjani, *A Mine of Her Own*, 33, 95.
9. Lynn Schuyler interview with Dawn Bruce, May 1980, Swartile Papers, Kamloops, BC.

Chap. 8

1. Grey Owl, *Pilgrims of the Wild*, 189-192.
2. Ibid., 192-195.

Endnotes

3. Ibid., 213.
4. Ibid., 223.
5. Ibid., 225.
6. Ibid., 226-227.
7. Smith, *From the Land of the Shadows*, 89.
8. Grey Owl, *Pilgrims of the Wild*, 240; Dickson, *Wilderness Man*, 206-207; National Parks Board, *Beaver People*, summer 1930.
9. To view the film see www.paddlinginstructor.com/video/canoeing-videos/1626-beaver-people-grey-owlfilm.html, (accessed 7 March 2010).
10. Anahareo *Devil in Deerskins*, 135.
11. Smith, *From the Land of Shadows*, 89; Anahareo, *Devil in Deerskins*, 135. 12.
12. Ibid., 136-137.
13. Smith, *From the Land of Shadows*, 89-90; Anahareo, *Devil in Deerskins*, 137.
14. "Grey Owl Devotes Life to Protection of Beaver," *Montreal Star* 24 January 1931 in Smith, *From the Land of the Shadows*, 91.
15. See Smith, *From the Land of Shadows*.
16. Smith, *From the Land of Shadows*, 18.
17. For a deeper discussion of the nostalgic depictions of Aboriginals see Vine DeLoria, *Playing Indian*, (New Haven, CT: Yale U. Press, 1998).
18. See Smith, *From the Land of the Shadows*. Archie was mistaken for Aboriginal on occasion and treated badly.
19. Smith, *From the Land of the Shadows*, 91,97,99; Anahareo, *Devil in Deerskins*, 180.
20. Ibid., 139-142.
21. Smith, *From the Land of the Shadows*, 90-91; "Significant Events in the History of Parks Canada," Canadian Geographic Magazine, www.canadiangeographic.-

ca/Magazine/MA03/Etcetera/parkstimeline.asp, (accessed 28 June 2007).
22. Ibid., 105; www.sierraclub.org, accessed 8 March 2010.
23. "Significant Events in the History of Parks Canada."
24. 24. Ibid., 89, 105.
25. For a more detailed exploration of this idea see Philip Deloria, *Indians in Unexpected Places*.
26. Ibid.

Chap. 9

1. The Colliery Engineer Co., *Placer Mining: A Handbook for Klondike and Other Miners and Prospectors*, (Scranton, PA: The Colliery Engineer Co. 1897, Facsimile Reproduction 1965, Seattle: Shorey Bookstore), 17-21.
2. Smith, *From Land of the Shadows*, 101.
3. "Quest For Gold to Buy Airplane Takes Mohawk Girl Prospecting Alone," Manitoba *Free Press*, 10 Oct. 1931.
4. Zanjani, *A Mine of Her Own*, 158.
5. "Quest For Gold to Buy Airplane Takes Mohawk Girl Prospecting Alone."
6. Ibid.
7. Ibid.
8. Ibid.
9. Ibid. For further reading on images of Aboriginals see Philip Deloria, *Indians in Unexpected Places*.
10. Frank H. Williams, "Archie Grey Owl Issues Warning That Housing of Beaver Must be Changed," Manitoba *Free Press*, 5 October 1931 in Smith, *From the Land of Shadows*, 109.
11. Lloyd Roberts, *Grey Owl—The Man*, unpublished manuscript 8pp.

Endnotes

12. Smith, *From the Land of the Shadows*, 108; Anahareo, *Devil in Deerskins*, 146.
13. Smith, *From the Land of the Shadows*, 104; Dickson, *Wilderness Man*, 227.
14. Smith, *From the Land of Shadows*, 105.

Chap. 10

1. For a history of Prince Albert National Park see Bill Waiser, *Saskatchewan's Playground: A History of Prince Albert National Park*, (Saskatoon: Fifth House Publishers, 1989) and Graham A. MacDonald and Grit McCreath, *Wakesiu and Its Neighbours: A Casual Illustrated History*, (Altoona, Manitoba: Friesens Corporation, 2008).
2. Waiser, *Saskatchewan's Playground*, 8,10; Brock Silversides, *Gateway to the North: Pictorial History of Prince Albert*, (Saskatoon: Western Producer Prairie Books, 1989), 12,14; Gary Adams, *Prince Albert: First Century, 1866-1966*, (Saskatoon: Modern Press 1966), 323.
3. MacDonald and McCreath, *Waskesiu and its Neighbours*,15-25.
4. 4. Ibid., 26, 32.
5. Smith, *From the Land of Shadows*, 110; Waiser, *Saskatchewan's Playground*, 40.
6. Smith, *From the Land of Shadows*, 110; Silversides, *Gateway to the North*, 14; Waiser, *Saskatchewan's Playground*, 43-46, Ian Barrie, "Memories of Terrace Gardens" *Waskesiu Memories, v.2*, Dorell Taylor, ed., (Victoria, BC: Classic Memoirs, 1999), 22.
7. Waiser, *Saskatchewan's Playground*, 51.
8. MacDonald and McCreath, *Waskesiu and its Neighbours*, 41; Anahareo, *Devil in Deerskins*, 146.

9. Anahareo, *Devil in Deerskins,* 148.
10. Author phone interview with Katherine Swartile, 14 July 2010.
11. Dickson, *Wilderness Man,* 222; Georgeann Short, Ajawaan, "Report on Investigations, Grey Owl Project," U. of Saskatchewan, 1971, Smith *Grey Owl Collection.*
12. Karl Clark to Sid [S.M. Blair], Edmonton, Nov. 16, 1932, S.M. Blair Papers, U. of Alberta Archives, 85-31: 46/2/211/3 cited in Smith, *From the Land of Shadows,* 111.
13. Short, Ajawaan, "Report on Investigations;" Waiser, *Saskatchewan's Playground,* 80.
14. Margaret Winters Charko to author, 24 July 2006, email.
15. Margaret Winters Charko to author, 24 July 2006, 14 November 2009, email. Anahareo, *Devil in Deerskins,* 151.
16. Ibid.
17. Margaret Winters Charko to author, 24 July 2006, email.
18. Doug Mackey interview with Johanna Bernard Murphy 1 January 1971, in possession of the author; Margaret Winters Charko to author, 3 November 2009, email; Robert Martin, "Anahareo: Out of the Wilds to explain Grey Owl," Toronto *Globe & Mail,* 6 September 1971.
19. Anahareo, *Devil in Deerskins,* 151, Margaret Winters Charko to author, 24 July 2006, 7 August 2006, email; Margaret Charko, "My Memories of Grey Owl," *Waskesiu Memories, v.2,* Dorell Taylor ed. (Victoria, BC: Classic Memoirs, 1999), 102.
20. Anahareo, *Devil in Deerskins,* 153; Short, Ajawaan, "Report on Investigations."

Chap. 11

Endnotes

1. Zanjani, *A Mine of Her Own*, 196; Backhouse, *Women of the Klondike*, 4.
2. Schuyler, "Still Bucking the Wind."
3. Dawn to Nancy, 7 February 1979, Swartile Papers.
4. Archie Belaney, Beaver Lodge to Gertie, 29 June 1933, MG30 D147, National Library and Archives of Canada, Ottawa, Ontario.
5. Ibid.
6. Ibid.
7. Ibid.
8. Grey Owl speaks of having had cross words with her before she left in a letter he wrote to her Madame, the Woman Prospector of Algoma, 24 August 1933, MG30 D147, National Library and Archives of Canada.
9. "Indian Squaw Turns From Kitchen Duties to Gold Prospecting," *Christian Science Monitor,* September 11, 1933; "Grey Owl's Wife Leaves Alone on Search for Gold," *Calgary Herald*, 12 September 1933.
10. Ibid.
11. [Grey Owl], Beaver Lodge to Madame the Woman Prospector of Algona, Algona Ontario, 24 August 1933, MG30 D147, National Library & Archives of Canada.
12. Ibid.
13. Ibid.
14. Ibid.
15. Archie, Beaver Lodge, to Mrs. Winters, 21 August 1933, 28 August 1933, 3 September 1933, MG 30 D147, National Library and Archives of Canada.
16. Archie, Beaver Lodge to Mrs. Winters, 27 September 1933 and Anahareo, *Devil in Deerskins*, 158.
17. Anahareo, *Devil in Deerskins*, 158-159.
18. Archie, Beaver Lodge to Gertie, 4 October 1933, MG30 D147, National Library & Archives of Canada.
19. Anahareo, *Devil in Deerskins*, 160.

Endnotes

20. [Archie to Gertie], letter fragment, c. December 1933, photocopy, Smith Grey Owl Collection.
21. Margaret Winters Charko, *Waskesiu Memories*, p.103.
22. Archie to Gertrude, Beaver Lodge, 15 May 1934, MG30 D147, National Library and Archives of Canada.
23. Ibid.
24. Ibid.
25. Ibid.
26. Anahareo, *Devil in Deerskins*, 160 and Archie to Gertie, 24 June 1934, MG30 D147, National Library and Archives of Canada.
27. *Canadian Press*, June 13, 1934, Smith, Grey Owl Collection.
28. rey Owl, *Pilgrims of the Wild*, 15; Genealogical records, Anne Gaskell Papers.
29. Grey Owl, *Pilgrims of the Wild*, 16, 17.

Chap. 12

1. Anahareo, *Devil in Deerskins,* 161.
2. Ibid.
3. Archie to Gertie, 24 June 1934, MG30 D147, National Library and Archives of Canada.
4. Ibid.
5. Archie to The Indian Woman (Ojibway) Prospector, Beaver Lodge, 11 July 1934, MG 30 D147, National Library and Archives of Canada.
6. Ibid.
7. Archie to Gertrude, Beaver Lodge, 20 July 1934, MG30 D147, National Library and Archives of Canada.
8. Ibid.
9. This letter is not in the archives collection and is only recounted in *Devil in Deerskins*, p. 164, but later letters

Endnotes

from him support the summary Anahareo recorded in her book.

10. Anahareo, *Devil in Deerskins*, 164; Gertrude Grey Owl, Flin Flon to Mr. Wood, 29 August 1934; Gertrude Grey Owl, Amisk Lake to Mr. Wood, 21 September 1934, written summaries in Smith, Grey Owl Collection.
11. Archie, Beaver Lodge to "Dear Kid," 27 September 1934, MG30 D147, National Library and Archives of Canada.
12. Ibid.
13. Ibid.
14. Ibid.
15. Archie, Beaver Lodge to Gertrude, 17 October 1934, MG30 D147, National Library and Archives of Canada.
16. Ibid.
17. Archie, Beaver Lodge to Gertrude, 28 October 1934, MG30 D147, National Library and Archives of Canada.
18. Archie—bald (not yet) to Gertrude, 17 November 1934, MG30 D147, National Library and Archives of Canada.
19. Archie, Beaver Lodge to Gertrude, n.d., MG30 D147, National Library and Archives of Canada.
20. Ibid.
21. Grey Owl to Hugh Eayrs, 20 July 1935, Smith, Grey Owl Collecton; Anahareo, *Devil Deerskins*, 171.

Chap. 13

1. Smith, *From the Land of the Shadows*, 115.
2. Grey Owl to Ellen Elliot, 24 March, 1935, MacMillan Archive, in Smith, *From the Land of Shadows*, 122.
3. Anahareo, *Devil in Deerskins*, 172-173.
4. See Smith, *From the Land of the Shadows*, 121.
5. Ibid.
6. Ibid.

7. Doug Mackey interview with Johanna Bernard Murphy, DATE; D. Smith interview with Emma Dufond, May 1973.
8. "Mrs. Grey Owl Aids Husband; Has Ambition," Waskesiu, Sask. 28 December 1935, no paper cited, Grey Owl and Family, Clipping File, Glenbow Archives.
9. Ibid.
10. Smith, *From the Land of Shadows*, 123-125, 129.
11. Ibid., 126.
12. Ibid., 128-130.
13. Ibid., 130-131.
14. Ibid.
15. Ibid., 145.
16. Ibid., 145-146.
17. Ibid., 149-151.
18. Ibid., 156.
19. Ibid.
20. Smith, *From the Land of Shadows,* 157; James Woods, Superintendent to J.C.[Campbell] 9 April 1936, Smith, *Grey Owl Collection*; Grey Owl, Beaver Lodge to Hugh & Rache 9 May 1936, Smith, *Grey Owl Collection*.
21. Smith, *From the Land of Shadows*, 158.
22. Margaret Winters Charko to author, 21 August 2007, 23 September 2006; and 5 July 2008 email; Short, "Report on Investigations;" Margaret Winters Charko, *Waskesiu Memories*.
23. Excerpt from "Thousands Flock to Northland's Vacation Centres for Summer," Prince Albert *Daily Herald*, 7 October 1936 in *Waskesiu Memories*, 218.
24. William A. Weber, *Theodore Dru Alison Cockerell*, University of Colorado Studies Series in Bibliography, No. 1 (Boulder, CO: U. of Colorado Press, 1965); D. Smith *From the Land of the Shadows*, 2-3, 226.

Endnotes

25. J.A. Wood to J.B. Harkin, 3 September 1936 and RCMP Report 2 September 1936 in Waiser, *Sasktachewan's Playground*, 57; [Betty Somervell to Kristin Somervell] c. 1950s, extract of photocopy in Smith, Grey Owl Collection.
26. Anahareo, *Devil in Deerskins*, 175; [Betty Somervell to Kristin Somervell] c. 1950s, extract of photocopy and Betty Somervell Diary, September 1936, photocopy, in Smith, Grey Owl Collection.
27. Smith, *From the Land of Shadows*, 160-161.
28. [Betty Somervell to Kristin Somervell] c. 1950s, extract of photocopy in Smith, Grey Owl Collection.
29. Ibid.
30. Ibid.
31. Ibid.
32. Ibid.
33. Ibid.
34. Ibid.; Betty Somervell Diary, September 1936.
35. Ibid.
36. Ibid; Margaret Winters Charko to author, email 3 November 2009.
37. Ibid.
38. Ibid.; Smith, *From the Land of Shadows*, 163.

Chap. 14

1. Waiser, *Saskatchewan's Playground*, 76, 77, 79, 82; MacDonald & McCreath, *Waskesiu and its Neighbours*, 48.
2. "Mrs. Grey Owl's Amazing Life Story," 6 October 1936, *Vancouver Sun*, Smith Grey Owl Collection.
3. Dawn Bruce to Ellen Burstyn, The Stone House, Palisades NY, n.d. draft letter [c. 1978] Swartile Collection.

4. Deloria, *Indians in Unexpected Places*, 78; 104-105. Hollywood, as Deloria notes, has never been a friendly place for Native Americans.
5. Extract of letters from enclosed in letter from Lovat Dickson to Hugh Ayrs, 27 April 1937 in Grey Owl Manuscript File, Macmillan Publishers Archives, typed copy in Smith, Grey Owl Collection.
6. Ibid.; Dawn to Nancy, 7 February 1979; Leslie Sara, "Could She Not Take Over Work Her Husband Commenced in Prince Albert National Park," Calgary *Daily Herald*, 23 April 1938, Glenbow Archives Clipping File; Registration of Birth for Ann, Gaskell Collection. This copy contains no recorded name for the father.
7. Smith, *From the Land of the Shadows*, 170-171.
8. Sara, "Work Her Husband Commenced in Prince Albert National Park."
9. Ibid.
10. Ibid.
11. Ibid.
12. Ibid.
13. Ibid.
14. Dickson, *Wilderness Man*, 247.
15. Ibid.; Smith, *From the Land of Shadows*, 170-171
16. Margaret Charko Winters to author, email 14 November 2009.
17. Sara, "Work Her Husband Commenced in Prince Albert National Park;" information on Moore was gleaned from letters and other materials in Swartile Collection and also from Katherine Swartile.
18. Joan Sangster, "Native Women and the Law," *In the Days of Our Grandmothers*, 301.
19. Ibid., 319.
20. Ibid., 310, 317.

21. Ibid., 316.
22. Author interview with Anne Gaskell, May 2008 and 2 February 2009.
23. Ibid.
24. Ibid.
25. Margaret Winters to author, email 14 November 2009.

Chap. 15

1. Smith, *From the Land of the Shadows*, 173-180.
2. Ibid.
3. Ibid., 181-194.
4. Ibid., 195-210; Margaret Winters Charko to author, email 23 September 2006.
5. Ibid.
6. Smith, *From the Land of the Shadows*, 211-216; Robert Martin "Out of the Wilds to Explain Anahareo", 16 September 1971, *Toronto Globe and Mail*.
7. See Albert Braz, "The White Indian: Armand Garnet Ruffo's *Grey Owl* and the Spectre of Authenticity," Journal of Canadian Studies, 36:4 (2001/2002), 171-184, among others who pose this theory he mentions Gary Potts, former chief of the Bear Island Anishnabe.
8. Anonymous, "Grey Owl's Deserted Wife is found in Poverty," 22 April 1938, *Daily Express*, in Smith, Grey Owl Collection.
9. Lovat Dickson to Major Wood, 26 April 1938, Lovat Dickson to Major Wood, 12 May 1938, Lovat Dickson to Major Wood, 20 May 1938, Lovat Dickson to Hugh Eayrs, 14 June 1938, Lovat Dickson to Yvonne Perrier, 14 June 1938, copies in Smith, Grey Owl Collection.
10. Ibid.
11. Isobel LeDuc to Hugh Eayrs, Macmillan Publishers, 28 April 1938, copy in Smith, Grey Owl Collection.

12. F. Williamson to Major Wood, 30 April 1938, Major Wood to F. Williamson, 2 May 1938, F. Williamson to Major Wood, 31 May 1938, copies in Smith, Grey Owl Collection; Waiser, *Saskatchewan's Playground*, 76,84.
13. Waiser, *Saskatchewan's Playground*, 84.
14. Anahareo, *Devil in Deerskins*, 187; "Grey Owl's Former Wife Unravels Mystery of Archie Belaney's Life," *Winnipeg Free Press*, 27 July 1938.
15. "Grey Owl's Former Wife Unravels Mystery of Archie Belaney's Life,"*Winnipeg Free Press*, 27 July 1938.
16. Anahareo, *Devil in Deerskins*, 187.
17. Lynne Schuyler, "One Spunky Lady," *BC Outdoors*, February 1981.
18. Short, "Anahareo- Report on Investigations," 6, Smith, Grey Owl Collection.
19. Ibid; Kristin Somervell Bonny to author, 3 January 2009; Betty Somervell to Kristin Somervell, 1953, copies in Smith, Grey Owl Collection; Countess Gertrude Moltke to Mr. Kingsley Wing, 1 July 1961, Swartile Papers.
20. Betty Somervell to Kristin Somervell, 1953, copies in Smith, Grey Owl Collection.
21. Pony, Prince Albert, to Dearest Summy, 17 October 1938, Anahareo, Christopher Lake to Bim, Lay, 9 January 1939, [blank] for Superintendent to Anahareo, 12 January 1939, copies in Smith, Grey Owl Collection.

Chap. 16

1. Author interview with Katherine Swartile, March 2006, May 2008, Katherine Swartile to author, email 16 October 2007; Lynne Schuyler interview with Dawn Bruce, May 1980, Swartile Papers.
2. Ibid.

Endnotes

3. Robert F. Berkhofer, Jr. *The White Man's Indian: Images of the American Indian From Columbus to the Present*, (New York: Vintage Press, 1979),55-61.
4. Marriage Certificate, Eric, Kendal, Cumbria to Gertie, 1942, Eric to Gertie, 23 December 1944, Swartile Papers.
5. Gertie to Summy, [1940] extract in Smith, Grey Owl Collection.
6. Anahareo to Willis Kingsley Wing (agent), 1 July 1961, Swartile Papers.
7. Author interview with Katherine Swartile, Kamloops, June 2007.
8. Summy to Pony, 25 August 1964, Swartile Papers; Donald Smith to author, 8 November 2009, email. Margaret Winters, *Waskesiu Memories*, vol. 2, 108.
9. Ibid.
10. Smith, *Land of the Shadows*, 213; Dickson, *Wilderness Man*, 268.
11. Eric to Gertie 23 December 1944, Swartile Papers.
12. Author interview with Katherine Swartile, Kamloops, May 2008; author interview with Anne Gaskell, Kaslo, British Columbia, May 2008.
13. Author interview with Katherine Swartile, Kamloops, May 2008; Eric to Gertie, 23 September 1944. Swartile Papers.
14. Eric to Gertie, 23 December 1944, Swartile Papers.
15. Author interview with Katherine Swartile, May 2008; see Wilna Moore correspondence with Anahareo, Swatile Papers.
16. Eric to Gertie, 23 September 1944, Swartile Papers; Author interview with Katherine Swartile, May 2008.
17. Author interview with Katherine Swartile, Kamloops, May 2008.
18. Ibid.

Endnotes

19. Ibid.
20. Ibid.; Mudder to Dawn, 4 December 1947, Swartile Papers.
21. Wilna to Gertie, 22 July 1947, Swartile Papers.
22. Mudder to Dawn, 1 May 1948, Swartile Papers.
23. Ibid.
24. Mudder to Dawn, 8 August 1972, Swartile Papers.
25. Maida, Christopher Lake to My Dear Gertrude, 20 August 1954, Swartile Papers; Author interview with Katherine Swartile, Kamloops, May 2008; photos, Swartile Papers.
26. Robert Remington, "Landmark's Future Uncertain" *Calgary Herald*, 5 December 2005; Katherine Swartile to author, 16 August 2008, email; author interview with Katherine Swartile, 16 November 2009; Edna Appleby, *Canmore, Story of an Era,* (Canmore: Edna Appelby, 1975), 7-26, 29, 34, 133.
27. See Chief John Snow, *These Mountains Are Our Sacred Places,* (Calgary: Fifth House Publications, 2005).
28. Charko, *Waskesiu Memories,* v.2, 103; author interview with Katherine Swartile, May 2008.
29. Author interview with Katherine Swartile, May 2008.
30. Ibid.
31. Author telephone interview with Katherine Swartile, Kamloops 1 December 2009.
32. Ibid.; author interview with Katherine Swartile, May 2008.
33. Ibid.
34. Ibid.
35. Wilna Moore, Muskody Indian Reserve, to Mr. Gray, Macmillan & co., 15 December 1952, copy in Smith, Grey Owl Collection.
36. Ibid.

Endnotes

37. Wilna Moore, Banff to Mr. Gray, undated, Smith, Grey Owl Collection.
38. Miss Wilna Moore to Mr. Gray, 31 December 1952, copy in Smith, Grey Owl Collection.
39. Wilna Moore to Mr. Gray, 7 February 1953, copy in Smith, Grey Owl Collection. t
40. Miss Moore to Mr. Gray, 12 February 1953, copy in Smith, Grey Owl Collection.
41. B.D. Sandwell, "Report," 23 February 1953, copy in Smith, Grey Owl Collection.
42. Ibid.
43. Smith, *From the Land of the Shadows*, 216.

Chap. 17

1. Author interview with Katherine Swartile, May 2008; Author interview with Duncan McKeller, May 2008, Park Warden near Canmore c.1952-1954.
2. Author interview with Katherine Swartile, Kamloops, British Columbia, May 2008; Mudder to Dawn, [c.1953].
3. Author interview with Katherine Swartile, Kamloops, British Columbia, May 2008.
4. Author phone interview with Katherine Swartile, 1 December 2009.
5. Mudder to Dawn, 5 August [1953], Swartile Papers [now in Gaskell Papers].
6. Author interview with Anne Gaskell, Kaslo, British Columbia, May 2008; author phone interview with Anne Gaskell, 14 November 2009.
7. Author interview with Anne Gaskell, Kaslo, British Columbia, May 2008.
8. Ibid.

Endnotes

9. Mudder to Dawn, 5 August [1953], Swartile Papers [now in Gaskell Papers].
10. Author interview with Anne Gaskell, May 2008, 14 November 2009.
11. Author interview with Anne Gaskell, Kaslo, British Columbia, May 2008; author phone interview with Anne Gaskell, 14 November 2009.
12. Ibid.; Author interview with Katherine Swartile, May 2008.
13. Author interview with Anne Gaskell, Kaslo, British Columbia, May 2008.
14. Mudder to Dawn, [fall 1953], Swartile Papers.
15. Author interview with Katherine Swartile, May 2008.
16. Dawn to Mudder and Kate, [Fall 1953], Swartile Papers.
17. Ibid.; author interview with Mitzi Whalen, Mattawa, June 2007
18. Author interview with Katherine Swartile, May 2008; Don Buckley, "Plain Dealing Around the Loop," *North Bay* Nugget, 29 December 1960; author interview with Mitzi Whalen, June 2007.
19. Author interview with Katherine Swartile, June 2007; Katherine to author, 2 August 2008, email.
20. Author interview with Mitzi Whalen, June 2007; Katherine to author, 2 August 2008, email.
21. Mudder to Dawn, 31 March 1954, Dawn to Mudder, 31 March 1954, Swartile Papers; Buckley, "Plain Dealing Around the Loop."
22. Wilna, Hotel Marlboro, Prince Albert, to Gertie, 20 April 1954, Swartile Papers
23. Ibid.
24. Ibid.
25. Ibid.
26. Ibid.

Endnotes

27. Eric, Calgary to Gertie, 1 May 1954, Swartile Papers; author interview with Katherine Swartile.
28. Dawn to Mudder, August 1954 and Grammy, Christopher Lake to Gertie, 11 August 1954, Swartile Papers.
29. Maida, Christopher Lake, to My Dear Gertrude, 20 August 1954, Swartile Papers.
30. Ibid.
31. Summy and Lovat Dickson addressed her as Pony in their letters to her and she often signed herself that way in her replies.
32. Mudder to Dawn 12 September 1954, Swartile Papers.
33. Mudder to Dawn, 12 September 1954, Dawn to Katherine, September 1954, Swartile Papers; author interview with Katherine Swartile.
34. Appleby, *Canmore, The Story of an Era*, 133; author interview with Katherine Swartile, May 2008.
35. Author interview with Katherine Swartile, Kamloops, May 2008 and author phone interview with Katherine Swartile, 16 November 2009; letters from Gertie to Eric, 1962, Swartile Papers.
36. Kristin Bonney to author, email 7 February 2008; Summy to Pony, 25 August 1964, Swartile Papers.

Chap. 18

1. Gertie to Eric [1962], Swartile Papers; author interview with Katherine Swartile, May 2008.
2. Author interview with Katherine Swartile, May 2008; Dawn Bruce Richardson Papers with Swartile Papers.
3. Mrs. Eric Moltke, Calgary to Mr. Richard Gregson, John Redway Assoc., London, 30 November 1959, Swartile Papers.
4. Ibid.

5. Ibid.
6. Deirdre Dalgano, John Redway Assoc., London, to Mrs. Gertrude Moltke, 10 February 1961, Swartile Papers.
7. See Jacquelyn Kilpatrick, *Celluloid Indians: Native Americans and Film*, (Lincoln: U. of Nebraska Press, 1999), Angela Aleiss, *Making the white Man's Indian: Native Americans and Hollywood Movies*, (Wesport, CT: Praeger, 2005) and Philip J. Deloria, *Indians in Unexpected Places*.
8. Berkhoffer, *The White Man's Indian*, 103-104.
9. Anahareo (Countess Gertrude Moltke Huitfeldt), Toronto, to Mr. Kingsley Wing, New York, 1 July 1961, Swartile Papers.
10. Ibid.
11. Author interview with Katherine Swartile, May 2008; Robert Lewis to Thos. McHugh, Jack Douglas Productions, 23 March 1963, Swartile Papers.
12. Disney Corporation to Dawn Bruce, 25 May 1964, Swartile Papers; Smith, *From the Land of the Shadows*, 216; M.U. Bateman, "The Story of Grey Owl," *The Canadian Outdoorsman,* January/February, 1967; "Daughter of Grey Owl Honored Festival Guest," *Daily Herald Tribune*, 24 February 1967, Grey Owl, Clipping File, Glenbow Archives.
13. M.U. Bateman, "The Story of Grey Owl", *The Canadian Outdoorsman,* January/February, 1967, Grey Owl, Clipping File, Glenbow Archives.
14. Ibid.
15. Smith, *From the Land of the Shadows*, 216; Ken Nelson, "Daughter of Grey Owl Honored Festival Guest," *Daily Herald Tribune*, 24 February 1967, Grey Owl, Clipping File, Glenbow Archives; Pony (Anahareo), Dawson Creek to Rache (Lovat Dickson) 4 December 1966, MG30 D237, National Library and Archives of Canada.

Endnotes

16. Author interview with Katherine Swartile, May 2008; Lynne Schuyler interview with Dawn Bruce, May 1980, Swartile Papers; Dawn to Nancy Ryley (CBC presenter) 7 February 1979 Swartile Papers; Anahareo to Lovat Dickson, 4 December 1966, MG30 D237, National Library and Archives of Canada.
17. Ibid.
18. Robert Martin, "Anahareo: Out of the Wilds to Explain Grey Owl," *Globe and Mail*, 16 September 1971, Grey Owl Clipping File, Glenbow Archives.
19. Shirley T. Popham, Chief Conservation Group, Information Services, Dept. of Indian Affairs and Northern Development to Rod Gadsby, North Burbaby, BC, 30 August 1971, Swartile Papers.
20. Ibid.
21. Smith, *From the Land of the Shadows*, 217.
22. Shirley Popham, Conservation Group, Dept. of Indian Affairs and Northern Development to Ron Gadsby, 30 August 1971, Shirley Popham to Shirley Dawn Bruce, 30 August 1971, Anahareo to Mr. Reglin, 18 June 1975, Swartile Papers.
23. Anahareo to Mr. Reglin, 18 June 1975.
24. Short, "Report on Investigations."
25. Ibid.
26. Ibid.
27. Ibid.
28. Ibid.
29. Ibid.
30. Ibid.
31. Ibid.
32. Ibid.
33. Dawn to Rache [Lovat Dickson], 12 December 1972, MG30 D237, Library and Archives of Canada; Barry Penhale, "Grey Owl—Englishman, Canadian Indian,

Endnotes

Conservationist," *The Forest Scene*, [1972], Swartile Papers; Barry Penhale interview with Mrs. Winters, 1972, Smith, Grey Owl Collection; Smith, *From the Land of the Shadows*, 216.

Chap. 19

1. Short, "Report on Investigations."
2. Anahareo, *Devil in Deerskins*, 1-2.
3. Ibid, 35.
4. Wayne Landen to author, 23 August 2011, email. There is no listing for Mary Robinson in Emma Lewis Coleman's exhaustive 1925 work, *New England Captives Carried to Canada Between 1677 and 1760* (Portland, Maine) though that is not to say she could have been captured after 1760.
5. Dawn recounted the story again in the May 1980 interview with journalist Lynne Schuyler and explained that the book containing the story was lost somewhere in the family.
6. Lynne Schuyler interview with Dawn, May 1980, Swartile Papers; Helen Worthington, *Toronto Star*, 9 June 1972.
7. Dickson, *Wilderness Man*, 124-125.
8. Lynne Schuyler interview with Dawn, May 1980, Swartile Papers; Rache to Pony, 23 November 1972, MG30 D237, Library and Archives of Canada.
9. Smith, *From the Land of Shadows*, 217.
10. Robert Martin, "Anaharco: Out of the Wilds to Explain Grey Owl," *Globe and Mail*, 16 September 1971, Grey Owl Clipping File, Glenbow Archives.
11. Pony to Rache, 1973 MG30 D237, Library and Archives of Canada.

12. Martin, "Anahareo: Out of the Wilds to Explain Grey Owl."
13. Anahareo to Editor, The Winnipeg Tribune, 26 April 1975, Swartile Papers.
14. Anahareo to Editor, Winnipeg Tribune, 26 April 1975, Swartile Papers; Dawn to Rache, 18 June 1975, MG30 D237, Library and Archives of Canada; Ken Hinkins, "She's Still Fighting," *The Victorian*, 9 April 1975, Swartile Papers.
15. Ibid.
16. Dawn to Nancy [Ryley], 7 February 1979, Swartile Papers.
17. Berkhoffer, *The Whiteman's Indian*, 103, 110.
18. Dawn to Rache, 25 January 1976, Swartile Papers; Jack Miller, "Brando Sought for Canadian Indian Film," Toronto *Star*, 4 February 1977; Pony to Rache, 9 January 1975, Rache to Dawn, 20 February, 1976, MG30 D237, Library and Archives of Canada.
19. Author phone interview with Katherine Swartile, June 2007.
20. "A Mohawk: a Legend in Her own Time," Toronto *Native Times*, Nov/Dec, 1975 and Dawn to Rache, 25 January 1976, Swartile Papers; Rache to Dawn, 20 February 1976, MG30 D237, Library and Archives of Canada.
21. "A Mohawk: a Legend in Her own Time."
22. Jean Johnston, *Wilderness Women: Canada's Forgotten History*, (Toronto: Peter Martin Press, 1973).
23. Grant MacEwan, *And Mighty Women Too*, (Vancouver: Douglas & McIntyre Press, 1976).
24. Dawn to Nancy [Ryley], 7 February 1979, Swartile Papers.
25. Ibid; Smith, *From the Land of the Shadows*, 217.

Endnotes

26. Citation, 14 October, 1979, International League for Animal Rights; Lynne Schuyler, "One Spunky Lady," *BC Outdoors,* February 1981; Dawn Richardson to Roger de Nantel, Director, Chancellery of Canadian Orders and Decorations, 18 May 1983, Swartile Papers.
27. Dawn, Kamloops, BC to Nancy, 7 February 1979, Swartile Papers.
28. Ibid.
29. Lynne Schuyler, "One Spunky Lady."
30. "Grey Owl's Widow Speaks Out Against Poisoning Wolves," Vancouver *Sun,* 21 March 1980; F.E. Murray, Chair, Pesticide Control Appeal Board, to Anahareo Grey Owl, 1 May 1980, Swartile Papers.
31. Lynne Schuyler, "One Spunky Lady."
32. Lynne Schuyler, "Still Bucking the Wind," Vancouver *Weekend Sun, Today,* 24 May 1980.
33. Ibid.
34. Ibid.; Lynne Schuyler, "One Spunky Lady."
35. Val Gislason to Dawn, 14 June 1980, Swartile Papers.
36. Dawn Richardson, Heffley Creek, BC, to Ellen Burnstyn, Palisades, NY, 29 May 1980, Swartile Papers. t
37. Ibid.
38. Dawn to Nancy, 7 February 1979, Dawn Richardson to Ellen Burstyn, 29 May 1980.
39. Author interview with Katherine Swartile, May 1980; Alan MacRae, "Anahareo, O.C., Still Espousing Conservation," Kamloop *News,* 25 July 1983.

Epilogue

1. Dawn to Ellen Burstyn, Palisades New York (draft letter c. 1980), Swartile Papers.

Acknowledgments

I am especially indebted to Katherine Swartile and Anne Gaskell for their trust and for opening their homes and their hearts to me. I am also very grateful to Don Smith for his support and enthusiasm, for all the bits and pieces he sent on to me, and for his unfailing hospitality. I also owe many thanks to Doug Mackey, who provided the initial contacts and acted as a wonderful host and escort around the Mattawa area, for introducing me to Albert Lalonde, Grey Owl's grandson, who sadly passed away only months afterwards.

I also owe many thanks to all the people who I met or corresponded with while pursuing this project, including Wayne Landen, Kristin Bonney, Margaret Winters Charko, Betty Taylor of the Grey Owl Society, Lynne Schuyler, Louise Montreuil, Dolly Bernard, Doug Cass of Glenbow Museum Archives, René LaMarsh of the Mattawa Museum, librarian Ebhlín ní Laoghaire and the staff of the Library and Archives of Canada.

PUBLISHED RESOURCES

Adams, Gary, *Prince Albert, First Century, 1866-1966*, Saskatoon: Modern Press, 1966.

Anahareo, *Devil in Deerskins, My Life With Grey Owl*, Toronto: New Press, 1972.

_____, *My Life With Grey Owl*, London: Peter Davies, 1940.

Applebee, Edna, *Canmore, Story of an Era*, Canmore: Edna Appleby, 1975.

Berkhoffer, Robert E., *The Whiteman's Indian: Images of the American Indian From Columbus to the Present*, New York: Vintage Books, 1979.

Backhouse, Frances, *Women of the Klondike*, Vancouver: Whitecap Books, 1995.

Black, M. Jean, "Nineteenth Century Algonquin Culture Change," in *Actes du Vingtieme Congres des Algonistes*, ed. By William Cowan, Ottawa: Carleton University Press, 1989.

_____, "A Tale of Two Ethnicities: Identity and Ethnicity at Lake of Two Mountains, 1721-1850," in *Papers of the Twenty-Fourth Algonquin Conference*, ed. by William Cowan, Ottawa: Carleton University Press, 1993.

Braz, Albert, "The White Indian: Armand Garnet Ruffo's *Grey Owl* and the Spectre of Authenticity," *Journal of Canadian Studies*, 36:4 (2001/2002).

Published Resources

Cameron, Jim, *The Canadian Beaver Book,* Burnstown, ON: General Store Publishing House, 1991.

Carriere, Gaston, *Jean-Marie Nédélec,* Sudbury, ON: La Societé Historique du Nouvel-Ontario, University of Sudbury 1957.

Carter Sarah, *Capturing Women: Manipulation of Cultural Imagery in Canada's Prairie West,* Montreal, McGill –Queen's University Press, 1997.

The Colliery Engineer Company, *Placer Mining: A Handbook for Klondike and Other Miners and Prospectors,* Scranton, PA: The Colliery Engineer Company, 1897, reprinted Seattle, WA: Facsimile Reproduction, Shorey Bookstore, 1965.

Deloria, Philip J., *Playing Indian,* New Haven, CT: Yale University Press, 1998.

_____, *Indians in Unexpected Places,* Lawrence, KS: University of Kansas Press, 2004.

Dickson, Lovat, *Wilderness Man: The Strange Story of Grey Owl,* New York: Atheneum, 1973.

Duncan, Jennifer, *Frontier Spirit,* Vancouver: Doubleday, 2003.

Edwards, Frederick, "Small Town, Big Men," *Macleans,* 15 September 1939.

Grey Owl, *The Men of the Last Frontier,* in *The Collected Works of Grey Owl,* reprinted from Macmillan 1931 edition, Toronto: Key Porter Books, 2004.

_____, *Pilgrims of the Wild,* Toronto: Macmillan, 1935.

Published Resources

Handley, Anent Michael J.: *The Life and Times of Michael J. Rodden in Northern Ontario,* Cobolt, ON: Highway Bookshop, 1995.

Innis, H.A., *The Fur Trade of Canada,* Toronto: Oxford University Press, 1927.

Johnston, Jean, *Wilderness Women: Canada's Forgotten History,* Toronto: Peter Martin Press, 1973.

Kelm, Mary Ellen and Lorna Townsend, *In the Days of Our Grandmothers: A Reader in Aboriginal Women's History in Canada,* ed. by Mary Ellen Kelm and Lorna Townsend, Toronto, University of Toronto Press, 2006.

Kilpatrick, Jacqueline, *Celluloid Indians: Native Americans and Film,* Lincoln NB: University of Nebraska Press, 1999.

Kruzich, Noreen, *The Ancestors Are Arranging Things, A Journey On the Algonkin Trail,* Ottawa, Borealis Press, 2011.

La Sentninelle (Mattawa, Ontario), 1895, nos.10-52, Library and Archives Canada AMICUS *catalogue no.*782101210.

Legree, Rev. Joseph C., *Lift Up Your Hearts: A History of the Roman Catholic Diocese of Pembroke,* Combermere, ON: Brown & Martin Ltd., 1988.

MacDonald, Graham A. and Grit McCreath, *Wakesiu and Its Neighbours: A Casual Illustrated History,* Altoona, Manitoba: Friesens Corporation, 2008.

MacEwan, Grant, *And Mighty Women Too,* Vancouver: Douglas & McIntyre Press, 1976.

Published Resources

Marks, Lynne, *Revivals and Roller Rinks: Religion, Leisure and Identity in late Nineteenth Century Small Town Ontario,* Toronto: University of Toronto Press, 1996.

Moore, Kermot A., *Kipawa: Portrait of a People,* Cobolt ON: Highway Bookshop, 1982.

Morel, Leo, *Mattawa: Meeting of the Waters,* Mattawa: Mattawa Historical Society, 1980.

Murphy, Clare Rudolph and Jane G. Haigh, *Gold Rush Women,* Anchorage: AK, Alaska Northwest Books, 1997.

Murray, Florence B. ed. *Muskoka and Haliburton, A Collection of Documents, 1615-1875,* Toronto: University of Toronto Press, 1963.

Novak, Milan, *Beaver in Ontario,* Ontario: Ministry of National Resources, 1972.

Pickles, Katie and Myra Rutherdale, ed. *Contact Zones, Aboriginal and Settler Women in Canada's Colonial Past,* Toronto: University of British Columbia Press, 2005.

Pink, Hal, *Bill Guppy: King of the Woodsmen,* London: Hutchinson, 1940.

Silversides, Brock, *Gateway to the North: Pictorial History of Prince Albert,* Saskatoon: Western Producer Prairie Books, 1989.

Smith, Cyndi, *Off the Beaten Track: Women Adventurers and Mountaineers in Western Canada,* Lake Louise, BC: Coyote Books, 1989.

Published Resources

Smith, Donald P. *From the Land of Shadows: The Making of Grey Owl*, Saskatoon: Western Producer Prairie Books, 1990.

Snow, Chief John, *These Mountains Are Our Sacred Places*, Calgary: Fifth House Publications, 2005.

Taylor, Dorell, ed., *Waskesiu Memories*, Victoria, BC: Classic Memoirs, 1999.

Tulchinsky, G.J.J., *River and the Bush: The Timber Trade in the Ottawa Valley, 1800-1900,* Montreal: McCord Museum and McGill University Press, 1981.

Waiser, Bill, *Saskatchewan's Playground: A History of Prince Albert National Park,* Saskatoon: Fifth House Publishers, 1989.

Wall, Sharaon, "Totem Poles, Teepees and Token Traditions: Playing Indian at Ontario Summer Camps, 1920-1955," *Canadian Historical Review*, 3 September 2005, 513-544.

Weber, William A. *Theodore Dru Alison Cockerell,* University of Colorado Studies Series in Bibliography, No.1, Boulder, CO: University of Colorado Press, 1965.

Zanjani, Sally, *A Mine of Her Own: Women prospectors in The American West, 1850-1950,* Lincoln, NB: University of Nebraska Press, 2002.

ARCHIVAL COLLECTIONS

Grey Owl Collection, MG30 D47, Library and Archives of Canada, Ottawa.

Anne Gaskell Papers (private collection).

Katherine Moltke Swartile Papers (update 2024) Glenbow Western Research Centre, U. Of Calgary, Canada.

Don Smith Grey Owl Collection, (update 2024) now in Glenbow Western Research Centre, U. Of Calgary, Calgary, Canada.

Isobel LeDuc Papers, Sherry Guppy/Temagami Library, Temagami Ontario, Canada.

INTERVIEWS AND CORRESPONDENCES

Bernard, Dolly, (Anahareo's cousin) author interview, Mattawa, June, 2007.

Bonney, Kristin Somervell, (daughter of Grey Owl & Anahareo's friend), emails 2007-2009.

Boyle, Father, (priest in Mattawa), author interview, Mattawa, June 2007.

Charko, Margaret Winters, (Anahareo's friend, mother looked after Dawn), emails 2006-2009.

Gaskell, Anne (Anahareo's daughter), author interview, Kaslo, May 2008 and numerous emails and phone conversations 2006-2011.

Landen, Wayne, (father cousin to Anahareo), extensive emails, 2009-2010.

McKellar, Duncan, (Park warden near Canmore and acquaintance of Eric Moltke), phone interview, May 2008.

Montreuil, Angie, (Anahareo's great-great niece), author interview, Mattawa, June 2007.

Montreuil, Louise, (Anahareo's great niece), local historian Doug Mackey interview, Mattawa, 2010.

Murphy, Johanna Bernard, (Anahareo's sister), local historian Doug Mackey interview, Mattawa, 1987.

Swartile, Katherine Moltke, author interview, Kamloops, May 2008 and numerous emails and phone conversations 2006-2011.

Interviews and Correspondence

Whalen, Mitzi, (neighbour and friend of Katherine as child), author interview, Mattawa, June 2007.

PERIODICALS

BC *Outdoors*, February 1981.

Calgary *Daily Herald*, 12 September 1933; 23 April 1938; 5 December 2005.
Canadian Outdoorsman, Jan/Feb 1967.

Christian Science Monitor, 11 September 1933.

Daily Express, 22 April 1938.

The Forest Scene, 1972. Kamloops *News*, 25 July 1983.

La Sentinnelle, Mattawa, Ontario 1895 nos. 10-52. Manitoba *Free Press*, 10 October 1931; 5 October 1931.

North Bay *Nugget*, 29 December 1960. Toronto *Globe & Mail*, 16 September 1971. Toronto *Native Times*, Nov/Dec 1975.

Toronto *Star* 9 June 1972; 4 February 1977.

Vancouver *Sun* 21 March 1980.

Vancouver *Weekend Sun/Today*, 24 May 1980.

The Victorian, 9 April 1975.

Winnipeg *Free Press*, 27 July 1938.

Winnipeg *Tribune*, 26 April 1975.

WEBSITES

www.aafna.ca/history, Ardoch Algonquin First Nation

www.ancestry.com

www.biographi.ca Dictionary of Canadian Biography

www.canadiangeographic.ca/Magazine/MA03/Etcetera/parkstimeline.asp

www.paddlinginstructor.com/video/canoeing-videos/1626-beaver-people-greyowlfilm.html

www.sierraclub.org

www.voyageurdays.com/history.htm (Mattawa)

www.ingramcontent.com/pod-product-compliance
Lightning Source LLC
Chambersburg PA
CBHW052132070526
44585CB00017B/1795